Comments on Reading
Volume I: Science and History

Chris Berry
Data Scientist, CBC

From Chris Berry's "Eyes on Web Analytics"[b]

I read the first 120 pages of Joseph Carrabis' new book "Reading Virtual Minds Volume 1" last night and polished it off this morning while sitting at the airport.

The book certainly forced me to think about being really aware of being aware of how hard I was thinking. I was engaged the whole way though, and in the end, I asked "wholly sh?t, what just happened there?"

I spent the better part of the night dreaming about it (always a sign that something upstairs is getting restructured).

I'll write about the experience without spoiling it for you.

Joseph tells the story about how NeuroCognitive-PsychoLingualAnthropology came to be. In spite of how long that word is, the book is very accessible, readable, useful, and intensely personal. The love leaps off many pages. (And one page where the middle finger literally leaps off the page. It's not directed at the reader and it's refreshingly honest.)

I'm taking away more than a few things that'll become part of my every day speech.

The first is how NextStage's machine runs. Joseph explains the principles of how it works specifically and uses accessible metaphors to expand. Those with an appreciation for collective intelligence and algorithm design will want to pay attention to how he explains it: it's superior.

---

a – Just so everyone knows, I never correct someone's writing when I'm quoting them. Too much a forensic linguist, me.
b – http://nlb.pub/K

The second relates to political science and some of the social ills (suppressed political participation) that a good colleague has been trying to understand for the better part of a decade. There are applications of the technology that could explain what we think we're seeing in the Canadian Election Study (CES). While I hope that Elections Canada and SSHIRC continue to fund the CES, NextStage offers a method of predicting a breakout election and perhaps a compelling explanation for turnout suppression. I haven't been more inspired since reading "How Institutions Evolve".

The third goes to marketing. It's generally accepted that people think differently. But how differently? And do those differences matter? And if so in which contexts? The book gives a concrete example of how much and how it matters to marketers. The notion of intensity channels is a useful and accessible schema for quantifying those differences and acting upon them.

The fourth goes to changes to how we define experience design. On this point, you really need to read the book for yourself.

The next three takeaways are far more personal.

The first deals with a preference of mediums. One NextStage dimension is 'visual', and it explains a lot about me. I'd sooner go over to somebody's desk and talk before writing an email before sending a text message before picking up the phone. In that preference order. And this includes literally hunting somebody own in a large office to find them in person. If the person is remote, I'd much rather use email. I'm that visual. So whether that means looking a digital signal, composed entirely of words with no tone: at least I can see the shapes of the words and the patterns. Thankfully the world is coming around with video chat.

The second deals with being intuitive and filters. Thankfully, Joseph uses as much common vocabulary as possible. We all know what we're talking about when it comes to filters. There's a reason why it's acceptable to fart in certain social situations and it's utterly unacceptable to so happen so much as speak a run-on sentence in another: even though they're both forms of passing gas. There's a certain degree of self-awareness that goes with it:

that a big part of understanding how others are reacting also involves the kinds of signals that you're giving off.

The third will be the subject of future blog posts.

Just go get the book. It's a very good read and most of the people I know who read this space will find it valuable.

Holly Buchanan
CEO, Buchanan Marketing, LLC, Co-Author of The Soccer Mom Myth - Today's Female Consumer: Who She Really Is, Why She Really Buys

From Marketing to Women Online[c]

I'm a long-time fan of NextStage's Joseph Carrabis. I was lucky enough to spend some time with Joseph in New York and it was one of the more interesting hours I've spent. We're talking big brain here folks. But without the ego - a rare combination.

What I enjoy most about the work Joseph Carrabis does is that he focuses not just on the what, but on the why. Many in the website conversion arena can tell you what website, landing page, banner ad, etc. performed the best. But they can't always tell you why.

That's what Reading Virtual Minds - Volume I: Science and History is all about - not only what people do online, but why they do it. I love Joseph's approach because he uses a combination of many different scientific approaches: Neurology, Psychology, Sociology, Anthropology, Semiotics, Linguistics and many more.

Book Review

Imagine if you could create a website that was more persuasive then even your very top sales person? Imagine that website could adjust the messaging and customer experience

---

[c] – http://nlb.pub/L

based on feedback from each individual customer. And best of all imagine it could make those adjustments not just from the customer's conscious feedback, but from their unconscious feedback as well?

How cool would that be? How much money could you make from such a website?

This is the end result of the science and technology behind "ET", an interface designed by NextStage to learn from website visitor behavior. Or, as author Joseph Carrabis puts it, "Technically, such an interface would be called a Symbiotic CyberSemiotic System, and who in their right mind wants to read that more than once in a book?"

In Reading Virtual Minds, Volume I: Science and History, Joseph Carrabis, CEO and founder of NextStage explores the science and history behind ET and understanding human behavior.

The premise of the book is:

"An interesting thing about behaviors is that people engage in thousands of behaviors without realizing they are doing so. These thousands of behaviors are little things that mean nothing by themselves, but added up give us a pretty detailed picture of who we are."

"If you know how to isolate and read these behaviors, and you know what information is being presented (such as a web page, a software interface, a brochure, a leave-behind, a PPT slide...), then you know how to predict what people are going to do and how to persuade them to do what you want, online and off, whether they're sitting in front of you, sitting in front of a computer half a world away, or responding to their emails on the iPhone sitting in Starbucks."

Thanks to ET, two people could be in the same room, surfing the same website, yet having two very different experiences, seeing different content served up based on their behavior. This is the ultimate customizable experience everyone's been talking about, but no-one's really been able to deliver.

I've done a lot of work with segmentation and personas and have seen the huge impact they can have on site performance and conversion. But the results ET can deliver are like personas times one hundred.

For me, the sign of a good book is one that gets you thinking, that raises questions, that makes you yearn for more. This book does exactly that. My copy is marked up, highlighted and filled with my own thoughts and notations.

The other sign of a good book is that there are concrete steps I can take back and apply directly to my life and my work. There are some incredible take-aways that are worth the price of the book, but not as many as I would have liked. But this volume is "Volume I: Science and History" In future volumes, Joseph promises to share how to implement these learnings.

If you're interested in improving your website, or overall customer experience, I highly recommend you read Reading Virtual Minds Volume 1: Science and History. It will get your brain spinning with possibility and will whet your appetite for more to come from this series. I personally can barely wait for the rest of the material to be published. (And just to get you salivating, there is a whole section on gender.)

Vicky Brock
Forbes.com & Bloomberg Top 9 female tech CEOs to watch, CEO, Clear Returns

I have been reading your book and feeling inclined to go off and be a perpetual student of new and interesting things. (A little visit to Stanford the other week also helped with that). I hope you take it as a compliment that the book is a delight in learning how little I know.

Jennifer Day
Product R&D Manager at OrderDynamics

Aah, now I am starting to get it!

For me, reading this book crystallized many of the concepts that underpin NextStage technology, and I feel like I am better able to articulate its promise. As I read, a foundation was built – barely perceptible – it wasn't just a string of "aha moments"; it was more like pieces falling into place and gaps being filled. Clearly if you've ever wondered what the technology is all about or how it came to be, this book is for you. However, it's perfectly obvious that this book is a must-read for anybody who has heard Joseph speak about the NextStage technology over the years. What is less obvious, perhaps, is that this is not a book only for web analysts or other web technologists. I believe this book will appeal also to anyone fascinated by human behavior, invention, science, and technology. If you happen to be a web analyst who also happens to be fascinated by those things, congratulations: you have found your ideal weekend reading. I very much look forward to the next volume.

Stephane Hamel
Creator of WASP, WAMM and OAMM, Immeria Consulting Services inc.

Just a quick note to let you know I've read your book! Some areas I especially liked, those where you explain why we react the way we do, and where you explain why it can be measured...Thrilling, chilling, amazing...the writing is excellent...

Gaby Flatt
CEO, One Eyed Blind Dog, LLC

Fascinating and frightening, but real magic!

What started as an exploration into how I might provide a better user experience to website visitors quickly turned into a journey of self exploration. Joseph Carrabis is able to explain complex subjects in simple and easy to understand text. This book solidified so many connections for me that on more than one occasion I thought to myself "WOW, so that's why people do that!"

As you get to the end of the book it becomes clear that ET in the wrong hands could be a bad thing. Yet, it's exciting to think of all the positive and good uses for this sophisticated technology. The book really sparked my imagination and I can't wait for volume II!

Claudiu Murariu
Founder, InnerTrends[d]

From Claudiu Murariu's Padicode Blog: Reading Virtual Minds – mind blowing book review

Online behavior is not offline behavior done online. This is what Joseph Carrabis explains with a scientific rigour in his book: Reading Virtual Minds, Volume I. He takes the reader through a journey from the basics of human behavior and communication to how do users interact with the online world. Once the scientific basis is understood he takes the reader through a set of experiments and case studies on how online behavioral targeting can be used for increasing performance

---

[d] – http://nlb.pub/M

What I loved the most about the book is that it comes with a scientific approach towards web analytics and behavioral targeting. On one side, Joseph has a strong background in sociology, anthropology, psychology and many other interconnected sciences. On the other side he loves the web. It was just a matter of time before putting them together (around 15 years of research, actually). The Internet is a very complex communication medium. He really treats it as such.

The book is mind blowing. At every page you find yourself saying out loud "Ohh Common, that can't be real!" just that at the next page everything is explained and becomes common sense. Imagine this: the behavioral targeting software he built manages to identify if a user who logs in to his account really is him or is it somebody else having access to his login credentials based only by the way the user interacted with the website. What about managing to identify the field of interest of the visitors just by the way they browsing through a website. Mind blowing, I tell you.

While many web analytics and behavioral targeting books out there are rather about cookies, numbers and statistics, for Joseph everything is about people. That's why this book was so different than anything I have read so far.

Another thing that strikes about the book are the reviews that come from people like Jim Sterne, Anil Batra, Bryan Eisenberg, Robbin Steif and Angie Brown. These guys are worldwide top notch when it comes to web communication and analytics.

How come the book is not in top 10 web marketing best sellers on Amazon, you might ask. I really have no idea as it really should be there. The only explanation I can find is that the book is some sort of the "Ace in the sleeve" for many top marketers. It's part of their secret of why they are so good at what they do. I don't like cheating in poker (unless I am the only one doing it :)) so I highly recommend this book to everybody. It will put some science facts in your work.

Clarissa Sawyer
Consultant I Coach I Bentley University Adjunct Faculty

Clear and Enlightening!

I read this as someone who is a novice user of social media. Ok, I have a web-site, and use LinkedIn and Facebook, and just began writing for a blog that Joseph writes for, too. But I still say I'm a novice. Why? My simple web-site went up 15 months ago, I started using LinkedIn 12 months ago, and 9 months ago I became a some-time user of FaceBook with a few close family and friends. Until I met Joseph and heard him give a presentation on social media, even though I used these tools, I really didn't understand their power to connect people to each other (and here's the good part) to me. Intrigued, I decided to buy his book and read it. I was surprised, unnerved actually, to learn how much can be inferred about me from my on-line presence using text choices, images, language, even interaction patterns (such as where I point and click on the screen and for how long). Having a background in psychology and organizational behavior, I was familiar with the idea that humans are interpreters and creators of symbolic communication. My effectiveness as a consultant, researcher, and teacher, depends on me being able to be a good reader of people. What I didn't realize until I read this book was how well my mind could be read "virtually." An excellent, easy to read, and fascinating introduction to this topic by a noted expert.

Todd A. Sullivan
Managing Partner at Hayes Soloway PC

Pardon my bias

As a friend and counsel for Joseph, I'd have given him 5 stars for selling an alphabetical listing of his personal library, so understand I have a bias here.

Through the teachings in his book and other publications, Joseph has taught me to better appreciate the hidden messages communicated by others in their body language, word choice, and emphasis. And he has taught me to better understand the messages I am communicating. And it is that unintentional communication that is always the most honest. If you want to better understand what people are communicating, if you need to have your message heard, I'd encourage you to read Joseph's work.

Adam Laughlin
Senior Software Engineer at Attend.com

Reading Virtual Minds - A world-changing blend of 120 disciplines

Think of every science fiction movie and television show you've ever seen. Remember every scene where any physical object, from a robot to a chair, interacts with an individual according to their size, preferences, mood, etc.

Evolution Technology ("ET" for short), is the technology behind Reading Virtual Minds. The scenes you're remembering? ET makes them possible. All of them.

To sum up the book, "The human brain is wired in a specific way and is bound by the rules of that wiring. Anything which can't be attributed to direct cause and effect of that wiring must be unique to the individual using the computer [or any object]."

Age is unique.
Gender is unique.
Emotional engagement is unique.
Excitement is unique.
Frustration is unique.
Confusion is unique.

The threshold required to reach any of those emotional states is unique for each individual, and that barely scratches the surface. The list seems to be limited by the number of times someone asks "Can ET _____?".

The answer? Yes. It can. Further, Evolution technology is small, fast, and works with any human/object interface.

Re-stated so you don't miss that. It applies to -any human/object interface-.

- Education: Imagine being able to know the learning potential of any student in the classroom, and the moment any get confused.
- Education2: PCs (or iPads): Imagine eBooks that tailor themselves to the way your brain learns, so you can instantly recall what you read six months earlier.
- Human Resources/Management: Imagine live measurements of every departments' staff satisfaction level.
- Marketing: Imagine knowing which pages of your website bored your visitors before they decided to leave.
- Business: Imagine an alarm clock that reminds you of what you're doing every time you get distracted.
- Medical/Behavioral: Imagine diagnosing neurological & psychological disorders over the web.
- Automotive: Imagine your car recognizing you by touch, and your seats adjusting without controls until they sense you're comfortable.

Evolution Technology isn't just a dream. It's here. Today. Working. Many of my colleagues and I have used it and been amazed (and sometimes humbled) by the insights it provides. New ET-based tools seem to pop up in the NextStage Knowledgeshop[e] every month - presents for the endlessly curious.

Like a cloud, ET has the potential to bring peaceful and refreshing mist, and it has the potential to bring oak-shattering lightning. NextStage tools' license agreements retain the right to refuse anyone in order to prevent harmful outcomes. Regardless of how it's used, however, Evolution Technology exists, and its existence will change your world.

As I said, I'm barely scratching the surface. Reading Virtual Minds, dimmed by its marketing-esque cover, heralds an age where our environment, our books, our possessions, understand what we need before we can ask for them. It also heralds an age of prejudices that have never before been possible. You owe it to yourself and those you care about to read it and explain it. I personally bought ten copies for family and friends.

Dr. Richard Lent
Author, Meeting for Results Tool Kit: Make Your Meetings Work and Leading Great Meetings: How to Structure Yours for Success, and Partner, Meeting for Results

Reading Joseph's Mind

I have been learning from Joseph in various ways for several years - sometimes in person, often through his writing. We have worked together on various projects together. His humor, stories and patience have been great aids to me as a novice in navigating social media in various forms. That humor, the story telling, insight and patience all come through in this book. It is

---

[e] – Everything that was in the NextStage KnowledgeShop is now available to NextStage Members. See http://nlb.pub/4

not a "how-to," but rather an engaging introduction to his very original way of thinking about how individuals reveal themselves through their behaviors. My only critique is that at times I wish he had written a longer book: Some short paragraph would cause me to think about something in a new way and I wanted to explore what he meant and what I thought about it. Fortunately, he cross references his many writings elsewhere and promises a second volume. Through this book, I'm still learning from him, and that's the highest recommendation I can give anyone's (nonfiction) book.

(and)

Joseph is one of the best teachers I know ... particularly in his fields. Spending time with him through a book or in a class is a learning journey. He shows you things you didn't know you could know-about yourself and others, in your real and virtual lives. He's a true polymath bringing together many disciplines in new ways through his observations and the tools he creates to "see" others and ourselves in the on-line world. I recommend this book highly, but warn you that it is worth more than one reading!

**Chett Rubenstein
Founder & CTO at insightXM LLC on Amazon.com 30 Sep 2014**

Great neuroscience primer

Great read by the brilliant and ever irreverent Joseph Carrabis.

CJD[f]

Not Very Informative

While this book shows a history of one guy's exploration into a certain kind of AI, and his opinions about doing business with folks interested in his technology, the book doesn't actually SAY anything...If you actually want to learn about how to do user segmentation or human behavior, this book isn't for you. He says things like "We learned a lot", but doesn't actually say what he learned. He learned that his software is a decent predictor, but doesn't explain anything about how it works.

---

[f] – Some readers questioned why I included this review. Simply for completeness sake: It was one of the reviews and I believe one can not accept the positive unless one is willing to accept the negative. Besides, this review may be helpful for someone who's looking for another kind of book.

Reading Virtual Minds
Volume II: Experience and Expectation

Joseph Carrabis
Chief Research Officer & Founder
The NextStage Companies

First Edition Publication Dec 2015
Northern Lights Publishing
Nashua, NH, USA

Book cover, back cover photo and all logos by John Scullin –
http://www.skolenimation.com.

Reading Virtual Minds Volume II: Experience and Expectation
1st Edition
all material copyright © 1999-2015 Joseph Carrabis.
All rights reserved.

Sections of this book were previously published on
The Hungry Peasant, http://www.hungrypeasant.com

ISBN: 978-0-9841403-5-0

When was the last time you experienced something for the first time?

Dedication

For Susan
ever patient, ever watchful, ever caring.

I can live in a universe with only her
but not in a universe without her.

Second to AJ
(because he was AJ)

Acknowledgements

Many people took part in the work on this book. Special thanks go to:

Jennifer Day
Dolores Fallon
Holly Buchanan

To those who put up with questions and research,
To those who listened and debated,

And especially to those who got me out from behind the keyboard,

Boo and Ghost,

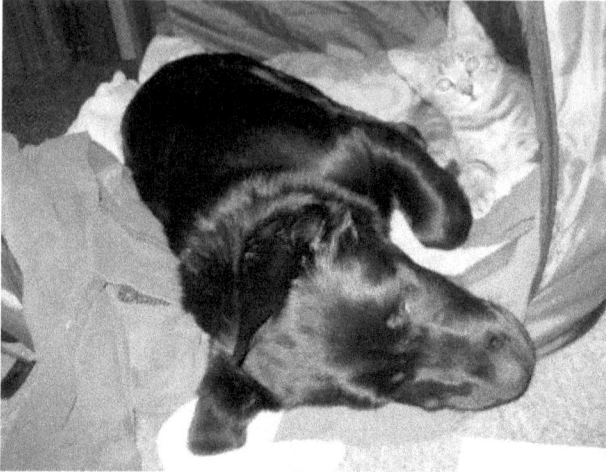

Thanks to you all.

To appreciate what has happened, you will have to abandon cherished notions and open your mind.
— Matt Ridley, Nature vs Nurture

Table of Contents

TakeAways

Digital Resources for the Reading Virtual Minds *Series*

Some of the images in the *Reading Virtual Minds* series print editions are dark and difficult to read due to grayscaling and sizing issues. You can find high resolution, full color images of most charts and graphs used in this series at http://nlb.pub/rvm

Evolution Technology™ (ET), the technology described in this book and the external demonstration of much described in this series, is the foundation of several tools used for a variety of purposes by people ranging from lovers to politicians to businesspeople to researchers and more. You can watch a video explaining and using many of the tools developed from ET at http://nlb.pub/3

Please note that case matters ("A" isn't the same as "a") with all nlb.pub urls.

Scientific findings typically come in two flavours: explanations for things we already knew occurred but had no idea why, or new phenomena that are clearly important but still mysterious.

— Yael Niv

About the Cover

Are you like the majority of people on this planet?

Here's a quick test to find out.

When you picked up this book (assuming you picked it up at some point) and after you looked at the front cover, did you turn the binding towards you or did you turn the open pages towards you? Did you go to the back cover first or did you browse the pages first?

In a world where "short attention span" is synonymous with "digital consumer" and attention spans have gone from hours to minutes to six seconds or less (and Vine[a] is making money on this very aspect of online attention), it's more about creating distractions that pull your audience towards you and avoiding distractions that push them away, about distracting them from what they're already doing and not letting anything else distract them from what you want them to do.[396,441,479,564,590,611]

Distractions and attractions. Create the right kind of distraction and you grab and keep your audience's attention. People are finding it increasingly difficult to focus on anything in our information-rich world so their minds and eyes are going to wander. Prevent that wandering for as long as possible and you're walking the razor's edge of attraction/distraction. You can only walk that razor's edge safely by knowing what kind of experiences your audience has had and what your audience expects.

This book's front cover, being white with gray text and black & white imagery that's almost milky in contrast, is free of distractions. Nothing fights for your attention. This book's back cover is more of the same.

But then there's that kitten picture on the bottom of the back cover. Cat pictures and videos are a big deal on the Internet right now. Websites like Toocute, all the Dailycute variations and Twitter accounts are there to distract you with a variety of kitten, puppy and similar images and videos. Perhaps you subscribe to

---

[a] – "Vine is a short-form video sharing service where users can share six-second-long looping video clips." - https://en.wikipedia.org/wiki/Vine_(service)

these sites and accounts or know someone who does or have had someone send you links to them. Maybe your Facebook feed is filled with them. Researchers actively study the online kitty effect[411] and crowdsource their funding:

> Soon, fans of the Internet-famous Lil Bub may get the chance to know what scientifically makes this kitty so darn cute. Thanks to a recent crowdfunding campaign conducted by scientists Daniel M. Ibrahim, Darío G. Lupiáñez and Uschi Symmons, the team plans on sequencing Lil Bub's genome in hopes to reveal the genetic reasons behind Bub's adorable features. The main interest for the study lies in Bub's extra digit on all four paws – a mutation scientifically referred to as polydactyly--however, the test could also bring to light further genetic explanation for Bub's unique short snout and small teeth. Since the campaign has recently reached its goal, Bub's blood will soon be shipped to the Max Planck Institute for Molecular Genetics in Berlin. We'll finally know if beauty, and cuteness, are more than just fur deep![b]

Have you ever wondered why you pay attention...to anything? To give these things your attention means you stop giving something else your attention, meaning you're allowing yourself to be distracted from whatever you're doing.

But the only way your brain and mind will allow you to be distracted for any recognizable period of time is if it determines the distraction will 1) provide a greater reward than what you're being distracted from doing and b) that any immediate and long-term deficit is acceptable. You non-consciously yet willingly shift your attention because you non-consciously believe the reward of the distraction is greater than the reward of the task at hand. Note this: it's not reward and cost, it's relative rewards. How do you do this? What mechanism are you using to measure these rewards?

First you non-consciously calculate that the cost in neural resources and time is a *fair-exchange*[c] for the semiotic

---

[b] – http://on.mash.to/1Klb6VK
[c] – covered in *Reading Virtual Minds Volume III: Fair-Exchange and Social Networks.*

information content payoff of the distraction. Next you determine the distraction's *concept price* (ditto), i.e., the psycho-emotional, -social and -behavioral load the distraction will place on you.

It's amazing what your brain knows how to do without you knowing what it's doing, isn't it?[d]

I wrote about environmental distractions in *Reading Virtual Minds Volume I: Science and History*'s[e] *About the Cover* section and provided Figure AC.1 (page 31) as a visual example.

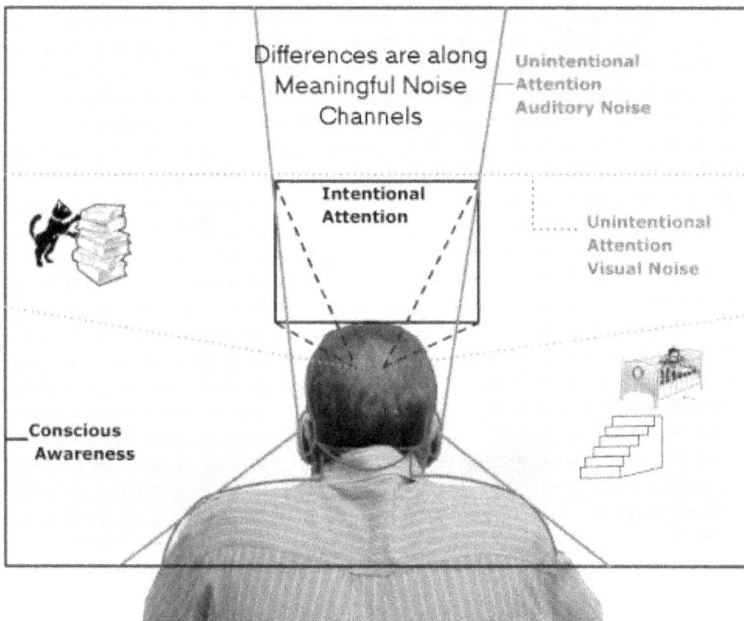

AC.1 – The neural effort required to focus our attention on any one information source is proportional to the amount and intensity of all information sources in our immediate internal and external environments.

This book deals with environmental and digital distractions, and specifically how our experience of these

---

[d] – The reward I mentioned is not having to pay attention. The picture is of a little kitty. Your mind and brain can relax and that relaxation is at a premium in an information-rich, digitally divisive world. The kitty gives us a chance to "not know".
[e] – http://nlb.pub/RVMV14th

distractions affect our expectations in general and more directly in the digital, online world. Both NextStage's and others' research demonstrate that people behave quite differently and have very different expectations when intentional attention is focused on a mobile interface than when it's focused on other information sources, for example.[25,28,57,173,277,407,446,505]

Back to the test; which way did you turn the book the first time (assuming you'd never had any experience of it prior to holding it in your hands)? There is no right or wrong answer, there rarely is in such things.

But this book's cover proves a point and to learn what that point is, you'll have to read the book.

AC.2 – More powerful than a curiously colored dress,
faster than a cat walking either up or down stairs,
able to be intelligent, compassionate and accessible or intelligent,
distant and disturbing simply by adding or removing a cat, ...

Most people who pick up the book and flip it over to see the back cover (versus scanning internal pages) are going to focus on the kitten picture, smile and ignore all back cover written content at first. NextStage's graphic artist could have placed any text on there and most people wouldn't have noticed because most people will look at the kitten picture before doing anything else. If our graphic artist and I have done our jobs correctly then the cover of the book already proves the book's point. In fact, we showed a test audience the cover mockup and they responded as we calculated; they all had a positive experience of the back cover content because of the kitten. Here's another tickler for you; there were several author images available, the test audience chose the one we're using (Figure AC.2, page 32 and, of course, the back cover) because (the test audience offered that) I looked intelligent, compassionate and accessible.

But when the kitten picture was removed? Then, I looked intelligent, distant and disturbing. One person wrote "I think he's looking at me evaluating me, that he doesn't like me." NextStage's and others' facial cognition studies reinforce this image-content dichotomy greatly.[3,5,7,9,10,32,46,49,60,63,174,187, 192,193,195,199,205-210,235,238,241,246,264,285,298,307,313,314,318,325-327,335,343,348,365,388,427,429,443,447,457,461,480,547,552,560,568,571,572,581,589, 591,608]

What doesn't change is that experience and expectation are governed by a multitude of factors and the number of factors grows exponentially as we age. Our experiences – the nurture part of the nature-nurture question – are so powerful that they influence regulatory genes that influence neural pathways that are tied to long-term memory.[268] People who've lived lives at the extremes – and this includes anyone who's had experiences outside the norm such as combat, dramatic religious conversion, trauma, near-death, terrorism, profound loss, profound love, long-term abuse – have much richer memories than those without such experiences. Sometimes this is good, sometimes not.

But only if you're willing to take your eyes off the cat.

Foreword

by Holly Buchanan
CEO, Buchanan Marketing, LLC
Author, *Selling Financial Services To Women*
Co-Author, *The Soccer Mom Myth - Today's Female Consumer: Who She Really Is, Why She Really Buys*

After inhaling *Reading Virtual Minds Volume I* I was like an antsy 3-year old waiting for *Reading Virtual Minds Volume II*. It did not disappoint.

I love the way Joseph Carrabis thinks. He has a unique ability to share broad rich theory with actionable specifics. Unlike many technical writers, he has a unique voice that is both approachable and humorous. It makes for an enjoyable read.

But what's the main reason why you should read *Reading Virtual Minds Volume II: Experiences and Expectations*? Because where most companies and designers fail is on the expectation front.

Humans are designed as expectation engines.

This is, perhaps, the most important sentence in this book. One of the main points Joseph makes in this volume is this – Understand your audiences' *whys* and you'll design near perfect *whats*.

Design failures come from getting the *whys* wrong. That can lead to failures on the experience side, but also on the expectation side. And that can be the bigger problem.

> Expectation is a top-down process. Higher-level information informs lower-level processing. Experience is a bottom-up process. Sensory information goes into higher-level processing for evaluation. Humans are designed as expectation engines. Topdown connections out number bottom-up connections by about 10:1.

Why is this so important?

> In language, more than anywhere else, we see or hear what we expect to hear, not necessarily what is said or written. Across all cultures and languages, neurophysiologists and psychologists estimate that what we experience is as much as 85% what we expect to experience, not necessarily what is real or 'environmentally available'.

And

> When people expect A and get B they go through a few moments of fugue. External reality is not synching up with internal reality and the mind and brain will, if allowed, burn themselves out making the two mesh.

Get your consumer/visitor/user experience AND expectation right, get their *why* right, and you'll be exponentially more successful.

Here are just a few of the goodies you'll find in this book:

> Privacy vs. value exchange and when to ask for what information. Joseph has some actionable specifics on this that will surprise you.
>
> Why we design for false attractors rather than the real problem.
>
> The importance of understanding convincer strategies. Convincer strategies are the internal processes people go through in order to convince themselves they should or should not do something.
>
> Companies spend a lot of time trying to convince consumers to trust them. But what may be even more important is understanding how to let consumers you know you trust *them*. This book has ideas on how to show your customers/users/visitors, *"I believe in you"*.

How often our own experience influence our designs. Unless you're able to throw all your experience out, and let the user's experience in, get out of the usability and design business.

How to allow your visitors easy Anonymous-Expressive Identity and make them yours forever.

Regarding new material, design, interface, the importance of making sure your suggestions provide a clear path to the past (thus being risk averse while providing marketable innovation).

As always, *Reading Virtual Minds* provides specific actionable ideas. But it will also make you think and approach your work in a new way. And I think that's the best reason to treat yourself to this book and the inner workings of NextStage and Joseph Carrabis.

Chance favors the prepared mind.
— Louis Pasteur

Author's Foreword

Hello.

It's me again, Joseph, the author.

Did you enjoy *Reading Virtual Minds Volume I: Science and History*[a]? You really shouldn't be reading this book unless you've read Volume 1. Or at least have Volume 1 handy. It provides the background and foundation for what is presented here and in the rest of the *Reading Virtual Minds* series.

For example, *memetic signatures*[20,37,72,155,162,222,265,370,376,412] were introduced in Chapter II "History". More detail (again without naming them as such) was given in Chapter IV "Anecdotes of Learning". They were described when I wrote about {C,B/e,M}s, the neuromathematical matrices of *C*ognitive, *B*ehavioral/*e*ffective, *M*otivational values that explain why we do the things we do the way we do them when we do them, why we do them one way here and another way there, [55,58,79,81,86, 90,92,100,102,118,121,122,132,136,139,140,142-146,148,150,157,158,160,161, 164,203,225,243,282,344,383,426,432,440,448,471,544] and how they are like fingerprints or signatures of thought.

{C,B/e,M}s are the basis for NextStage's Rich Personae™[91, 96,101,102,114,118-121,128,131,136,137,155,157,158,433,434] codification system[b] (think "audience classification" or "segmentation", and I'll mostly use "Rich Personae™" interchangeably from here on out) and this is where we run into the reasons Volume 1 came first (aside from numeracy).

Memetic signatures are to the emotional-spiritual-psychological being what fingerprints and DNA are to the physical being, with a difference. You can replicate fingerprints (any biomarkers, really) and you can replicate DNA (cloning, for example) and it would be exponentially difficult to replicate a full memetic signature (you'd currently[c] need to solve an 80^{80}

---

[a] – You can get copies at http://nlb.pub/RVMV14th
[b] – Rich Personae™ are behind many of our tools (NextStage members have full use of most of our tools. Some tools require training, some no training, some advanced training). All member benefits can be found at http://nlb.pub/4
[c] – as of 04 Jan 2015, anyway.

hyperdimensional matrix and there's not a lot of mathematics designed to support such things).

Just as lots of people have *similar* but not *identical* DNA, lots of people will have similar but not identical Rich Personae™. Most people have the same DNA for commonly shared physical attributes (five fingers, for example). Include the DNA for five fingers and masculinization and sexual orientation,[364,367,387] or for five fingers and certain types of disease[317] or five fingers and various ethnic markers[364,387] or five fingers and spatial abilities[458] or five fingers and exceptional athletic ability[198] and you're effectively culling the human herd along increasingly specific DNA markers. The same is true for increasingly specific Rich Personae™ markers. Someone may be highly visual, for example, but are they strongly attracted to visual stimuli or repelled by visual stimuli, and does the type of visual stimuli matter?[54,205,237,242,243,250,332,360,368,375,398,529,609] Such questions may seem trivial or obsessive, and in today's information-rich world if you want to drive someone's eyes to what you want them to do such questions are paramount.

NextStage and its clients use increasingly specific Rich Personae™ in applications from marketing to security to identity development and recognition tools and more. Marketing material can be designed so that everyone with a given Rich Personae™ of (for example) two factors ("everyone within a given audience") will respond the same way. Know ahead of time how some percentage of a given population is going to respond to your creative content and suddenly manufacturing, marketing, logistics, product distribution, supply chain, etc., are so much easier to deal with. You can select who will respond and when with surgical accuracy. NextStage's Evolution Technology™ (ET) borrows heavily from immunology, virology and related studies and is designed to immunize entire populations towards what you want them to do and away from what you don't want them to do.[d]

---

[d] – Computer- and neuro-scientists would recognize ET as a *parallel-distributed system*, or "PDPs", that works using Sternbergian models, meaning it determines the steps individuals need to go through to solve a problem, not just whether or not they could solve the problem.[258,531-540] Its original purpose was in education and it serves that purpose quite well. It turns out this methodology serves many other needs quite well, too.

Rich Personae™ with sufficient granularity are indistinguishable from {C,B/e,M} matrices and {C,B/e,M} matrices with sufficient granularity become memetic signatures. This means you can "immunize" large populations at some yield and smaller populations at a higher yield and even smaller populations at even higher yields...it all depends on what you want them to do, when, where you want them to do it, how you want them to do it and what you want them to think regarding why they're doing it.

Reading Virtual Minds Volume I: Science and History demonstrated this increasing granularity with the image shown here as Figure AF.1 on page 40.

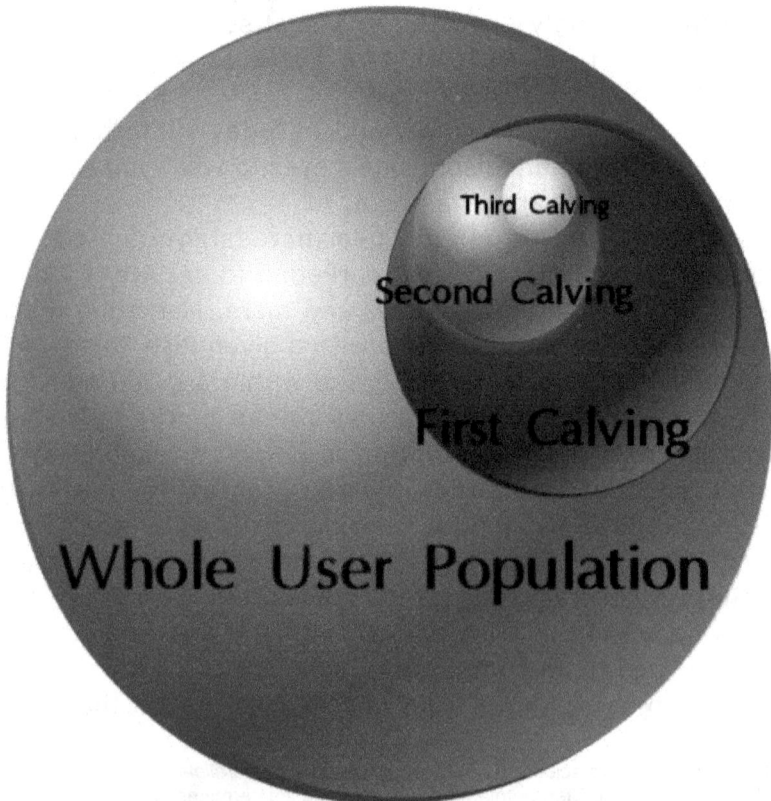

Figure AF.1 - Culling the herd from Reading Virtual Minds Volume 1: Science and History, Section III.2, "Summing the Parts"

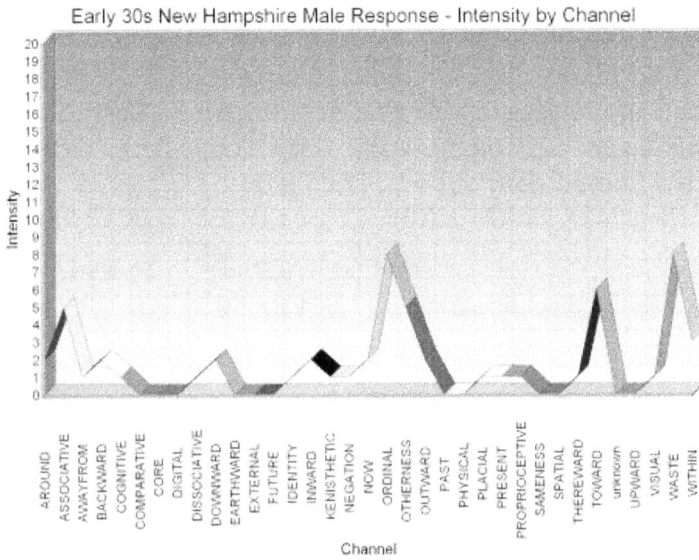

Figure AF.2 - The Mid 40s SC Male Response

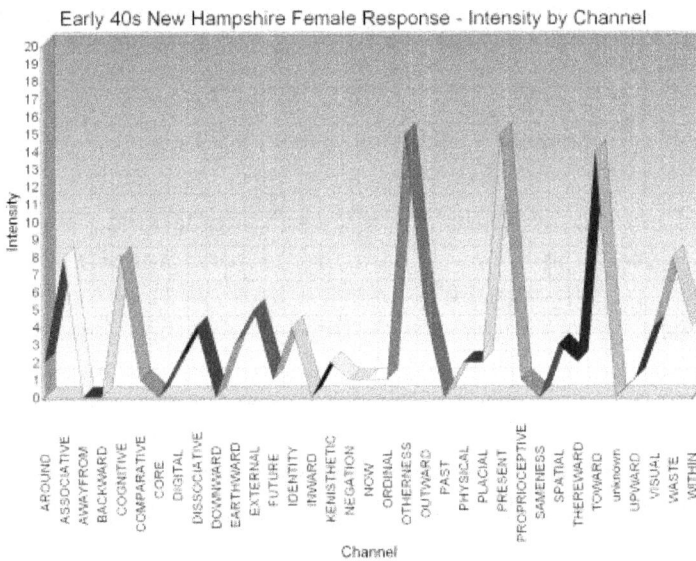

Figure AF.3 - The Early 40s NH Female Response

Unique memetic signatures were demonstrated in *Reading Virtual Minds Volume I, Section IV.5, "Mark Broth Discovers What Makes a Lawyer a Lawyer"* and shown here in Figures AF.2 through AF.4 on pages 41-42. Figures AF.2-AF.4 show the different responses a South Carolina mid-40s male, a New Hampshire mid-40s female and a New Hampshire mid-30s male had to the same information (a print ad).

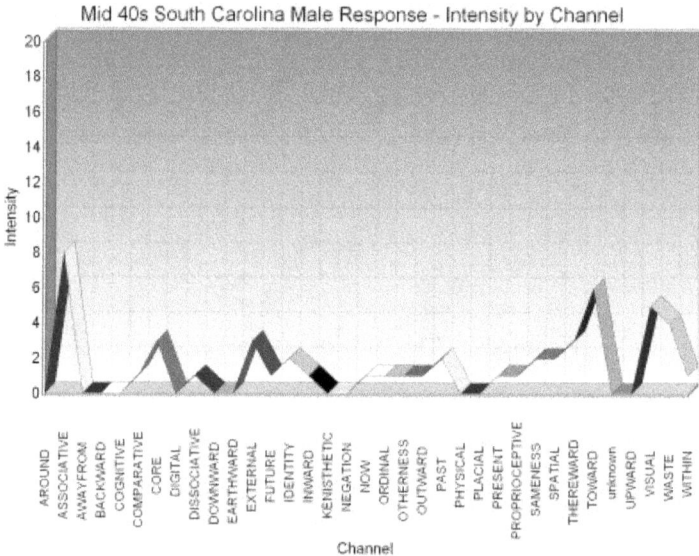

Figure AF.4 - The Early 30s NH Male Response

This book deals with how different populations ("audiences") respond to certain types of information. Specifically, what different populations experience and what they expect to experience. Psycholinguistically, this is "what has happened" and "what is happening" – both recognized as *experience* – and "what will happen" – recognizable as *expectation*. Humans keep themselves sane by learning to predict what will happen with a fairly high degree of accuracy (within a given culture. Transplant them to a completely foreign culture and they'll get frustrated without social tools or psychosocial training to cope). This is why people who live in terrorist environments tend to be depressed and have little hope for the future; they can't predict what will happen with any level of accuracy other than "we're not sure what will happen when", not good if you're planning a life for yourself and your family.

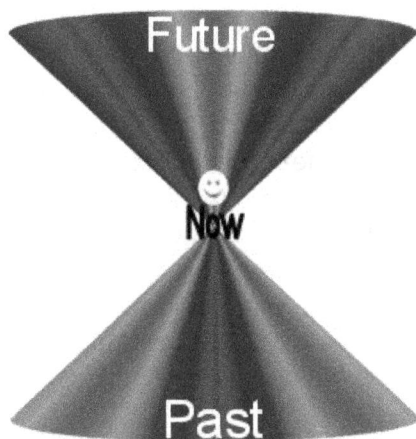

Figure AF.5 - The Traditional Minkowski's Cones

Most people with Western educations non-consciously consider time as a kind of line or funnel that goes from their past through their present, thus making their near future a predictable point on that line (or the vertex of a funnel) and leaving their far future open to conjecture. Western societies have fostered that belief since the onset of the industrial revolution and Hermann Minkowski diagrammed it as shown in Figure AF.5 (page 43, traditionally called "Minkowski's Cones"). In Minkowski's Cones, the Past is everything that's ever happened to the observer (the lower cone underneath the vertex), the Future is everything that ever will happen to the observer (the portion of the upper cone above the smiley face), Now is the vertex where Future becomes

Past and whatever's outside of the cones simply doesn't exist for the observer. It may exist in the multiverse but this individual observer will never know of it.

Sound like some of your best marketing efforts, that "...will never know of it" part? Then congrats, you're reading the correct book to find out why.

What Minkowski realized was that the point where Future flows into Past isn't "Now", it's slightly behind or below "Now" in the observer's frame of reference because the observer's past can only become the Past once it's left the observer's Now. Our Future becomes our Past only after we've experienced it in the Now. What Minkowski further conjectured was that the observer (us) actually exists slightly ahead or in front of Now because it takes our brains and minds a few moments of time to recognize, internalize, understand and respond to what's going on. In other words, we react to events that are already in our Past and our responses are only in the Now for less time than it took the Big Bang to occur. Brings a whole new meaning to "We are stardust, we are golden, we are billion year old carbon, ..."[e], doesn't it?

Figure AF.6 - Minkowski's Cones for the Digital Age

But Minkowski created those cones before the digital age was even considered. The closest realization to what we now recognize as the Internet was probably in the film *Until the End of the World*[f]. Now and thanks to the Internet's ability to provide everyone with all the information that exists instantaneously (barring drops and buffering issues), Minkowski's Cones are squished ever flatter as shown in Figure AF.6 (page 44). Our pasts are documented on social networks for all the world to see whenever the world wants to see them. Our futures are decided and redecided continuously and surreptitiously based on what our social networks deem important or worthy. Our pasts and our

---

[e] – Joni Mitchell, *Woodstock*, 1969
[f] – http://en.wikipedia.org/wiki/Until_the_End_of_the_World

futures are so intruding on our nows that we don't even have time to respond to events as they occur before responding to the next event, resulting in chronic fatigue and confusion because our brains, continually firing PPSETS against MMNs (see page 92), are continually exhausted. We are becoming increasingly exafferent – passive observers – to our own lives because we have no time to react or consider our reaction. Our nows don't have any time to exist, for us to be in the experience of them, in the moment, and our pasts and futures are flattened by information's accessibility. And even if we do respond, we no longer have the social training to know how. We're more apt to ignore an event or "change the channel" than be reafferent (interact with). We have become like Peter Sellers' Chance the Gardener character in *Being There*[g], only knowing what comes to us through our digital device. How many people have you seen walking down city streets with their earphones or bluetooths in, their thumbs going wild because it's more important to communicate with someone in their virtual environment than to be aware of their immediate environment? Consider this Facebook exchange from mid-July 2011 and written by noted social media guru Paul Gillin:

> Last night I walked right by Shel Holtz, a social media expert whose work I greatly admire, and didn't even notice till he was a hundred yards away. The reason: My nose was buried in my smart phone.

My response?

> Paul wrote "Last night I walked right by Shel Holtz...My nose was buried in my smart phone." An example of too social to be social. May I suggest "Reading Virtual Minds V1" by yours truly, specifically the sections on how humans create community with whatever's in front of them and to the exclusion of all else?

---

[g] – http://en.wikipedia.org/wiki/Being_there

Humans are also losing their abilities to remember, plan and more.

> If you're noticing that you remember less and less about past events, you're not the only one. Studies have found that technology is having a negative impact on our memories. Since we know that technology will always have our backs, whether it's a search engine query or photos we uploaded to social media, we don't commit as much to memory and in turn, our listening skills and abilities to work productively are being affected. To combat this, take the time to disconnect. If you're in an important meeting, turn off your phone, and don't bring your laptop. This will keep distractions to a minimum so you can focus on remembering the central aspects of the meeting at hand.[h]

The tendency to categorize our sensory environment is the rule,[295] and if more and more of our reality is digitally based we may be sowing the seeds of our own extinction (see the discussion of Florida being west of Ohio, page 65). The pushback to this is prevalent enough that it's made its way into mainstream media. The movie *While We're Young* has two couples from two different generations meeting and sharing, and it's the younger couple not wanting to use the 'net and stay offline. The phrase used is "We don't need to know. Let's just not know it. Let's not know what it is" and demonstrates a willingness to be satisfied with a lack of knowledge. This is a call to the mythic, to mystery, and away from digital, sensory reality. More myth, less fact. Still wanting to be involved, but in a way that is more satisfying to their Core than to their Personality.

A second pushback also comes from the younger audience, although this time younger still; the younger generation is making a return to *owning* things, especially what has recently been labeled "cloud-based content". Youth want to own their own content rather than leaving it in the cloud or fog because losing the signal and buffering is not a satisfactory experience[i].

---

[h] – http://bit.ly/1J8Wl4s
[i] – another bow to *Reading Virtual Minds Volume III: Fair-Exchange and Social Networks*.

> Photograph technology has come a very, very long way
> since the first camera. Pictures had to be taken in just the
> right amount of light and the less light there was, the longer
> you had to sit and wait. These days we're all about DSLRs,
> Photoshop, and filters. (Speaking of, have you seen the
> new Instagram color highlight tool? Way cool.)
> Photographer Victoria Will is bringing the old tech back,
> however. Check out these photos she took at the 2015
> Sundance Film Festival using a vintage tintype camera.
> Stars attending the festival lined up to have their picture
> taken and we have to say we prefer this to the overly edited
> look we're so accustomed to today.[j]

And if you're a good behavioral ethologist, you know the above statement is flawed. Whatever's happening on the digital device *is* the individual's immediate environment, whatever's happening on the street, to the person beside them, is outside of Minkowski's Cones regardless if they're conic or planar as far as this person walking down the street is concerned. Makes one wonder if the Darwin Award should be given to the individual who walks into traffic or fountains or to the people who created the technology that allows such things to occur.

Two things fall from all this. One is a sense of *digital entitlement*; seeing it happen digitally or learning of it as it happens or before anybody else knows it happens is better than being there first-person when it does happen. The immediacy of real-time experience is subsumed by the repeatability of virtual experience, as noted in the Huffington Post's article on a man so busy on his mobile that he missed the whale surfacing in front of him (and as shown in Figure AF.7, page 48).[k] I had a socio-culturally similar experience when I got into a discussion of the value of family photograph albums. A fellow in his mid-20s saw no need for them. All the images could be digitized and stored on his mobile for easy access. Less space and less maintenance. My argument was along the lines of "...but just think of holding in your hands what your family held in theirs, of remembering being

---

[j] – http://nlb.pub/R
[k] – http://www.huffingtonpost.com/2015/02/05/phone-humpback-whale_n_6619166.html

in your grandmother's lap when she told you of coming to America and the pictures she took along the way...", a nod to Faith Popcorn's "We are hungry for things that have touched human hands."

Figure AF.7 - A man so busy on his mobile that he misses seeing a whale a few feet away. Let's hope he's not working for NASA monitoring when an ELE comes around.

The response? "How long did it take your grandmother to fly over?" This could be a generational response and I think not.

The first-hand experience is no longer valued as necessary for complete understanding. Stephen Colbert was quite correct when he said "It used to be, everyone was entitled to their own opinion, but not their own facts. But that's not the case anymore. Facts matter not at all. Perception is everything. It's certainty that counts."[1] It gets worse when the non-conscious is considered.

---

[1] – http://en.wikipedia.org/wiki/Truthiness

That sense of digital entitlement leads to *unintentional recklessness*[374,439] as evidenced by the increasing need for DWD (Driving While Distracted) laws.[m]

The other fall from this causes cultural anthropologists and ethnographers to grow anxious. Historically, those who had instantaneous access to information, who basically could know all there was to know, were considered gods.

How do you design when your audience has the experience of gods? How do you manage expectations when the gods have been taught to expect everything instantaneously?

And a final note before leaving the *Reading Virtual Minds Author's Foreword*: I still use personal examples and anecdotes (as noted in *Reading Virtual Minds Volume I*). Some readers were challenged by that. *Reading Virtual Minds Volume I* readers who've gotten this far, welcome. You're on the road to understanding why using personal examples and anecdotes is important and how that understanding can empower your personal and design experiences greatly.

---

[m] – Most people can't multitask regardless of what they believe. However, the belief that they can perform multiple operations simultaneously leads to performing one task while attending to another task, i.e., unintentional recklessness regarding the task being performed.

The untrained man reads a paper on natural science and thinks; 'Now why couldn't he explain that in simple language?' He can't seem to realize that what he tried to read was the simplest possible language — for that subject matter. In fact, a great deal of natural philosophy is simply a process of linguistic simplification — an effort to invent language in which half a page of equations can express an idea which could not be stated in less than a thousand pages of so-called 'simple' language.

— Walter M. Miller, Jr., A Canticle For Leibowitz

Using this Book

As I write this, people have come to accept the Internet as part of their daily lives. Neither phones, cars, radios nor TV – not even personal computers themselves – insinuated themselves into our everyday existence so quickly or cleanly. Access to the Internet has become such a requirement that schools and libraries have public access terminals, not for people to learn programming or write resumes or do research in local archives but simply to get people in the door because logging onto the 'net is now the draw. Coffee shops, airport terminals, buses and subway systems proudly advertise WiFi, Wireless, and other connection standards[a]. Public school systems assume students will be TXTing during class and logging in to do homework (and I'm talking all grades, K-12[b]). The child without 'net access via mobile, laptop, tablet or some such device is considered disadvantaged in today's learning environment.

It's the rare cellphone that isn't net-enabled, all so that we can get that email, browse a website, send a quick reply, TXT while we drive... .

Has anything been adopted more quickly, become more ubiquitous than the 'net?

Cellphones and all forms of mobiles owe their ubiquity to the 'net. Groups now use mobile connectivity to organize rallies, protests, terrorist attacks, ...[97,108,130,270] Both Flashmobs and

---

[a] – Verizon turned Paul Macarelli into a cultural icon via their "Can you hear me now?" campaign and dropped both Macarelli and that campaign in April 2011 after nine years according to Reuters (http://nlb.pub/N). "Can you hear me now?" spawned some wonderful parodies and perhaps the greatest single reason Verizon changed its marketing direction was due to a major shift in public consciousness. The "Can you hear me now?" campaign arrived when "being connected" was considered a necessity and a must have. Now a need to "get off the grid" is de rigueur and being unreachable is the desired state.[89,99,110,133,226,356,382, 413,414,430,541] A pre Jan 2012 automotive commercial has a group of mid-20s males driving further and further away from civilization, routinely holding up their mobiles and reporting, "Not yet". The common wisdom is that they're looking for some kind of connectivity. The commercial ends with one of the cast proudly displaying that they've finally reached a place where there is no signal, hence they can do what they want uninterrupted. What? There's no off-button on that mobile?

[b] – and even more so school districts that have adopted Google Classroom™ as their standard. I have to wonder if such underbudgeted school districts are familiar with Andrew Lewis' "If you're not paying for it, you're not the customer. You're the product being sold."

Community Response Grids[108,125,130] rely on them. Data transmission volume eclipsed voice transmission volume for the first time in Dec 2010 and it doesn't look like its going to turn around. Cisco stated that "...global mobile-data traffic reached 2.5 exabytes (2.5 billion gigabytes) per month..." at the end of 2014.[21] Mobiles, more than anything in recent history, demonstrate "The history of technology is the study of placing the most power in the most hands economically."[16,105,134,141,143,149,154, 163,417]

But economical power comes with a price and that price stems from Lord Acton's "Power tends to corrupt, and absolute power corrupts absolutely."[c]

Give human beings power of any kind and they lose social concepts of time. Power is something all human beings crave since they started their infant crawlings because those infant crawlings are the first time we, as humans, began exerting our independence from our primary gods, Mom and Dad.

Exerting independence is demonstrating power. First we demonstrate power over self – we no longer need to be carried. Chances are we're also doing a rudimentary job of putting food into our mouths and using a toilet. Next we demonstrate power over our environment. This is the period parents often call The Terrible Twos.

Let me tell you, it ain't no fun for children, neither. They are experiencing power over the big, complex world and all they hear is "no, No, NO!" or "come here, Come here Come Here COME HERE COMEHERECOMEHERECOMEHERE!"

Then, after we've done a fair job of exerting power over our environment, we see how well we do exerting power over others. This is fairly easy for the child with much younger siblings, not so much so for single children and all hell for children from dysfunctional families. The child whose parent demonstrates power over his or her family by yelling at them, berating them, emotionally and physically abusing them, take these elements on as their model. They become abusers (the abused become

---

[c] – http://nlb.pub/O

abusers is a well-established phenomenon in psychological literature although there are some notable exceptions[172]) and the literature indicates that abuse whether physical, mental, emotional, spiritual, sexual (and these are just the dominant human-human forms) and so on all come down to different demonstrations of power abuse.[306,512]

Everybody wants power over others, few people can get it and only those with damaged egos publicly admit it.

So what's left? Power over the elemental forces of nature. Military forces have been hunting ways to use weather as a weapon throughout history.[39,385,495,593] The desire for weather as a weapon is in our mythologies as thundergods and gods hurling lightning bolts, from weather witches and wizards to the X-Men™'s Storm.

Modern humans are not terribly far removed from our huddling-in-cave ancestors who were terrified of the lightning and screamed at the dark sounds stalking us in the night. Unchecked and uneducated, human beings become what they fear and we learned early in societal history to fear our gods – the elements. Much of Western science stems from the Judeo-Christian adage "And God said, Let us make man in our image, after our likeness: and let them have dominion over the fish of the sea, and over the fowl of the air, and over the cattle, and over all the Earth, and over every creeping thing that creepeth upon the Earth."[d] There you have it in one sentence; we are close to gods and we should have power over everything.

Do remember that Adam and Eve were kicked out of Eden for wanting knowledge not allowed them (and we hear children worldwide bemoaning the same injustice from their parents, citizens from their governments, penitents from their religions and so on), specifically knowledge of the primary elementals, good and evil. Eating the apple was merely the demonstration of that desire for knowledge. The Judeo-Christian god said, "...the man has become like one of us, knowing good and evil; and now,

---

[d] – Genesis 1:26

lest he put forth his hand and take also of the tree of life, and eat, and live for ever".[e]

People who can understand good and evil can control good and evil, control the gods themselves, and few parents willingly give control of themselves into their children's hands. After all, those children might remember all those "no, No, NO!"s and "come here, Come here Come Here COME HERE COMEHERECOMEHERECOMEHERE!"s and what parent wants that?

Thus from time immemorial humans have been wanting more and more power in their hands and, if you can't have power over your lovers, neighbors, family, friends and enemies, the best power is power over the elements themselves.

But until we can call down rain, raise the earth, stop the tides, boil the ocean and darken the sun (imagine the weaponry in that!), let's exercise dominion over the Elementals' two idiot cousins, Time and Distance. Time and distance are far more active in our psyches than the elements themselves because we're almost *reafferent* with them. We interact with them and they respond in metricable quantities we recognize. More fascinating (and useful when designing human-machine interactions) is that the brain's hippocampus and *grid cells* are specifically designed to help us understand and interact with temporal and spatial relationships.[11,26,33,36,48,50,51,233,249,254,272,276, 279,281,294,303,305,328,333,354,358,372,384,438,477,493,519,530,562,575]

Will it take too long to walk downtown? Ride your bike. Weather too opposing? Take the bus or drive the car.

The distance covered remains the same. Maybe. Research demonstrates that the brain always selects the shortest visible route between two points regardless of any obstacles on that route. This is true whether someone is walking from point A to point B or navigating between two points on an interface.,[345f]

---

e – Genesis 3:22
f – The concept described is called *direct distance*. Imagine yourself coming out of a store or mall and see your car parked 2-300 feet away. Most people would walk the shortest, or "direct", distance to their car, possibly weaving through several parked vehicles to get there. Direct distance is not *optimal path*. You may be pushing a shopping cart full of groceries and cars along the direct distance are parked too closely for the cart to get through easily. But determining optimal path, even in interface design, requires calculating through several

Regardless of estimation errors (and perhaps because of them) time and distance are unequivocally linked in our psyches because we have some seven million years evolutionary history designing us to be cursorial hunters. De-linking time and distance is equivalent to...well...making us into gods. Walking versus biking versus driving decreases time involvement – we have power over time – by effectively shortening the distance because it takes less time to traverse it. Ask someone "Do you know how long it takes to walk to the supermarket?" and let them answer. Next ask "Is it closer if we take the car?" and there's a moment's hesitation in their reply. The mind goes into a mini-fugue because time and distance are linked in cognition (or were, anyway), so if we drive and it takes less time then the supermarket must be closer, but we logically know it's not and two parts of our brain – primitive (or lower) and higher – go into conflict. Expectation is a top-down process. Higher-level information informs lower-level processing. Experience is a bottom-up process. Sensory information goes into higher-level processing for evaluation. Humans are designed as expectation engines. Top-down connections outnumber bottom-up connections by about 10:1.

So we use technology to shorten the distance between things, like straight highways and bridges over unfordable rivers and planes to fly over oceans and uncrossable mountains and spaceships and transporters and who knows what else, and all to shorten the time it takes to travel between two points.

It's amazing how we'll use technology to shorten distance and therefore time. We build remote controls for TVs, stereos, home entertainment centers, garage doors, car starters and toys so we don't have to get up, go out, or move to interact with them, effectively shortening the distance traveled to achieve a goal, hence shortening the time required to realize that goal.

=====

factors. Direct distance is binary. Something is the shortest visual path or it isn't. People who chose direct distance paths regardless of all other factors tend to be *Towards* operators on the neuro-psychologic-behavioral axis of *Towards-AwayFrom*. These people are goal-oriented. The more goal oriented, the more direct distance oriented they are.

Our mobiles can start our cars and, as demonstrated recently, usurp our control over them[g]. They can check our homes, alert authorities that we've fallen down and can't get up from continents away and behold, distance and time are now equal and we're in Einstein's Universe, everything is immediately available to us (if we wish and the 'net is running where we are[h]) and we have truly become gods because we can make things appear and disappear with a snap of our fingers, a clap of our hands, a click of our mouse or a tap on our tablet.

We have power and marketing works very hard to convince us that our power is absolute.

They convince us by making things as usable as possible at the price of usability. By giving us experiences and decreasing our expectations.

Usable - experience, usability - expectation. These exist along axes that are worth remembering.[i] When something is usable but its usability is low or non-existent, our experience goes to average and eventually what we once considered nominal becomes our average. Think grade inflation and you've got the idea. Think of people who feel they should get a reward (such as a plaque) for merely showing up instead of being an exemplar to their workmates and you get the idea. When we experience a continuous average our expectation becomes minimal as well. We expect and eventually accept poor service, poor workmanship, shoddy handling and worse. Hence we are corrupted and the corruption exists due to the belief that we live in an instantaneous world, whatever we want we should have. We got it immediately and (what we recognize as) payment occurs in that same virtual realm, also instantaneously. Don't like what we

---

[g] – See 'Car hacking' just got real: In experiment, hackers disable SUV on busy highway, http://nlb.pub/P, and Researchers prove self-driving cars can be hacked, http://nlb.pub/Q
[h] – An interesting note: On a recent vacation the 'net went down where we were staying due to a lightning strike. People spent the first day walking around in a daze, asking each other "Are you okay?" and meaning "Can you get a signal?" The hotel proprietor noted that the staff, which had traditionally been very close-knit while coming from different corners of the globe and had stopped socializing as much, suddenly were spending time together and talking with each other. Amazing!
[i] – and we'll be covering them in detail in Reading Virtual Minds Volume IV: Use, Usable, Usability and Usage.

got? Get another, also immediately. There is no thought of what might happen at the end of the month, that's too far away, too distant in time, to have any consequence on our happiness now.

Now.

People want to do everything at once, a product of the Information Age and specifically this Digital Epoch, a function of time and distance becoming one in our psyches. T.S. Eliot wrote, "Where is the wisdom we have lost in knowledge? Where is the knowledge we have lost in information?" Information isn't knowledge and knowledge isn't wisdom.

I often tell students that people respond in the moment with a lifetime of experience. I think they forget that I, in my sixties (as I write this), have responded to a lot more moments than they, at twenty-one, have. Just because you can do a thing doesn't mean you should. Understand why a particular TakeAway described in this book brought about the results it did and you'll have much greater knowledge as to whether or not that particular technique is one you should employ in your current efforts.

I also encourage you to employ one method at a time. You're not obligated to do everything simply because you can, and points of diminishing return really do exist. A math professor once told me, "For god's sake, if you're going to make a mistake, make it at the beginning. They're so much easier to find that way," and I pass that on to you. Figure out which of these examples and suggestions best fits your immediate problem. Take one example and suggestion and apply it. Measure the results. If you're satisfied, apply another example's method. Measure the results. Keep on in this way until your immediate problem is solved. Now you've gained experience, developed some wisdom in the application and are ready to tackle some of your longer-term challenges. Science may progress by leaps and bounds, but it does so in excruciatingly tiny, little steps.

The rest of this book deals with individual aspects of people's interaction with information in their environment. We're going to focus tightly on the individual's (be they customer, visitor, user, etc.) point of view, their concepts of success, of completeness, of satisfaction.[151] What is included here is true regardless of interface because humans are designed by evolutionary forces. Until human eyes have a need to see infrared, human ears to hear ultrasonics, human noses to scent one molecule out of several million, ... you get the idea.

The examples and suggestions in this book will be targeted towards reafferent applications.

Reafferent applications?

Starting when the first drawing appeared on a cave wall and stopping around the dawn of the modern Internet, human information consumption was largely exafferent, meaning humans were passive and there was no real information *exchange* between the information's source and our response to that information or its source. We watched TV, read a newspaper, went to a movie. The most reafferent experiences we had were at meetings, rallies, movie houses, live theater, sporting events, ... all things where we as humans gathered together to interact with each other about a shared, real-time experience.

Reafference – humans taking an active part, an exchange of some kind, in their information consumption – is a direct product of the Internet[64,65,106,107,286,304,454,529,556,604] although technical reafference started with the Qube system[j]. Consider the following about the intersection of reafference, design and usability from award winning Graphic/UI designer John Scullin:

> Design and Usability shouldn't be confused because they're two fields that weren't meant to overlap. They do so on the web because it's the first interface where people are meant to do more than look and feel, they're suppose to interact. You have to make things understandable (that's the usability part) but you can only make things understandable if you know how they'll respond to what they see (that's the design part). You have kick-ass sites that nobody can use and completely usable sites that are so ugly nobody wants to navigate them. Most web designers tend towards usability and it shows in most sites. You know where to click but you don't want to. Design, and I mean making links and content elements appealing enough for people to

---

[j] – The Qube system was the precursor to the internet's marketing survey panels. See http://www.qube-tv.com/

> want to look at them and click, that's where you get kick-ass sites that visitors navigate easily and do business on.[115]

Historically, the degree of an individual's reafference was based on their social class and standing. The lower one was in the socio-economic scale the more exafferent they were to the daily activities of that society as a whole, the higher on the socio-economic scale the more reafferent. The Internet has changed all that, but the only reason the Internet is the marketing and advertising focus it is today is because the collective buying power of the middle class far outweighs the buying power of all other classes combined.

Again, a demonstration of the most power in the most people's hands economically.

The chapters in this book are based on past, current and ongoing studies of how people interact with information in their environment. Marketing and sales people recognize this as brochures, online sites, emails, leave-behinds, flyers, meetups, tweets, smartmobbing, flashmobbing, ... Generally collateral in any way, shape or form[k]. The studies themselves take the form of focus groups, investigators questioning/interrogating visitors in person or via email, online forms, phone calls, and/or asking selected individuals to perform some virtual (computer- or web-based) or real-world task. All of these studies were performed from an anthrolinguistic perspective, not a "how do I get more conversions?" perspective. In other words, the goal of the work is to learn how people interact with information in their environment. Specific to this volume, when the interaction is the basis of achieving a recognized and desired goal.

Virtual tasks and real-world tasks are often identical in nature but quite different in structure and outcome. The similarity of nature while different in structure is familiar to anthropologists as the difference between ceremony and ritual. The ceremony is the "why" or reason we do something, the ritual is the "what" we do.

---

[k] – You can measure and predict reafference via several NextStage's tools. See http://nlb.pub/s

An example of ceremony and ritual being used in modern marketing – and probably without the marketing/advertising agency even knowing what they were doing – is Proctor & Gamble's dominance in "mom cleaning" social marketing.

In this case, the use of ceremony and ritual starts with evolution, and the concepts of Place "placial" and Space "spatial". Some of the most primitive parts of the brain deal with concepts of place and space, as in territory and range and how these are tied to our experience and expectation.[6,11,15,26,33,36,48,50,51,180,233, 249,254,255,272,276,279,281,283,294,303,305,328,333,344,354,358,372,384,389,392,395, 409,438,477,493,511,515,516,519,520,530,562,575,597] Humans and most other life forms mark out their territory, defend their territory, have a home, hunting, grazing, foraging or migration range.[l]

Cleaning is an activity necessary to maintaining a healthy territory and all creatures that recognize territorial boundaries periodically "clean" their territories.[m]

Men and women clean differently, though, and the difference is one of place and space, or territory and range. Women clean a place, men clean a range. Cleaning is a positive activity for both.

Humans have elevated "cleaning" to ceremony status. This is demonstrated in language with such phrases as "Cleanliness is next to godliness". All ceremonies are demonstrated by rituals that are specific to culture and society, and all ceremonies are acts of honoring, the cleaning ceremony specific to "honoring our place". Belief systems do this by "sanctifying" things such as churches, burial grounds, etc. Modern language recognizes these sanctifications with phrases such as "xyz is a holy place", "only

---

[l] – Perhaps the most obvious demonstration of a *home* range in the online world is the "favorites" list on blogs and browser bookmarks. The blogs and sites frequently visited are the online equivalent of home ranges. Look through someone's frequented blogs or internet bookmarks and you can develop amazingly complete descriptions of their life up to that point in time.
[m] – Marking, arranging, basically any behavior that imparts a culturally recognized order to a place is a cleaning behavior. Examples range from your dog "hiding" toys around the house to bringing a favorite toy onto their bed to play with to your cat doing the same to a co-worker using things like a coffee cup, pen, notebook, tablet and mobile to mark out space at a conference table. NextStage teaches how to recognize the last item during negotiations and how to use such behavior to your advantage (as part of our *Know How Someone Is Thinking in 10 Seconds or Less* weekend intensive). You can get an idea about our trainings in **Comments from Live and Webinar Training Participants** (page 350). Contact NextStage for details.

the dead walk there", "that place is full of ghosts", "we honor our ghosts" and so on.

Culturally, one of the most prevalent female honoring ceremonies and sanctifying rituals is cleaning, again elevating their "place" to godly status. "Cleaning" is something that occurs in "their place". The "place" has to be a certain way. The woman who honors her "place" properly (by cleaning it) is socially and culturally rewarded by her friends. This reward takes the form of *social recognition* and with statements such as "What a beautiful home you have", "I love what you've done with the living room", "This is a great office", "This place has you all over it", "You've really left your mark here" and so on. Woman A telling Woman B that she's done a great job cleaning her "place" usually causes Woman B to feel *social acceptance*.

Men are "spatial" or "range" oriented, meaning they are more focused on the space around something rather than the space inside something. That does not mean however, they don't like cleaning. It just means they like cleaning in a different way, for example, washing the car, mowing the lawn, etc.[n]

Thus, it is this evolutionary and anthropological behavior that makes Proctor & Gamble's social media marketing perform so incredibly well, and often more so than other verticals.

The real- and virtual-world tasks that move between ceremony and ritual are *the hunt* and *the gathering*, a nod to our hunter-gatherer ancestors and something evolution has well adapted humans for as we are *cursorial hunters*, meaning we're designed to track and chase things down. We adapted ourselves to agrarian lifestyles and this shift is seen in the changes in the gods and rituals as humans shifted their consciousness from on-the-move hunter-gather mindsets to stationary, agrarian mindsets.

---

[n] – Ever see a man with a really neat garage or tool area or cubicle? Whatever you do, don't tell him that you're witnessing his feminine side come out unless you're sure he's comfortable with such concepts. Not all male egos can handle such information, although 'net-enabled male generations are more accepting of it. A fascinating aspect of evolutionary design is that men are physically spatial and women are placial, however move from physical reality to temporal reality and men are placial, women are spatial. Again, women are good determining long-term investments, men are good at solving problems now.

But those on-the-move, hunter-gatherer mindsets are still with us. Both real- and virtual-world demonstrations of this usually involve some aspect of searching for something, either online or in a mall (for example)[o], purchasing either a specific item or an item of the participant's own choosing, and/or evaluating some process for achieving desired outcomes (purchase, problem solve, "secret shopper" and the like). The size of studies to identify and explore such behaviors depends on time and resources. Most often a highly targeted and small sample size (10 CEOs of Fortune 500 companies, for example, or 15 Chicago-based working mothers with incomes between US$25-35k) is used to make a generalization for all working mothers nationwide or all Fortune 500 CEOs. There are some problems with these methods, however[p]:

- They primarily measure the investigator's interpretation of the participants' subjective experience.
- They do not measure the participants' direct, immediate, subjective experience of what is being investigated.
- They attempt to create objective statements of a subjective experience by pulling the person out of their experience to comment on that experience.
- They measure what's happening at the machine, not in the person (in the case of virtual surveys).[q]
- Small sample sizes are neither quantifiable nor distributable against larger populations.[595,596]

---

[o] – The etho-behavioral similarities between pack animals prowling and teens mall hopping is...alarming, really. A group of teenagers rejoicing and bonding over a "find" and a pack's synchronizing howl over a "find", a gang singling out a victim and a pack singling out the weakest member of a pack, ... sometimes what we study here at NextStage is discomfiting at best. This behavior is also a strong reason it is doubtful if traditional brick&mortar shopping will ever go away. Doing so would deny humans of too much of their evolutionary heritage.
[p] – Most of these are documented in *Reading Virtual Minds Volume I: Science and History*. It's now common to perform such studies via the internet and involve larger sample populations. NextStage was employing Internet-based, large-population studies as far back as 1996, something also documented in *Reading Virtual Minds Volume I: Science and History*.
[q] – NextStage Members (and why aren't you one yet? http://nlb.pub/4) have access to a NextStage Research Whitepaper, *A Demonstration of Professional Test-Taker Bias in Web-Based Panels and Applications*, another whoppin' fine read.

- Having individuals act in synthetic situations most often produces synthetic results and few studies are designed to identify, isolate and remove the effects of synthetic situations to produce natural results.
- They most often rely on individuals being cognitive about their behavior although it is recognized that emotion, not cognition, is the precursor to behavior (this was stated eloquently by Berger and Schenk, "Humans are not thinking machines that feel, but rather *feeling* machines that think."[29]).
- They require people to feel a response in an unnatural setting, be self-aware enough to comprehend the response, and be honest and articulate enough to communicate that feeling in a manner that is clear and recordable.[r]
- Power Analysis[s] methods are not used or are unknown by the experimenters.

In the early 2000s, I took part in a panel discussion in which one of the panelists described some research his group conducted. They picked three groups of 25 site visitors each from a company's email list, contacted them and sent every person in the first group US$100 cash, everyone in the second group received a check for US$100 and people in the third group received an online gift certificate for US$100, redeemable on the company's website. In each case the money was given with "no strings attached."

People in the first group, when contacted a few weeks later, had spent the money on consumables and entertainment (food, movies, music). The second group deposited the check and the majority used it to pay bills. The third group purchased something they'd been interested in for a while but couldn't justify purchasing.

---

[r] – Many thanks to Todd Sullivan, Esquire and Toddness Factor Originator, supra, for this bullet.
[s] – http://en.wikipedia.org/wiki/Statistical_power

These results were surprising to the group doing the study. I wanted to know how such results could have been surprising. The results, with no other information, told me the income level of the groups he was working with, their educational background, their ages and so much more.

Information without knowledge is worthless. Knowledge without wisdom is useless.

Reading Virtual Minds Volume II: Experience and Expectation has three parts. The first part starts with **Digital Resources for the Reading Virtual Minds Series** on page 27. That first part is unnumbered and contains the usual drivel that most readers skim over because they don't appreciate its importance and usually have a pressing problem they want to solve and hope against hope that whatever book they're holding will solve that problem for them. If you're reading this, you're reading (at least part of) that first section. By the way, if you're in the "pressing problem, dear god please let this book solve it *now!*" camp, please read **The Magic Bullet Will Not Be Found On Page 396...**, page 66, before purchasing this book.

The second part starts with **Chapter 1 – Of Coin Tosses and Card Tricks** on page 71. It contains the meat of this volume and covers (probably) more about how our experiences affect our expectations and what that means for online communications than you'd care to know.

The last part starts with **Appendices** (page 234) and the Joseph-standard overdeveloped reference section, the glossary, the index, the bio, training information, the usual stuff.

NextStage Evolution (NSE), in the process of compiling the information in this book, did use interviews, observation and focus groups as part of its research paradigm, and did so for two specific purposes.

The first purpose is to create a data "seed" that ET uses to test against as it learns and incorporates information into its system. People who've seen presentations on ET have heard us talk about our Language Engines™ and how they're built. These Language Engines™ are an example of creating a data "seed" for ET to use as it grows and learns (think of a grain of sand becoming an oyster's pearl and you get the idea. More correctly, think of a child's babbling what it hears from siblings, parents and other relatives as prelingualizing speech and you've got the idea).

An example of this testing against a data seed would be starting out with the erroneous statement "Florida is west of Ohio" and then having ET observe people heading southeast from Ohio to get to Florida and returning from the same direction. ET keeps its knowledge of "Florida", "west" and "Ohio" and incorporates "southeast" into its information system to create the statement "Florida is southeast of Ohio".

In that sense ET is, like Wikipedia and "wisdom of the crowd" systems, subject to the whims of the masses;[112,168,234,542] if all it encounters is the belief that Florida is west of Ohio so shall it believe and so shall it act upon.[112] Encountering a single individual who thinks Florida is southeast of Ohio would cause ET, based on the information from the masses, to either mark the individual as an anomaly or ask for help depending on what behavioral rules (business or otherwise) were in place.[t]

And one of the most terrifying things we've learned about masses, knowledge and expertise is that the masses will consider the most knowledgeable resource the least expensive resource. Every day, more people visit Wikipedia – a free site – than visit Britannica Online – traditionally a for-pay site that changed to free to retain market relevance.

The second NSE purpose of interviews, observation and focus groups is to validate information gathered via ET. In both cases NSE uses the "Chinese General" solicitation to gather individuals' responses.[u]

---

[t] – Marketing can be a science provided one remembers that much of marketing relies on 2nd order logic. *Marketing Science* is often based on what are called "secondary information markets". Example: It is not logical that Florida is west of Ohio. However, if the market believes Florida is west of Ohio and the marketing goal is dominate the market, marketers must cater to that belief. Doing otherwise would cause loss of market share. It could be argued that not catering to the market's current belief – i.e., their Identity structure – would be an interesting study in debranding.[74,82,84,88,117,120,179,505,602] However, it would not be profitable. The goal of marketing is not to educate the market (unless doing so increases market share), it is to increase market share. Period. So don't use 1st order logic when talking marketing, only 2nd order logic applies. Unless the market requires 1st order logic be used...

[u] – The Chinese General Solicitation is based on an old story in which the Emperor called all his generals together and said that the country was going to be invaded. Each of them was to

Readers also need to know that this book, while quite a mindful in and of itself, is part of a triad that includes *Reading Virtual Minds Volume III: Fair-Exchange and Social Networks* and *Reading Virtual Minds Volume IV: Use, Usable, Usability and Usage*. Each volume is self-contained as they'll primarily appeal to different disciplines. My suggestion is to read them in order because this book builds a foundation, *Reading Virtual Minds Volume III: Fair-Exchange and Social Networks* applies to so many things and with good reason; it affects much of what people do even though most people are unfamiliar with the concept or how it manifests itself in our lives. Next comes *Reading Virtual Minds Volume IV: Use, Usable, Usability and Usage* because once you understand how experience and expectation guide our behaviors, and how fair-exchange determines successful social interactions, the next thing to study is how these apply to usability.

The Magic Bullet Will Not Be Found On Page 396...[v]

...or any other page, for that matter.

Since publishing *Volume I* and listening to and reading people's comments, I've learned that there's a significant audience who'll purchase this book (or any book, really) in the hopes of finding the magic bullet, the secret sauce, the missing link, the golden arrow, ..., and that these same people are convinced their targets are continent-wide bullseyes.

I'm convinced these same people believe The Fonz really did jump a motorcycle over a shark on *Happy Days*[w] and that Indiana Jones did survive a nuclear detonation in a refrigerator[x]. More

=====

explain to the Emperor why they were the best one to lead the troops into battle. The Emperor listened to each general separately and let them say any and every thing they wished. When they were through extolling their own virtues, the Emperor asked, "But if something happens to you, who would then lead my armies?" The individual whom the majority of the generals thought was second only to them was the one chosen by the Emperor to lead his armies.
[v] – The following conversation can be thought of as a precursor to the *Reading Virtual Minds Volume IV: Use, Usable, Usability and Usage*.
[w] – https://en.wikipedia.org/wiki/Happy_Days#.22Jumping_the_shark.22
[x] – http://youtu.be/M0upNuDNRSk

importantly, these same people are out to convince you that you should believe such nonsense, too!

So if you're one of the people who believes The Fonz did jump his motorcycle over a shark and that Indian Jones did survive a nuclear detonation in a refrigerator or that there's a magic bullet somewhere in this book **stop now, put the book down, walk away**. That's my best advice to you.

Magic bullets.

The problem with magic bullets is that they'll always find their way into a heart or head and they have amazing disregard as to whose heart or head they go into.

One comment I received about *Reading Virtual Minds Volume I: Science and History* was:

> The book is chock-a-block full of fascinating concepts, one right after another, and at each one I say, "Wow, this is cool and important. I can see its usefulness in some context or other." And I have no doubt that they are all of a piece in your head, organized in a most beautiful, internally consistent tapestry.
> And yet I find no straightforward way to organize them in my own head.

I appreciate that, truly I do. The majority of people will find the topics I present and the way I present them different in the extreme.

My advice to you is to ask yourself a question: Do I want to learn how to use these things repeatedly, how to synthesize this into new ways of doing things, or do I just want a one-off to get me out of my present jam and probably not touch the book again until I'm in a similar jam?

Are you looking for a one-off? Definitely buy the book. You'll most likely fail at fixing the one-off because you won't have learned what the problem really is or how to actually solve it without creating cascade errors, but you should definitely still buy the book because I like getting royalty checks and it's all about me anyway, isn't it?

Or are you looking to learn so that you can understand and be better at what you do, do you want another tool in your toolbox that you'll use in immediately obvious and increasingly unobvious ways to better yourself, your life and those around you?

Oh, well, you should definitely buy the book because that's what this book and all the *Reading Virtual Minds* series is about. You'll have gotten wisdom and I'll still get a royalty check.

Nice deal, that.

There are readers who "got" *V1* on the first read. One reader wrote to let me know that they'd read the book cover to cover each day for the first thirty days they had it, learning something new each time.

What did readers "who got it in one" have in common that readers "who couldn't get it in ten" lacked?

The ones that I interviewed had an open mind in one way, shape or form. They came to learn, not do. They came with curiosity and not specific questions. And they read the book when they were relaxed, not in a rush and needing to find a specific solution to a specific problem. In a neurophysiology perspective, the "in 1"s and "in 10"s had different parts of their brains active when they were reading the book.

So first, you should read this book relaxed. If not relaxed, then late at night before you go to bed, when your mind's tired and your conscious filters let more things through. The subjects (there's not one subject, there are several) covered in the *Reading Virtual Minds* series will baffle most people not trained in these disciplines because they'll apply filters that are irrelevant to the subjects covered.

Let your non-conscious, primitive mind have a go at it. The primitive mind's been around longer – from an evolutionary standpoint – than the conscious, higher mind and, in a tug of war, it will win. It won't tell you it's won, and you won't know it's won, but win it will. If you learn nothing else in this series learn this: emotion wins...and sells.

Second, leave your questions for later (preferably after you've finished reading the book). There are lots of answers in here and the best way to find them is to ask questions after you've learned the answer. That way you'll know what types of questions to ask and the answers will satisfy you.

Third, study, not do. Learn, then do. You will learn how to solve problems, how to isolate what you want to solve, how to recognize and define problem and solution states, how to determine if a given problem is currently solvable, how to solve it, how to recognize that the problem is solved, ... Basically how to define exactly, how to methodologize precisely and how to make sure your bullseyes are well within range of your bullets and arrows so that you'll hit your targets with remarkable regularity.

Still with me? Read on and enjoy!

To the untrained mind, everything is a wonder.

1 – Of Coin Tosses and Card Tricks

It can be tricky explaining *Experience* and *Expectation* when lots of people aren't completely sure what is meant by those terms. When I write "...what is meant by those terms" I mean in a scientific sense, not a marketing sense. Let's face it, marketing mungs up perfectly good words with no rhyme or reason at all, so the best thing we can do, right out of the gate, is put forward some definitions that are both workable and obvious; workable in the sense that you can use them to get things done and obvious in the sense that we're going to teach you a little kind-of card trick that demonstrates the difference between experience and expectation so-o-o well you'll want to share it with all your friends. Once we've mastered the little kind-of card trick we're going to spend a little time teaching you how to make money in bars by tossing a coin and getting people to bet on whether the toss will be heads or tails. It can be a lot of fun in the right bars, and it also teaches the workable and obvious differences between experience and expectation.

1.A – Experience, Expectation, Two Decks of Cards and Why Eye-Tracking Sucks[a]

Is it more important to know where somebody's eyes are or getting their eyes to focus on what you want them to see? This subchapter's title is provocative, yes, and I'll freely admit that eye-tracking studies have their place and that place isn't in the design of user experiences, interfaces, marketing material, so on and so forth. Study visual cognition and visual intelligence enough and you'll discover that people don't always look at what they're seeing, and where their eyes stop moving is really where the brain tells the optic ganglia "Okay, stop taking stuff in so I

---

[a] – Some of this material originally appeared in *Help visitors focus and reap the rewards*, http://www.imediaconnection.com/content/16533.asp

can figure out what we just saw".[18,113,219,220,252,260,404,421,483,484,522,524,548,566,617,619]

In other words, capturing where people's eyes stop moving is capturing where they stop paying attention to what they're looking at. People's eyes stop moving when the brain needs to catch up on what was just seen.

Now, let's demonstrate that. It's easy. Go get two decks of cards, same size, shape and thickness. Most importantly, make sure the backs of the cards have grossly distinct visual characteristics. The cards in Figure 1.1 are an example. They're exactly the same size, shape and thickness. The only real difference is that the back of one card is blue and white, the other is red and white. You can do this with decks having pictures on the cardbacks so long as the pictures are radically and easily identifiably different, like a snowman and ocean liner. Personally, I'd just go with a blue deck and a red deck.

Figure 1.1 - Got 'em? Great! Now for some fun with visual cognition, kenisthesiology, motion studies and, of course, experience and expectation!

Got 'em?

Great.

Now shuffle the two decks together three to four times so that you have a single deck of 104 cards. Get them nicely mixed. You know; red blue red red blue blue blue blue red blue red red blue blue red red red...

Pick up the mixed deck in one hand, card backs facing you, take the top card and put it on the tabletop. Make sure the hand holding the deck is out of your visual field. You want to keep your eyes on that tabletop card so that you're not seeing the deck (similar to Figure 1.2).

Figure 1.2 - Eyes on the cards on the table, not on the picture of the cat.

Now, making sure you keep your eyes on that tabletop card and as quickly as you can, Grasshopper, separate the cards into their two separate decks, red with red, blue with blue, by taking a card from the unseen deck and putting it on the tabletop. Make note of how easy it is to do.[b] Even better, if you happen to place a red card in the blue pile, leave it there, and if you happen to place a blue card in the red pile, leave it there. The goal is to be quick.

Now that you've separated the cards, shuffle them together again. Mix them up really well then take the shuffled deck in one hand, same as before.

This time we're going to do something different. Keep your eyes on the shuffled deck in your hand, not on the cards on the table, so that the cards on the tabletop will be out of your visual field (similar to Figure 1.3).

Figure 1.3 - This time keep your eyes on the cards in your hand, not on where you're placing them on the tabletop.

Now, as before, as quickly as you can and this time keeping your eyes on the card deck in your hands, separate the cards by their colors, red with red and blue with blue.

---

[b] – Children and people with certain types of autism are remarkably adept at this exercise.

About 85% of the people on the planet find the second method much simpler to do than the first method. Yes, there are other ways to separate the two decks by color and we can use them to demonstrate other neuroscience concepts some other time. This simple exercise has some very complex science behind it, and what's most important is that it's a demonstration of attentional focus[396,441,479,564] and eye-tracking. The first method is a demonstration of what the eye's looking at interfering with the brain-mind's ability to perform a task,[444] the second exercise is a demonstration of the brain-mind ability to perform a task optimally by focusing the eye on that task.[2,93,116,296,445,472,486]

Consider the first exercise again. Your eyes are focused on the end result (the piles on the table), not on what you need to know to get to the end result (the cards in your hands). Because you're focused on the piles on the table you have no knowledge of what color card is in your hand (and coming up next) until it's close to the piles on the table and the goal is to be as quick as you can separating the cards into all blue and all red piles.

But your expectation is based on the cards on the table top and the best you're going to do is 50/50 putting the correct card in the correct pile without correcting your motion once you see the card in your hand.

Get that. In the first exercise, *expectation* is based on the cards on the tabletop because that's where your focus is but you have no *experience* to guide that expectation until it's (almost) too late to act.

The second exercise allows your experience (you know the card color before placing it) to guide your expectation (where to place the card on the tabletop) before you have to act. Most people, if they let the cards fall where they may (*budda-boom*) in the first exercise, will have some red cards in the blue pile, some blue cards in the red pile and there's the lesson. Almost nobody will have red cards in blue piles or vice versa (or far fewer, if nothing else) in the second exercise.

Get that. When *experience* guides *expectation* people are more successful (and foreshadowing the rest of this volume, successful people are *satisfied* people).

1.B – Experience, Expectation, Tossed Coins and Social Probabilities[c]

We get into a little math in this section. Readers should feel free to ignore the math and focus on the results, kind of like "you don't need to know how cell towers work to use a mobile phone".

Okay, ready? Here we go...

Some people with a Bayesian bent might consider the above card trick an example of "the observer's state of knowledge of the system" (especially the second part of the trick and regarding the accuracy of placing a given card in the correct pile).

My response is "So?" It's a great little fact to dribble out at cocktail parties and it's only going to increase ROI if you're paying attention carefully.

Not so what comes next because some will call it frequentism, others Bayesian and in truth there's no probabilities involved. It's straight mathematics although the number of variables gives most people pause.

Which is why we're not going to worry about them.

We're going to win bar bets by tossing a coin.

Toss a coin and there's a 50/50 chance of getting heads or tails, correct?

Well, yes and no. What I didn't specify in the above is whether or not the coin was being tossed in an ideal world.

An ideal world?

Yes, a world where the only thing that exists is the coin. The coin is also perfectly balanced. There are no air currents to interfere with the toss, either. Nor any intersecting fields or forces. And lets not forget whatever's tossing the coin. It has to perfectly toss the coin each and every time, endlessly, ad infinitum, ad nauseam.

Probability – as most people think of it – does rule in that ideal world. Toss a coin 100 times and you should get a 50/50 split or amazingly close to. The more you toss, the closer you'll

---

[c] – Social probabilities were demonstrated in a audience-participation exercise given during NextStage's 2008 SNCR TS Eliot, Ezekiel, Beehives and Mighty Mouse presentation.147

get. Toss forever and it'll be a perfect 50/50 split. That "toss forever and it'll be a perfect 50/50 split" comes from statistics. Statistics works best when it deals with incredibly large data sets. Even when statistics are being used to determine if an individual walking down a grocery store aisle will pick item A or item B from the shelves, that determination is based on (one hopes for accuracy's sake) a study of thousands upon thousands of ideal individuals walking down a single yet ideal grocery store aisle picking items from identical and identically ideal shelves.

That's in the ideal world where coins, air, tosses, grocery store aisles, shelves, statistics and everything else is perfect.

Perfect.

How many worlds do you know like that?

Welcome to the real world, where how things are connected determines the probability of their happening, the world of social probabilities.[322,349,416] In this world the probability of a tossed coin being heads or tails is governed more by how strong or weak the connection is between the tosser and the coin than anything else.

Let me give you a well known example of this in the real world, the "Six Degrees of Separation" model so well publicized in popular media.[41,197,293,340,378,413,414,518,526,579,586,587,606,618] Without going into agonizing detail, the six degrees model works because everybody on the planet knows at least 47[165] other people and with a world population of about seven billion and my 47 people each knowing 47 other people who each also know 47 other people and with only a single point of connection between each group, everybody is connected to everybody else by at most six discrete points of connectivity.

It's that *connectivity* that's the killer. How strong is each connection? What's the guarantee that each *link* in the connection chain will act? More precisely (and no double entendre intended), what's the probability that each link will act? And how much will each link act?

Those questions take the form of equations. A guarantee that something will happen means you're 100% sure it will happen. If you're 100% sure, then you believe the probability, "P", of it happening is 100%. This looks like

$$P(\text{it will happen}) = 100\% \mid (\text{you're sure})$$

How much each link will act is where it gets tricky[d]. Will the next link in the connection contact all of their 47 people? Will they send emails or call? Check for valid email addresses, talk or leave a message? Get the request on their mobile, decide to do it when they get home and forget?[e]

Welcome to social probabilities.

But before going too far into this brave new world of social probabilities et al, let's investigate that coin toss in the real world and use it as a demonstration.

Series (100 tosses per series)	Heads	Tails
1	33	67
2	25	75
3	3	97
4	18	82
5	20	80

Wow. Rather amazing, isn't it? Five-hundred tosses and a majority of tails each and every time?

Here's the extra information that's obviously in the above yet not recognized in the unreal, simulated worlds where perfect coin tosses occur:

---

[d] – There are several mathematical techniques that can be used here and we're going with Logical Calculus for the simple reason that we know it gets us where we want to go.
[e] – One thing we've learned is that the more immediately and easily a message is to communicate to others, the more likely people are to communicate that message, hence the popularity of Twitter, TXTing and similar channels.

1) I "stacked the deck" in my favor. I'm very good at tossing a coin and getting the result I want because I once spent a year teaching myself how high to toss, how much spin, how much time to allow for flight before catching the coin, at what point in the coin's flight to catch it, ... to make sure I always got the outcome I wanted. A whole bunch of factors. In the above, I was consciously adjusting my toss and catch to favor tails over heads. That was conscious on my part. It now takes effort on my part to neutralize my conscious and non-conscious minds so that a coin toss is a genuinely arbitrary coin toss when I do it.[f]

2) Look at each series (see **Appendix B – Coin Toss Outcomes**, page 245) and you'll note that the unwanted results tend to clump. It takes me a few tosses at the start of each set to get the rhythm back and when I lose it in the middle there's a few tosses required to get it back. Even so, when I lose it, the tosses don't go random, they go to Heads.[g]

3) If you've read *Reading Virtual Minds Volume I*,[87] you know that if I have to make a conscious effort to neutralize my non-conscious mind, there's nothing non-conscious about it and the neutralizing effort will be more directed non-consciously towards getting random results. In other words, I'll see what I got on toss 1 and non-consciously adjust to get what I want on toss 2, etc.

4) Remember that we're talking about a human being working at a desired outcome. I "stacked the deck in my favor". Granted, not everyone is going to practice coin tossing the way I did. They'll practice pick-pocketing, slight-of-hand, parlor magic, card tricks,

---

[f] – By the way, I'm not the only one who can toss a coin and get the result they want. Harvard University math professor and self-taught magician Persi Diaconis, for example, gets the result he wants about 100% of the time.

[g] – Mathematicians note that the numbers don't correlate with Révész' recognizable randomness examples.497

investing, sales, management decisions, coming out
ahead in business dealings, ...

Whenever someone excels at something and whether they
did so intentionally or not, somewhere along the way they
practiced getting the result they wanted to ensure they have an
edge.,[231,234,263,295,416,431,502,506h] When humans negotiate they're
always wanting to stack the deck in their favor. People were
happy to bet me that I couldn't get more heads or tails or vice-
versa. They thought they knew the odds and would agree to a
"best out of 30" or "best out of 50" game, not realizing it
normally took me 5-10 tosses to get everything in sync. When
they challenged I would give them the coin and sure enough,
untrained they would get a close to 50/50 mix. Most laughed it off
and a few got very upset. In all cases, they said there had to be a
trick to it and they were correct, there was.

So item four is that anybody can perform this trick if they
have a little knowledge of human physiology and how
psychomotor behavioral cues work.[24,54,59,64-66,78,80,83,152,167,169,184-186,212,215,224,252,257,262,271,280,292,320,339,352,380,390,391,453,456,490,503,507,517,549,558,582,583,594,598-600,607,612]

I hadn't tossed a coin with a goal in mind for several years
when I did the experiment for this chapter. Notice that the
pattern is 67, 75, 97, 82, 80? Those numbers, if they had voices,
would be saying "He remembers how to do it", "He's increasing
his cognitive and psychomotor control to get the results he
wants", "Okay, he's got a lock on it" , "That increased cognitive
and psychomotor control is starting to cost him" and finally
"Yeah, he's tuckering". I'm guessing if I'd continued the numbers
would have started to hover around 75. Now we come to the
intersection of ideal and real worlds:

---

[h] – This is why venture capitalists are so rotten at picking winners – the cost of practicing is
exorbitantly high.This is also why they stack the deck as they do – 10% for the person who
came up with the idea, 90% to them if it succeeds. They have to pay for their failures
someway and without knowing how to repeat success there are few venues left for covering
loss after loss after loss.

TakeAway #1 - People do not function randomly regardless of how large a population you study.

Those "$\pm 2\sigma$" that appear in studies only exist as ± 2's because researchers neutralize everything else, throw out outliers, don't know how to isolate all the variables, all those usual tricks of the trade to get publishable results. Those tricks work perfectly well and should be encouraged in ideal and near-ideal environments (quantum chambers, stellar populations, etc.). But in the social world, the world where most people live, the world that is governed by intuitions and social mores and cultural trainings? That's the world of social probabilities, where coin toss results can be what you need them to be, the voting and buying behaviors of the masses don't act logically, and where "Big Data" forecasts can be hideously thrown off by a single unknown and unaccounted for variable. You can still create ideal situations in the social probabilities world and doing so requires knowing lots about real-world probabilities and all the factors that really effect personal and social outcomes. The usual and obvious demonstration of this is in neuroeconomics (Rational Actors Beware!).

So long story short, your intuition was right all along; if you toss a coin nine times and get nine heads, put your money on the tenth toss being heads.

So long as you're the one tossing the coin.

And provided you really want it to come out heads.

This isn't frequentism because there's lots of prior knowledge involved, and it's not Bayesian because after some time, t, the probability of getting other than what's intended drops to zero (0) and what remains is calculating the outcomes in the room. The room outcomes are dependent on the social outcomes of the toss and that changes the experimental frame considerably.

Now let's tie this back to experience and expectation.

In the above coin toss bar trick, I'm betting on *my* experience, others are betting on *their* expectation. Note the operative words in the previous sentence; "my" and "their", not "experience" and "expectation". *My* experience is based on a prior knowledge that greatly stacks the deck (my expectation of success) in my favor. *Their* expectation is based on experiences that are invalid in this situation.[i]

Prior knowledge and the lack thereof is the basis for so much that happens in the world, everything from gambling that's not gambling to combat victories that are decided before soldiers meet in the field to merger decisions to whether or not someone will be thrilled with a gift or not. My prior knowledge works strongly in my favor because I've done lots of work to isolate as many variables as possible, and mathematically any variable I isolate such that it's no longer dependent on other factors becomes a constant. Maximize the number of constants, minimize the number of variables and your equation moves from advanced mathematics to simple arithmetic.

People adept at these kinds of things can accurately predict outcomes a long ways out. I described this in Emer Kirrane's *Joseph Carrabis – Fear Álainn* Crepuscular Light interview:[331]

> Predicting the future isn't as difficult as some people claim it to be. Accurate predictions are based on planar orthogonal projections (imagine a line extending into forever, several planes intersecting that line and perpendicular to it. Each plane is a different event. Picking the correct event is determined by all the orthogonal intersections that happened before, hence have become fixed on the line). From this we recognize that it helps to know a lot about what's happened before and what makes "this time" different from "those times". The further out (in time) the prediction, the more orthogonalities exist between "now" and "then", and this is where most people encounter difficulties because probability mechanics get involved and there can be several "lines into forever" that intersect and curve around each other such that their orthogonalities intersect or become intertwined.

---

[i] – This is the neuromathematical equivalent of insider trading. Stanford University's Ron Howard, a presage of modern Decision Theory, demonstrated this by flipping a coin, keeping it covered and asking his class the probability of heads. He would then peek so that he knew if the coin was heads or tails and again asked his class, who had not peeked, the probability of heads. Who's gambling and who's investing? His class was gambling based on expectation, he was investing based on experience (fantasy sports trials hinge on this).

TakeAway #2 - The more experience you have, the more likely your expectations will be met.

TakeAway #3 - The more experience you have, the greater your surprise when expectations aren't met.

Need to get something done and can't? Your surprise is unpleasant. Need to get something done and can? Your surprise is pleasant

By the way, TakeAways 1, 2 and 3 are the basis for everything else in this book.

Anticipointment: when experience doesn't live up to expectations.
— Matthew Roche

2 – Experience and Expectation

People over a certain age, regardless of who they are or what they're doing, expect certain things to occur in certain ways. This process of "expecting what has been experienced" starts with birth and continues throughout life. The more varied someone's experiences are the less static their expectations, the less varied their experiences the more static their expectations. Someone who's never traveled beyond their town, village or neighborhood, is poorly-read and -educated, can only respond to new situations based on their town, village or neighborhood experiences. The individual who is well-traveled and/or well-read, who has opened themselves up to new experiences, is much more flexible in how they respond to new and novel situations.

Humans have many neural axes that help them function and probably the best-known is the Flight-Fight behavioral axis. Most axes exist along one neurological plane: Cognitive, Behavioral/effective or Motivational. The Experience-Expectation axis is interesting because it bridges Cognitive and Behavioral/effective and nowhere is this more obvious than in language. Native English speakers will experience a neurolexical challenge when they read the image in Figure 2.1 (page 86), non-native English speakers won't have any problem at all. The more idiomatic (natural) someone's English use, the more that image will be a challenge. In language, more than anywhere else, we see or hear what we expect to hear, not necessarily what is said or written[a]. Across all cultures and languages, neurophysiologists and psychologists estimate that what we experience is as much as 85% what we expect to experience, not necessarily what is real or "environmentally available". There is a truth in "Believing is Seeing" that goes well beyond childhood or people raised in mythic cultures. The paranoid delusional can't imagine why someone wouldn't be waiting to attack them, the PTSD sufferer

---

[a] – Much of misreading is because we see not what's written but what we expect to see written. This is also true in unintentional blindness studies.[311,337,366,371,393,420,423,442,466] For that matter, much of what we see, period, is based on what we believe we should see or want to see.[357]

can't escape threat, the egomaniac sees all things as either praise or attack, readers of this book are either awed by the tools made available or at a complete loss regarding others' praise of the content. We can only observe what we've been trained to observe (otherwise we don't know what we're looking at). To see something totally new, we have to be completely engaged in doing something we've never done before.

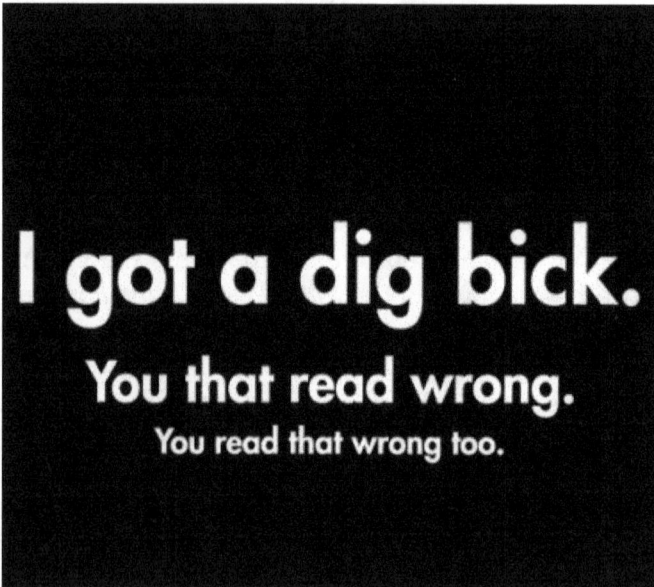

2.1 Exactly what is written, if you're a native English speaker.

What is the same in both the highly experienced and poorly experienced individuals' cases is that they will respond with tools first from their Personality, then from their Identity and lastly from their Core.[56,87,109,194,196,291,312,361,411,415,449,476,492,504,508,553,576,588,592,b] They will go deeper inside themselves to get a desired outcome – to have their expectation fulfilled – based on how any given immediate experience escalates. This is why some people, when they're involved in some kind of negotiation (it can

[b] – Core, Identity and Personality are discussed in detail in *Reading Virtual Minds Volume I: Science and History*, specifically in subchapter *II.3 – Core, Identity and Personality*.

be with a partner, a peer, their family and sometimes in business) and are repeatedly not getting what they want, resort to childhood personae; they are literally going back through their life to find the right emotional key for this experiential lock and when maturity fails, out comes the child. This can be anything from the obstreperous, annoying child to the coy, cloying child. Basically whatever worked with their parents and siblings, that's what they'll resort to when all else fails. It can be anything from pouting to raging to crying, and whatever it is it'll involve some form of acting out, of behaving in a way that belies their age and education and demonstrates the root of their familial background.

The poorly experienced person exhausts their Personality and Identity store fairly rapidly in new situations and, if they survive, this new experience modifies the last-used element in that store. The individual who exhausts their Personality and Identity store and survives a new experience with tools from their Core will have their Identity and Personality stores modified by the new experiential information. This appears in language as "They've learned to expect it" or "They've learned what to expect". The individual who exhausts their Core and survives has their Core changed. Core change occurs when people go through remission from major disease, faith or spiritual upheaval and the like. The Apostle Paul's falling off his donkey on the road to Damascus is an example of Core change.

Such shifts and changes literally mean the individual's life has acquired a new perceptual (cognitive) basis, new motivational drivers, new behavior patterns and ways of expressing their behaviors (effects) and if you've intuited that this means they've radically changed their {C,B/e,M} matrices, you're spot-on and congratulations! Whatever their previous "mission" was in life – to have a family, to gain wisdom, to get rich – they've acquired a new "mission", hence we use the term "*re*mission" and in language this becomes "He's not the person he used to be" or "She got a new lease on life", etc. Probably the best-known example from literature is Dickens' Scrooge in *A Christmas Carol*. If Scrooge's transformation isn't an example of a major shift in an individual's entire {C,B/e,M} matrix, nothing is.

Long ago I knew a young Christian woman who had an amazing faith in her god.[c] People loved to hear her testimony because she always had a positive, uplifting attitude, always a smile, always a kind, warming word for those around her. She often used the phrase "I'm a Little Princess and my Daddy owns the Universe" to describe herself and you could hear the capitalization in the way she said it.

Her faith was based on a belief that god always answered her prayers and not in a general, "god answers everybody's prayers" sense. Her faith came from a belief in a genuine two-way communication between parent and child. I questioned her about this once and realized she had never really asked god for anything in her prayers, they were always psalmic odes for god's will or statements of acceptance of immediate situations as demonstrations of god's will. Somehow she had redefined this general bottom-up prayer into a genuine bidirectional communication.

One day I noticed she was agitated. She was flushed, her normally bright eyes were fearful, her breathing shallow and oral, almost panting, her voice quiet and anxious. In short, a major conflict between Identity and Core, and Personality was the casualty.

What had caused this?

God hadn't answered one of her prayers.

But god always answered her prayers. That was the basis of her faith. What had happened?

What had happened was that the nature of her prayer had changed. This one time it wasn't psalmic or odic. She'd upped the ante. She'd asked her god to directly act for someone else's benefit. Her prayer asked for a recognizable outcome, a change in someone's immediate situation. Not for herself, of course, but for someone else.

I didn't ask what the prayer was and whatever it was, god's silence demonstrated to her a broken covenant. The god she worshipped faithfully and lovingly since childhood was now

---

[c] — *Reading Virtual Minds Volume I: Science and History, 4th edition* readers may remember this anecdote in the *Reading Virtual Minds Volume II Preview* at the end of the book.

ignoring her. Several people spoke to her about this. God was testing her faith, so on and so forth. She responded, "But God doesn't test us beyond what we can endure" and this was beyond her endurance. Because god had never failed her, she promised a response to this other person and when none came, experience, a Core experience that was fueling her Identity and Personality, failed. The Little Princess was thrown from her throne. The Loving Father loved her no more and because Loving Father-Little Princess was the mirror and echo she'd used as self-definition for so long, her voice could not be heard, her reflection not seen.

Experience had trained her to have certain expectations and now expectation-realized – what is known as "immediate experience" or "experience of the *Now*" to neuromathematicians and QBists – was not matching experience. Her agitation, fear, anxiety and especially frustration were all outward demonstrations of Personality, Identity and especially Core in chaos. The level of frustration, especially, was a demonstration of her Core in a high state of flux.

Frustration (as I use the term here) occurs when we've exhausted our repertoire of learned responses to a situation, when our solutions no longer work, when things aren't going as planned.

Children demonstrate frustration when their problem-solving skills aren't up to the challenge at hand. Give a child a puzzle beyond their problem-solving ability and, based on other factors in their environment,[258] they'll either rise to the challenge or start repeating their known problem-solving methods and continue failing. Good teachers watch for such things and intervene, demonstrating new problem-solving skills or encouraging the child to explore alternatives. Bad teachers know only one way to teach a subject and lack subject matter expertise. Such teachers often set students up for failure or blame students for the instructor's own failed teaching ability, thus demonstrating weaknesses in the teacher's own Personality, Identity and Core.

Users demonstrate frustration when their problem-solving skills aren't up to the challenge at hand. Present a new or modified interface during an otherwise mundane upgrade and, based on other factors in their environment, the user will either rise to the challenge or start looking for elements of the old interface (which usually no longer exist) and continue failing. Consider the following exchange from a Microsoft™ Help board:

> I am interested in reply which tells me the following:-
>
> "The ribbon is not going away - on the contrary, other software producers are adopting it "too.
> "As will all new things, it seems confusing and intimidating at first, but if you try it, you'll find that it quickly becomes familiar."
>
> As I have said, I work in IT and am very used to dealing with new products and with learning to exploit new functionality. There is however another side to the idea of "new". Think for a second on respecting previous customers, backwards functionality and here is a novel idea, giving customers what they actually want and not what is dreamed up by software developers, salesmen and senior managers who "think" they know what customers want. It is also interesting to note what big blue chip companies might make of a product which isn't immediately intuitive and would require tools and courses to help maintain staff productivity. Be aware that out there in the real world you will find many examples of companies using old software they are comfortable with, many IT companies still have NT boxes on the floor, we have just been given Office 2003 at work and are pleased to have that update and the company standard browser is I.E. version 6.
> Although I have downloaded a little patch to let me see a menu which helps me do my work, I would actually much prefer if Microsoft would just simply offer customers a choice. Here are ribbons but customers are able to customize product and if they prefer menus then what is wrong with that? Aren't they still loyal customers who deserve respect? Doesn't this sound more reasonable rather than "The ribbon is not going away - on the contrary, other software producers are adopting it too.".

I'm not sure if the people involved in the above exchange recognize it and they're talking about something called *adaptation method.* Basically, once people get used to doing something a certain way they become less vigorous with each repetition. The first time somebody does something, the action is "new". The second time, "less new" and eventually the action becomes known and requires less neural effort and energy to perform the action. Have you ever looked at a picture and couldn't figure out what it was, then once told, couldn't stop seeing what you were told it was? That's adaptation method working. Figure 2.2 (page 91) can cause anxiety or laughter depending what you're used to (adapted to).

Figure 2.2 - Any anxiety is due to conflicting neural processing. Do you believe what you see or what you read? Or does what you read convince you of what you see?

Adaptation method is why new interfaces to existing properties, platforms, software, etc., fail when released to the general user population. The old usage reflexes are no longer valid and a new reflex needs to be incorporated, essentially overwriting the existing reflex.[d] Adaptation method and its effects can be seen in sports professionals, professional musicians and anybody whose job is based on repetitive motions such as factory line workers. The difference is that factory line workers have to deal with motion fatigue and mind-numbing work while professional sportspeople and musicians practice movements, not scenarios. Each audience/game is new and often require learned skills to be used in new ways.

TakeAway #4 - Make each use memorable by moving minor interface features around.

Note that the above applies only to branding interfaces, not work interfaces.

The desire for the familiar affects more than the Microsoft™ example above. Soon after Firefox 29.01 was released – and essentially forced an interface upgrade on users – there was an app available designed to get the new Firefox interface back to the old Firefox™ look&feel. LinkedIn™ released its Pulse add-in and within minutes there were thirty-seven *suggestions* on how to use it (all written by LinkedIn™ staff) and forty-seven *threads*, many with several contributors, on how to get rid of it (all written by users).

Two things that happen when you introduce a new or modified interface without warning. The first deals with *preparation sets* or PPSETs,[274,341,359,444,456,485,565] the second is

---

[d] – Amusingly, user experience and design professionals could learn from people in the language learning fields. Adults learning a new language have a similar challenge, having to learn a new language "reflex" where a proven reflex already exists. The challenge is compounded by the need to retain the old language reflex while learning a new one. This is why people who become idiomatically fluent in multiple languages later in life will literally shift their position and sometimes posture when going from one language to another; they're shifting neural reflexes much the way a professional boxer shifts posture and position when moving from "this is just me" to "this is me boxing".

that the brain responds with what's called *mismatch negativity*, or MMN.[330,351,410]

PPSETs occur any time an individual does anything and are literally the brain's way of rehearsing something before it happens in reality. Going back to professional sportspeople, musicians and the like, they often intentionally practice their event or performance in their minds before actually doing it and there are lots of neurologic and somatic reasons why this is useful. Everybody does PPSETs, though, and some of the more gross (large-scale) examples are when we "practice" what we're going to say to someone before we say it in reality, how when we "practice" an important encounter before actually meeting the person or group (asking for a raise, a doctoral defense, confronting a spouse or co-worker and giving a presentation are common examples).

When we register shock, dismay, tension release, anxiety release, when we belly laugh or burst out laughing, etc., its because our PPSETs didn't prepare us properly for what actually happened. This is why we're awed by magicians and good jokes; we are *primed* (prepared or led to believe) one thing is going to happen, our PPSETs prepare us for the primed outcome and another outcome occurs. We respond with either a release (laugh) or increase (anxiety) of tension.[12,44,77,123,126,127,181,221,227,244,290,315, 350,355,406,545,554,565,610]

When it comes to interfaces, user experiences and just marketing in general, PPSETs are the user's or audience's learned responses to the interface, experience or content.

However, the more familiar we are with what we're doing, the more those PPSETs become part of our neural wiring, meaning once a response to an interface or content is set, it's tough to break that pattern, meaning familiar interfaces cause familiar responses.

Expectation is based more on context than content as far as PPSETs and MMNs are concerned. Something's funny or not depending on who says it.[295] Couple that with what's called the "ceiling effect"; if a task is too easy then the experimental results may be too hard to detect.

TakeAway #5 – To learn if your designs are effective, first test the edge of usability then pull back.

Now let's add in something called "categorical perception". Categorical perception causes humans to lump things into broad categories. Example: Take ten people and decide who's short and who's tall. If we see all ten at once, then the divide is based on the ten people's average height. If we see them one at a time we base the results on the first person we saw.

Put these all together and you get:

TakeAway #6 – Give visitors time to shop elsewhere and they will.

TakeAway #7 – If their experience with your interface/property is bad, everything else is good.

Let me give you a real-life example. I originally published my books through LuLu and was running into repeated problems. Not showstoppers individually but they were starting to put lots of +1's in the debranding column. Then, I had a problem that I knew was not difficult to solve from a customer service standpoint and was told it was impossible to solve.

So I performed an experiment. I took the same files to Amazon's CreateSpace system (they were all ready to publish) and was selling the book in about a day.

And here's the kicker. About a week later, I received an email from LuLu letting me know that the problem that drove me to Amazon's CreateSpace was solvable on LuLu and would I be interested.

Talk about "too little too late"!

These concepts go far beyond what most people think of as an "interface". Anything where humans interact with something is an interface.[e] Two friends chatting as they're walking down a sidewalk are communicating through the interface of language and shared experience. CSR officers take note!

TakeAway #8 - Don't like your numbers? A radical redesign is called for.

MMNs are a neural holdover from the time of our ancestors who had to quickly and accurately differentiate how the winds were moving the grasses, how the leaves were clustered in the trees, how the water was swirling around the rocks in rivers and lakes and so on. The function of MMNs is to bring our attention to the one thing that's different from everything else in the environment and are the source of the *Sameness-Difference Sorter* modality axis. The one or two stalks of grass that weren't moving with the wind signaled a lion, leopard, tiger, bear, wolf or some other predator preparing to pounce. Ditto leaves in trees and water in a pond, river, stream or lake. But MMNs don't stop there. Our ancestors were sensitive to animals growling, snakes rattling, hooves pounding, cold spots, warm spots, the changes in animal scents, the off taste of a berry, ... MMNs kept our ancestors safe by bringing their attention to the one thing that was different from all the other things they knew about.

Consider this a bit further and you'll appreciate that MMNs also signaled our ancestors when something was unique and good, too. Anyone who's seen a child's first taste of ice cream or chocolate has seen MMNs in action. That look of surprise then delight is the external, behavioral demonstration of "Wow! This is different! How can I get me some more of this delightful stuff?"[f]

---

[e] – with a nod to *Reading Virtual Minds Volume IV: Use, Usable, Usability and Usage*.
[f] – The Sameness-Difference Sorter modality axis is one of the major behavioral axes. It demonstrates itself most often in how people sort things and recognize what's out of place in their environment. Sameness sorters group all like things together and determine what's out of place by recognizing what doesn't fit in any of the groups. Difference sorters mentally ignore all similar items and what's left is what's different. Each methodology has its strengths and weaknesses. There are many pop culture quizzes that rely on the Sameness-Difference behavioral axis to demonstrate individual personality traits. One of our favorites is "What do a fork, a pile of dirty laundry and a menu have in common?" Silverware placement and dirty laundry sorting are demonstrations of whether or not someone is a sameness or a difference

MMNs come into play when there are interface changes that people aren't prepared for. The individual is used to one way of doing things and is prepared to do things that same way when *boom!* things aren't the way they were. Responses range from momentary confusion to frustration to rage, all dependent on how time-critical the task was when the modified interface popped up. Most people use word processors, spreadsheets and other software as tools[g]. Change the shape of a hammer when someone needs to drive a nail and you've set both the person and yourself up for failure. The best time to change interface design follows the same rule as getting a loan or looking for a new job; the best time to get a loan is when you don't need one. The best time to go looking for a new job is when you don't need one. The best time to modify or introduce a new interface is when the user doesn't need your software or device for daily productivity. And time-criticality is crucial. No one is interested in learning a new interface when they're falling off a cliff unless that interface lands them safely on the ground somewhere.

Fortunately there's a way around this "introduce when not being used" scenario.

TakeAway #9 - Change interfaces slowly over time so that users habituate to new features as they need them.

Most software goes through several maintenance upgrades between major upgrades. UXers should include minor interface modifications – starting with least-used interface options or menu items – with each maintenance upgrade. Existing users will have grown comfortable with the new interface through the upgrade cycle. New users won't notice any difference at all.

Good designers offer migration paths from old to new designs. Such migration paths demonstrate new problem-solving

=====

sorter. Sort all clothes at once - sameness sorter. Sort clothes as you go - difference sorter. Ditto where someone places their knife and fork to free their hands when dining. Sameness sorters search for commonality, difference sorters search for uniqueness.
[g] – covered in *Reading Virtual Minds Volume IV: Use, Usable, Usability and Usage*.

skills or encourage users to explore alternatives.[h] Bad designers set users up for failure, demonstrating weaknesses in the designer's own Personality, Identity and Core.[i]

> **TakeAway #10 - People will use a new interface when they believe it rewards them more than the old interface rewards them.**

This was mentioned briefly in ***About the Cover*** (page 29).

> **TakeAway #11 - People will use any interface when they believe there's a fair-exchange[j] between themselves and what's on the other side of the interface.**

That little princess whose daddy owned the universe had never been taught that sometimes god doesn't answer, that sometimes what we pray is a request and not simply a blind tribute, and she was psychologically, emotionally, physically and spiritually destroyed. What she had always thought (cognitive) no longer matched experience, therefore her behaviors towards people, places and things were in question because her behaviors were no longer producing the effects she'd learned to expect (behavioral/effective), hence her motivations for doing things were no longer valid.

And for those of you familiar with NextStage's work and writings, you know that we've just described what happens when

---

[h] – covered in *Reading Virtual Minds Volume IV: Use, Usable, Usability and Usage*.
[i] – Here's a bit of psychology for you. People set up other people to fail when they fear them. They may fear them as individuals, as group members, they may fear what they will or won't do. It takes a bit of digging to determine what the fear is about and you'll always find it there. So bad designers set up users to fail because they fear...what? There is no greater group with imposter syndrome than digital property designers, it seems. I've had more web/digital designers have emotional blow ups because nobody could use their interfaces than in any other field I know. Meanwhile, NextStage's sites have had two –2! – user usage failures in several tens of thousands of uses in the past sixteen or so years. One occurred when the user didn't read the directions, another occurred when another user didn't look at what she was clicking on. Laugh while-a you can, Monkey-Boy.
[j] – covered in detail in *Reading Virtual Minds Volume III: Fair-Exchange and Social Networks*.

the {C,B/e,M} matrix completely shifts and that such shifts are demonstrated in the Personality, Identity and Core correspondingly.

It's worth noting that everybody undergoes minor shifts during their day. NextStage's RichPersonae™ coding system designates {C,B/e,M} matrices with letters indicating the strongest sensory modality, so ET will recognize individuals as As, Es, Gs, Is, Ks, Ns, Os, Ps, Ts or Vs.[k] By the time someone is in midlife, their strongest modality tends to stay their strongest modality regardless of what's going on around them. They may have momentary shifts to other modalities and such momentary shifts are demonstrations of their using varied experiential references to address immediate situations. Once the immediate situation resolves itself the individual returns to their chosen major modality (depending on how much of an emotional, physical, spiritual or psychologic shock the situation is).

But someone in "mid-life crisis" or spiritual upheaval or going through remission or encountering a new interface when they don't have time to learn its intricacies, etc.? We sometimes say the individual went through something and came out a different person or say to the individual "You're a new you". The UX term is "uninstall". Marketing knows this as a "lost client".

Mid-life crisis, spiritual upheaval and disease remission are recognitions of major modality shifts, of permanent changes in the individual's {C,B/e,M} and the replacing of old Personality, Identity and Core with new Personality, Identity and Core that can better deal with their larger experiential inventory. Uninstalling software, deleting an app and lost clients are exemplary of users who don't have time to shift their {C,B/e,M}s around.

Let me give you an example of user experience crashing down on designer expectations, of visitors not having time or inclination to shift their {C,B/e,M}s for even a second. A friend

---

[k] – What, you thought there were only five senses? How mid-20th century of you. NextStage updates its system when there's definitive research that new sensory modalities exist. Sometimes ET recognizes a new sensory modality before research declares it exists. That's always fun.

sent me links to two sites, each containing a request for charitable giving, and asked for a quick review. Specifically, he wanted to know if the charitable giving requests were working.

I dutifully went to both sites and was immediately met with a lightbox popup, the first word my eyes locked on was "SWEEPSTAKES".

I immediately closed the lightbox, looked over the site and couldn't see anything about any charitable giving options.

I contacted my friend. The lightboxes were the charitable giving promos. 90% of the people closed the lightboxes as soon as they popped up. I have no idea how many of the remaining 10% gave anything. Evidently quite a few people wanted to know if this was some kind of scam. Such challenges have plagued online popup surveys for years.[120]

The above anecdote and story about the little princess might be interesting at best if it didn't demonstrate a major challenge in user experience and design. One major unmet expectation can change someone forever, lots of little unmet expectations can do the same thing. The difference is trickles of water over time versus a flood; both can change the course of rivers, the former simply does it without the landscape taking notice. If you're involved in usability, you want trickles of water over time. Users will easily accept minor changes accumulating over time. You can even rewrite a system's entire backend, leave the interface unchanged, and users will be thrilled. They may note decreases in execution time, faster loads, whatever, and most won't.

But heaven forbid you alter their interface one iota.

And you can work wonders on the backend that improve things a thousand fold, but change one thing on the front end that fails?

Whoa!

Introduce a complete interface rewrite with more than five (in most cases) bugs in most often used functionality and today's users will hang you in effigy. This is especially true with mobile interfaces. Research shows that mobile users, regardless of whether the interface flaw is hardware- or software-related, blame the software, the app, every time.[57,173,277,284,407,505,580] Too many minor failed expectations and people get jaded.

The question becomes "How jaded do people get?" Mobile users are notorious for giving up on a device because of repeated app failures (see *3.A – It's What, Not How: Marketing When the Time is Right*, page 116). Will people give up on Dell™, Microsoft™, SAS™, Comcast™, ConAgra™, 3M™, Avery-Dennison™ (most people have no idea how big that company is) and the like because some interface doesn't suit them? Probably not and such companies work their size and ubiquity to their advantage.

And now, if I may, a bit of a riff on size and ubiquity because, from an evolutionary standpoint, they are funny things.

Evolution, you see, doesn't naturally favor size and ubiquity.

Unless we're considering the evolution of an ecosystem. Then the bigger and more ubiquitous the better (for survival's sake), and the business example of an ecosystem is a company that diversifies and has many holdings.

Take Google as the example. Google's Fortune 500 rank was 46 in 2014, 55 in 2013 and 241 way back in 2007. That's nice but not from an evolutionary biology perspective because – if we just limit our study to humans and their organizations, what they build, what they create, what they think of as "theirs", what they own – the human species is the largest business on the planet with over 7.4 billion employees.[I] There're a lot of us out there and we're making more every second. At an amazing rate. Our nearest competitors are the US Department of Defense (DOD) with 3.2m employees, The People's Liberation Army (China) with 2.3m employees and then Walmart with 2.1m employees.

The human species as a business is over 3,000 times larger than the largest company.

And none of those businesses from US DOD down to Google and beyond are cloning themselves. Google isn't making any more googles and the US DOD isn't making any more US DODs.

[I] – as of 16 Dec 2015. See http://www.worldometers.info/world-population/ for something more up to date

How about net worth? The human population's value is about $219,000,000,000,000,000 (going by environmental replacement costs). The 2014 Global 1 company (based on capitalization) is Apple at $469,000,000,000. So if we're talking money, the world's largest company is 1/500,000 the size of Humanity Inc.

Nice numbers, huh?

What makes this analogy so interesting is that these numbers are only proxies for what humans, Google, Apple, Walmart, the US DOD and so on are really in business to do.

Take a guess. What do you think it might be?

Make money? Nope, that's a proxy.

Make more of themselves? Kind of, maybe. Businesses replicate by diversifying their portfolio and ingesting smaller companies. If anything, think of a smart amoeba and you have the idea.

The ultimate business is survival. As individuals? Meh. As a species? Definitely, oh yeah, you betcha! But to survive as a species, the best options are to be a species of small, nimble, quick and intelligent individuals. Of the world's oldest businesses, 89% have fewer than 300 employees.[m]

Now let's go back to Google because they fit the initial criterion; they're big and ubiquitous. And in the greater scheme of things, they're easier to think about.

From an evolutionary standpoint, Google is one of the largest predators on the planet. There are only 45 larger predators and lots – I mean lots and *lots* and **lots** of lesser predators.

It reminds me of a song I heard as a kid. About Big Bad Short Fat Irving, the 142nd fastest gun in the West. "There were 141 faster than he but was a'gunnin' for 143."

Large predators, the ones near the top of the food chain, are very vulnerable. Look at polar bears, wolves, lions, tigers. Top of the food chain doesn't get you much because to get to the top you tend to specialize and when you specialize you lose the ability to adapt "downward" so to speak.

---

[m] – from http://en.wikipedia.org/wiki/List_of_oldest_companies

Google "preys" (we're using metaphor here) on other companies. YouTube, for example.

Google also preys on us and with good reason. There's lots of us out there. About 7.4 billion, in fact.

Here's another evolutionary biology fact; the larger the predator the more prey it must consume. This is why the largest creatures tend to consume the smallest creatures – think whales and krill. The only way whales can satisfy their hunger is to devour massive amounts of little tiny krills. And if you think money is the de facto standard, you're not living in the 21st century. Money stopped making the world go round on 9/11. Information is the new collateral and it's going to stay that way for a while.

And where is the largest collection of information on anything these days?

But let's get back to money because it's easier for most people to think about as a form of collateral.

I look at my bank account and Google's and I'm...umm...tiny. I look around my neighborhood and all together, we're...umm...tiny. I don't think there's anything or anyone in my state (New Hampshire, at present) that's anywhere near #46 in the food chain.

Tiny.

Fortunately, I also know that the tiny creatures are also the most adaptive. We have to be. There's sooo many of us. And we're sooo tiny. By comparison. You don't see a lot of dinosaurs hanging around, do you? Nope. The smart dinosaurs turned into birds in order to survive. They got tiny (by comparison). T-Rex, in order to survive as a species, evolved into the modern chicken.[n]

Remember how Mick taught Rocky to be quick on his feet?

Catch the chicken.

And that was a domestic, barnyard chicken.

You don't even want to try catching a wild chicken.

So I'm not really worried about privacy. I'm not worried about becoming prey in any way, shape or form. I'm too tiny in

---

[n] – http://www.livescience.com/1410-rex-related-chickens.html

comparison. I can feel the bow wake of the whale before I become one of the many in the mouthful of krill, and if I stay away from where the lions, wolves, tigers and bears are, I'm good.

2.3 – Rocky learns to be quick and
nimble at the talons of a master.

Google is the one that's vulnerable. Their very size and position on the food chain means other creatures, able to evolve more rapidly (i.e., able to respond to market forces, pressures, demands, hostility, ...) will eventually deal with it. Why do you think Google became Alphabet? Remember the search engine wars of the late 1990s and early 2000s?

It'll be like those old dinosaur movies; the two great dinosaurs will wrestle their way over the cliff or into the lava flow and we, the clever *little* mammals, will scurry away, chuckling all the while.

Of course, if Galphabetoogle wants to come along and gobble up NextStage – I mean– if they want to come a' courting – I don't mind climbing a little higher on the food chain myself.

Remember Big Bad Short Fat Irving? Look out #143. I might be a' gunnin'.

2.A – The Ubiquity of Failed Expectations

Jading is becoming the norm because failed expectations plague the digital world; people are confusing entertainment with experience. People believe they're having lots of experiences and they aren't. Let me give you some examples:

> Seeing the Sistine Chapel on screen is nice. See it in person and you want to change faiths for an instant.
> Seeing the King's Table on the Isle of Skye on screen? So-so. Walking it? *Whoa!*
> Seeing a video of the moonglow on the Greenland ice cap from a jet flying 30,000 feet above? You think "That's been Photoshopped." Seeing it from the jet flying over the ice cap? You'll stop thinking for a while.
> Seeing the Grand Canyon, even in IMAX? Yeah, it's breathtaking. Seeing it from its own edge? You'll forget to breathe.
> Seeing the Aurora Borealis dance on the horizon in a YouTube video or some such? It's nice. Seeing it reach down to the far isles from our Nova Scotia mountaintop? You make plans for meeting SnowWalker[o].

So the 'net can bring me the world but the world is far too big to fit in that box sitting on my desk (and much worse if the box is in the palm of my hand!). The box of the mind, however? Infinite capacity. It's like the TARDIS.[p] Bigger on the inside than on the outside.

The difference between experienced and surrogated is causing problems in design because people believe they're having lots of experiences and they aren't. They're having surrogates of experience and mistaking the video for "being there". We're becoming a world of Chauncy Gardiners.[q]

––––––––––––

[o] – In Inuit myth, the Aurora Borealis were the souls of unborn children. SnowWalker carried these souls to earth and gathered them back up again at the end of life. SnowWalker's comings and goings caused the Aurora Borealis to dance on the horizon.

Because people are substituting entertainment for experience, even the simplest instructions must be simplified down to the point of only having entertainment value. If people's experience of interaction is primarily through entertainment and not reality then the instructions of what to do must be based on their experience of entertainment, not their experience of reality. This is witnessed by any "how to" instructions for any goods sold internationally. Open the box and the first thing encountered is a brilliantly designed infographic with no words, only images, of how to put the purchase together with each step clearly and cleanly separated from the steps before and steps after, one operation per step. Nothing to confuse or confound. Such instructions are brilliant and even more so because they're often cartoonish in character. Again, we must entertain if we wish to provide experience.

> **TakeAway #12 - The less action required in each step in a process, the more likely the user/visitor/audience will succeed in the overall process.**

This experience to expectation gauge goes negative even faster when we, the users, have more experience in a given field than the designer does. Let me give you some literary examples of how having more experience than the designer can cause problems.

I knew an author who wrote a book with a female detective as the central character. She did the normal detectivish things – found clues, trailed red herrings, had arguments with police and other government officials, practiced her markspersonship, interrogated suspects, ... – until at one point she got into some hand-to-hand combat with a highly skilled opponent. She came out of it with busted ribs, a punctured lung, a broken arm, a dislocated shoulder and severe bruising.

=====

[p] – http://en.wikipedia.org/wiki/TARDIS
[q] – http://en.wikipedia.org/wiki/Being_There

She limped home (literally) where she was met by her police detective lover and, before she had any medical attention, they had sex.

The author had asked me to critique his book and when I got to that part I stopped, looked up at him and asked, "You've never really been in a fight before, have you. I'm talking about a fight where you weren't sure you were going to survive, a fight where you needed help just to pick yourself up and get away before the police showed up to survey the damage." I wasn't asking questions, I was stating facts.

He admitted this was true. With his permission, I applied mild pressure to one of his nerve plexis. Mild pressure and he fell to the ground, gasping for air, his face ashen, his body sweating. I gave him a minute of shaking then helped him back up. "Now imagine if I had wanted to hurt you seriously. Imagine that level of pain ten- to twenty-fold, all over your body. Are you going to be up for sex?"

He rewrote that section of his novel.

Another author was a college freshman when I met him. He asked me to critique a story that contained a passionate love scene. Except it was neither passionate nor love and only because the author, despite his authorial skill, was only eighteen years old and had never really experienced either passion or love in the way his mid-thirties protagonists would have experienced it.

Perhaps you've experienced reading a book or watching a movie or TV show only to be pulled out of the story because the author or scriptwriter, even for the briefest moment, didn't know what they were writing about and you did. I've watched some excellent episodic television with bank tellers and been amazed at the flaws they'll catch in scenes where money is exchanged, or with horse riders who notice that the horse someone rides in on isn't the horse they're sitting on when they get to the stable and so on. Monitoring such things is called "continuity". Continuity used to be the purview of copy editors in writing, in scriptwriting they were handled by script or continuity supervisors.

Interface and user experience designers don't have such people watching their backs. Even in writing, screen and video production it's a dying art.

But here's the catch and the point to these authorial anecdotes as they apply to user experience and design, and it goes back to the discussion that started this chapter regarding how experience drives Core, Identity and Personality: if all I've ever had is surrogate experiences, then surrogate experiences are my reality and I'll recognize these surrogate experiences as valid for everyone because my social network will contain people who've had similar surrogate experiences (gamers, for example). Pop culture fans are notorious for believing that surrogate experiences are the same as real experiences. This false belief is why commercials and such now have disclaimers such as "You will never be allowed to do this on a test drive. Ever." and "Closed course. Professional Drivers. Safety systems deactivated. Do not attempt".

So experience is never flawed. It may be wanting and it's never flawed.

And experience fuels our expectations. PPSETs and MMNs are all over the place.

Experience is what you get when you did not get what you wanted.
— Randy Paush

3 - Expectation versus Satisfaction

3.1 from http://thechive.com/2011/01/17/things-real-people-dont-say-about-advertising-23-photos/

When was the last time somebody opened up a solicitation email or browsed a company site and said, "My God, this is beautiful! I'm so glad I opened/read/saw this! I'll just have to tell all my friends!"

Chances are you've never heard those types of comments. Chances are that you view these types of activities with the same sense of boredom and frustration that you used to view salespeople who didn't know when to quit.

The next time you are in one of these situations take a minute and do a little self-monitoring. Are you tensing, perhaps a little, perhaps a lot? Is your brow furrowed or smooth? Are you blinking less than you normally do? Are you breathing from your chest or from your abdomen? And your big thigh muscles, the quadriceps and biceps femoris, are they tensed, maybe a little maybe a lot?

In short, are you anxious or relaxed? You'd be amazed at the number of people who go through minuscule to mightyscule anxiety responses when they engage in these relatively innocuous online activities.

The question for NextStage was, "How come?"

Before the proliferation of mobiles, people were in safe if not comfortable environments when they opened emails or browsed websites, usually in home or office settings. This is no longer the case. People TXT, tweet, post, chat, pin, email, message and browse while walking, driving, eating, ... you name the bodily function, people are online doing it.

And is anybody safe from being YouTubed?

But barring external stimuli such as vehicular and pedestrian traffic, what caused someone to experience anxiety when they opened an email or browsed a website?

Expectation.

When people expect A and get B they go through a few moments of fugue. External reality (experience) is not synching up with internal reality (expectation) and the mind and brain will, if allowed, burn themselves out making the two mesh. One extreme end of fugue responses is insanity, the other extreme end is denial (which is, of course, just another form of insanity – what is called "ignoring the elephant in the living room")[a]. Most people just go through a few moments of confusion before incorporation or experience "instantaneous" incorporation, both of which lead to acknowledgement and integration of the conflicting information. Note that "acknowledgement" isn't "acceptance" so much as it means the information is integrated with existing knowledge to create a greater knowledge- and information-base. The extremes of this are something similar to a *petite mal* and

---

[a] – Insanity and denial are *polarity responses* to the same stimuli. In both cases, the stimuli is not integrated into the individual's psyche.

more often hypnotic attention – the primary learning strategy employed when moving from Stage 1 to Stage 2 learning.[b]

People are changing their behaviors both in response to and to respond to new information channels. This "in response to and to respond to new information channels" is an important distinction that many people are missing. The types of information people are accessing is the same as always – gossip, news, warnings, requests for help – it's only the method of access that is changing. We long ago stopped meeting at the town's general store[c], we now meet online but what we talk about is the same.

When eLearning and eCommerce audiences are asked "Do you really expect a great experience when you're on some site?" The response was hugely negative. Specific to mobiles, NextStage research demonstrated that the overwhelming majority of mobile users load a "desktop" site on their mobiles because the mobile-designed experience is so poor.[57]

Let's expand the discussion beyond digital properties. Do you expect a truly engaging experience when you read a PDF file on screen? Have you gotten to the point in your business or personal email where you've apologized to someone because their email got stopped by your spam filter so you didn't know you were supposed to do whatever it is you're apologizing about? Do you list yourself as "unavailable" on Skype and choose to proactively engage with others whom you have a more than casual attachment to? I've had numerous people email me that I forgot to send them something only to explain that yes, I did send what they requested, it was in the very email they were responding to.

---

[b] – There are two basic times that people enjoy the unexpected; 1) when the unexpected is an anticipated element of the environment (like a magic show, carnival ride, plot twist, i.e., there's some entertainment value or other reward associated with the unexpected event73,269,509) and 2) when they're moving from Stage 1 to Stage 2 learning.501,525 These are the only two situations where the unexpected is satisfying.
[c] – People in the United States, when interviewed during the first half of the 20th century and asked what was the one event that changed their life the most, almost universally answered RFD or "rural free delivery". Mail coming to their door meant they no longer had to go to a central location where they'd interact with their neighbors, gossip, share ideas, discuss current events and so on.

Most of them don't read their emails "below the fold". Especially on mobile devices.[d]

Pick a site or tool interface, any site or tool interface, even ones that you're familiar with and use regularly, perhaps a site you already have bookmarked or a tool that you use so often you've iconized it on your desktop: the question becomes "Is going to that site or using that tool something you consider during your other daily activities?" With an opt-in email newsletter or list-server, will you be talking about what you read or saw the next day? Will you even remember it in the next five minutes? Or do you, like most people, have a separate email account that collects such things and that you periodically clean out without reading?

Are you more likely to share an amusing video or joke or are you more likely to wax poetic about how easily you could navigate some site or interface? Or are you yourself or do you know someone whose social constraints are so relaxed that you event yourself for the whole world to see then suffer disappointment when no one plays along?[60,109-111,124,175,561] Therapeutic caregivers have a term for this; attention seeking behavior.[42,309,465,527,601]

Let's put those questions into context. There are people who will take time out of their day to contact their significant other for no reason other than to say hello, exchange some gossip, so on and so forth. There is nothing objectively crucial to their day which requires this activity and subjectively their day isn't complete without it. Likewise there are people who can't wait to get back to a book they're reading. Such people find great *satisfaction* in relatively mundane activities.

And if you've been paying attention you realize immediately that objectivity is relative, cruciality is imperative and satisfaction is a one-way bridge from the latter to the former.

---

[d] – Likewise, I've had people apologize to me with "Sorry, I forgot you actually read everything in an email."

TakeAway #13 - The first design is for what the user believes is imperative (crucial) and for how they want to do it.

TakeAway 14 - Satisfy a crucial need first and they'll accept anything else you give them.

In these and similar cases the individual has an *expectation* which, if unmet, leaves them unfulfilled and wanting, i.e., *unsatisfied*. Now let me share a statistic that is damning to information designers regardless of what they're designing (interface, tool, digital property, ...): People normally attempt things three times. If there's no satisfaction after three attempts then it doesn't matter when they're successful, they will not experience pleasure in the act and they will lose interest in the act.[268]

Good thing few information designers know that bit of neuroscience, I guess.

Satisfaction occurs when we feel the outcome of some action is positive. The outcome doesn't have to be what we wanted as the outcome – although the closer the better and if the need is emotionally based, the outcome better be on the far side of 90% – all that matters is that we *feel* the outcome is positive. It's psycho-emotive, belief-based, not psycho-cognitive, logic-based, and brings us back to the differences between acceptance and acknowledgement. We may accept and acknowledge an outcome is for the best and still not be satisfied. Satisfaction comes when Core values[e] are met or exceeded. Acceptance and

---

[e] – Core values are those concepts of what's right and wrong, good and bad that we learned as children and, once our innocence is lost, remain but with different names. We give them different names because modern society requires it. We can't hit people when we feel hurt, even though hitting them again and again and again may be exactly what we want to do to satisfy our sense of "justice". Another example comes from people celebrating in some way, shape or form upon signing a momentous contract, closing a deal, etc. The phrase most often used is "*We won* the deal". The sense of "winning" comes from being in competition with other businesses. That winning sense is based on the endorphin rush that comes from knowing *we*'ve been selected for something good, something beneficial to *us*, something wonderful that others will congratulate *us* for, envy *us* for and so on. That endorphin rush is the brain registering a Core value, Acceptance, under a new name, "Winning the deal".

acknowledgement are projections of the Identity and Personality.

And the greatest Core value is placed on the Positive-Negative axis. It is the first one we learn as a child and the most long-lived one in our evolutionary ancestry. Single-celled creatures don't feel pleasure, they experience Positivity. They don't feel pain, they experience Negativity. The Positive-Negative axis is the first thing we sense in the womb and the last thing we sense in life.

The wonderful thing about this axis is that all other modalities are built upon it to some degree or other. What is the difference between warm and hot? Sensorially, warm and hot are both positive and negative and both are positive and negative in the same direction. The difference occurs when we're too far along the cool-warm axis to be comfortable. Then, whether warm or hot, the sensory experience is negative.

It is the kinship that all modalities bear with Positive and Negative that make them so useful in causing desired outcomes. Is someone having a positive experience? That's the best time to invite them to do something you want them to do. Is someone being successful doing something trivial? Psychologically, they're much more prone to take on risk because success creates a euphoria that's hard to beat.[14,43,213,214,222,230,263,300,302,346,362,399, 468,474,476,487,494,510,551,574,578,581]

This is a boon for ad designers and companies selling space in their games, personal advancement sites, ...

TakeAway #15 - Guarantee player wins when specific ads display and revenues will skyrocket.

Do you finance your game app development by running ads while people play your game? Do you want to make some real money? Tell your ad-based clients that you'll guarantee players win when your clients' ads display. Your client's revenues will climb and so will yours. Clients don't want to pay for the guarantee? Then player ad buy-in will be based on player success in your game.

So make your game challenging enough to be unobvious in player wins. Make the player work for it and just make sure they do win. Again, your revenue will skyrocket.

> **TakeAway #16 - Create branded, addictive behaviors with no-cost rewards when specific ads display and revenues will skyrocket.**

Have you ever heard the expression "Close only counts in horseshoes and hand grenades?" An interesting feature of the primitive brain is that it enjoys horseshoes and hand grenades because the higher brain recognizes "close to" as "I'm getting better" and opens a reward channel in the lower brain.[13, 30,31,38,53,68,183,218,253,286,300,308,324,362,400,422,481,496,513,521,523,528,543,546, 584,614] Studies show people feel just as good when they get nearer to perfect as they do when they get to perfect, and often getting to perfect causes a kind of post-partum depression that needs to be avoided at all costs. After you've achieved your goal you can get psychologically lost until you find another goal. Sending an intermittent signal that a gamer is getting better (a brief text message on the screen, a sound, an haptic (vibration) are all valid reward signals once the gamer recognizes their meaning) is sufficient reward to create branded, addictive behaviors.

> **TakeAway #17 - Add a few symmetrical visual, audio and haptic enhancements to each game level or navigated page on a digital property to keep users/visitors engaged.**

The brain remembers patterns more easily than irregularities.[35,201,251,478,605] Both Sameness and Difference sorters[297,472] rely on pattern recognition to find what they're looking for. Experience designers can use these neural artifacts to create highly memorable (and we hope pleasant) game and usage experiences by adding sensory enhancements as users/visitors continue through different experiential levels. The brain remembers the enhanced experience and seeks to repeat it because it is the most easily remembered. Do this to conversion pages and checkout pages and you make use of a little piece of neural wiring that helps you achieve your goals.

3.A — It's What, Not How: Marketing When the Time is Right

Regular readers know two of my favorite quotes are Steve Jobs' "...people don't know what they want until you show it to them." and Henry Ford's "If I'd asked my customers what they wanted, they'd have said a faster horse." Lots of people point to Steve Jobs' and Apple™'s success with a RahRah attitude that (in my opinion) belies a lot of ignorance of society and culture at most or an amazingly narrow view of success at the least. They seem to forget that Steve Jobs and Apple™ – and I'm not denying their success – were introducing technology (the Macintosh computer and all that followed it, save the Newton. People seem to forget the Newton) to an existing market, not to mention one that existed largely due to technologies developed through public dollars.[386]

Apple™ was established before the advent of PCs. Apple's founders, The Two Steves, had established themselves as being outside the corporate world. But PCs were filling a market that the Apple™ IIe, III (I think it was "III") failed to touch. The Lisa made an attempt but there was no "there" there when it was released. Apple™ aficionados were waiting for Apple to come up with something to strike back and the Macintosh was it. All that market needed was a reason to demonstrate just how different the Macintosh was from the PC. Culture and society met marketing and technology head-on and the two have lived happily together ever since. At least for 13% of the market.

But all this is academic and history. The battle is no longer for device or operating system, it is for *What*. People long ago gave up caring *How* they got something done (device and methodology), the battleground is "What can I do?"[f]. Henry Ford understood this; people wanted to travel faster. They didn't understand and couldn't imagine an automobile, so they said "faster horse". Steve Jobs' audience knew what it wanted to do, they didn't understand and couldn't imagine being able to do it beyond the paradigm they were familiar with.

This *What* versus *How* is a critical factor when doing experience and expectation audience studies. Few studies investigate *protention* and (my belief is that) expectation studies are worthless without such investigations. Protention is to expectation what hope is to belief and what emotion is to logic. Protention is what we really, really, really want to have happen, Expectation is what we think will really happen. President Obama's message – Change – is a protentious message. Voters (I'll offer) expect some kind of change to occur regardless of who gets into office. But a young african-american male is so different from an old white guy that protentious change is obvious if not evident. Some will ask why a white female wouldn't protend change. I'm quite sure some white females would have been protentious and had a good shot at the White House. Hillary[g], the white female we're talking about without naming names, did not signal herself as being different enough from the old white guy network, indeed many believed she was part of it, to signal protentious change.

Study user/visitor/audience protention and you'll discover the necessary "What" and "How" elements for your interfaces and designs.

TakeAway #18 - Design audience studies so that you learn what people want to do, then design products that achieve the "What" via a beautifully elegant "How".

---

[f] – covered in agonizing detail in *Reading Virtual Minds Volume IV: Use, Usable, Usability and Usage*.
[g] – And what a wonderful example of a personal brand. She's not *Hillary Rodham Clinton*, she's simply *Hillary* and few people in the modern world have to ask, "Who?"

Remember Clarke's Third Law, "Any sufficiently advanced technology is indistinguishable from magic."? Demonstrate *what* people can do, show them that *how* to do the *what* is simple, and you've demonstrated magic.

3.B – What, How, Experience and Expectation

The sad fact is that most people we interviewed don't expect a great or even a good online experience regardless of device used. After several repeat visits to a favorite digital property they might be neutral, or they may be enthusiastic about getting emails, TXTing, tweeting, updating their profile or Facebook page, chatting with friends online, but here we separate the *experience* from the *expectation* and learn that most people's expectation is rather low (see Chapter 2, *Experience versus Expectation*, page 85).

Consider Figures 3.2-3.7 (pages 119-124). All represent data collected over a fifteen day period from thirty sites in NextStage's inventory. Red is low, yellow is medium and green is high in these figures and each indicates a slightly different aspect of how visitors interact with digital properties.

Figure 3.2 (page 119) shows that a majority of visitors to digital properties don't expect much from their experience. NextStage first encountered this *Meh* attitude in the early 2000s. The excitement of the 'net had worn off, the dot.com boom had busted years earlier, Internet wunderkinds were turning in their Birkenstocks for Maybachs and the unexplored territory of the 'net had become another business vector. There was a bubble with the advent of mobile apps and advanced screen and network systems that made real-time mobile gaming workable and that bubble has been corralled by those who game for a living. Or as someone we interviewed who confessed to being a one-time binge-gamer said, "It's incredible and then you have to work to pay the bills for all the gaming you do. Unless you're Johnathan Wendel[h], work wins."

Now consider how much of our day involves being online. Imagine spending your entire day with the expectation that your day is going to be mediocre, humdrum, uneventful. In some demographics, that's a good thing.

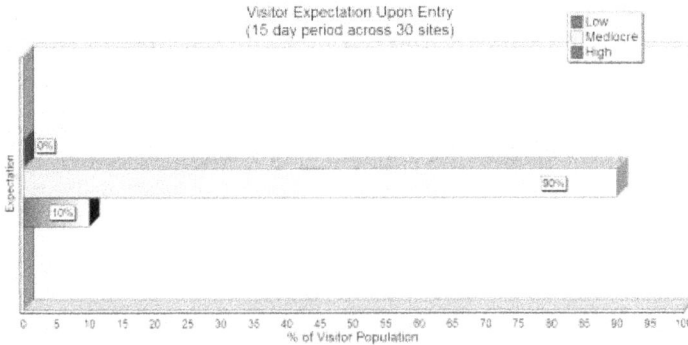

3.2 - Visitor Expectation of their digital property interaction upon entering that property.

A good thing? Yes. NextStage conducted a two-year study with an odd purpose: We wanted to find the average experience. One thing we learned was the answer to "Who wants an average experience?"

Oddly enough, most people do. Extreme experiences can be rewarding, demanding, invigorating and the majority of people on the planet aren't adrenaline junkies. They simply want to make it through their day and into their beds at night, preparing to awake to the monotony of another day. If their experience *of* – not *on* but *of* – your interface is way above average, it'll get in the way of their living their lives. People stop and stare at horrible accidents and great beauty but only a few interact with such things. Your interface needs to be average and then a little more; enough to remain in several different types of memory

---

[h] – Johnathan Wendel, aka "Fatal1ty", is the fourth richest video gamer (based on winnings) in the world. Johnathan Wendel's pseudonym, "Fatal1ty", is a nod to what we wrote about pseudonyms on page 197.

(immediate memory so that the user can get their task done, long-term memory so that the user becomes branded to your interface, episodic memory ditto, procedural memory so that the user can achieve their goal with little cognitive effort and propositional memory so that the user knows your interface will help them achieve their goal), not so much that it stops them from living their lives.

But that study was years ago in Internet time. Now imagine you're a Millennial who expects to be entertained. You have two basic options; deal with the fact that your day is going to be uneventful or convince yourself that mediocrity is exciting and do what used to be called "acting out" and more recently "attention seeking behavior" in psychological circles (as was written on page 112).

I.E., you event yourself.[8,71,98,200,236,259,275,305,307,310,312,319,323, 329,330,342,369,375,394,408,410,419,428,450,514,528]

YouTube, Instagram, Vine, Pinterest, Facebook, FourSquare, social platforms that no one's thought of yet and those that have long since died (SecondLife,[23,98,129,451] anyone?). You make yourself the story. And when you're not the story you do something even more outlandish to make yourself the center of attention once again.

But human attention is a commodity that evolves according to the environment it is in. What caught our attention yesterday is not even noticed today. Anybody remember when webcams first came out? Anybody remember the shock and outrage associated with some of those "most downloaded on the Internet" news stories? Now, who cares? I doubt if anybody notices.

Figure 3.3 (page 121) shows an even more interesting statistic. The number of visitors who left a digital property satisfied is less than 40%.

This is also where fun with statistics comes in. Some readers will look at Figure 3.3 and conclude "At least more are leaving satisfied than are leaving with medium to low satisfaction". Let me share a statistics anecdote from NextStage's Quotes file:

Please, take care of yourself this holiday season. A recent joint study conducted by the Department of Health and the Department of Motor Vehicles indicates that 23% of traffic accidents are alcohol related.

This means that the remaining 77% are caused by idiots that just drink coffee, carbonated drinks, juices, milk, water, and stuff like that.

Therefore, beware of those who do not drink alcohol. They cause three times as many accidents.

This message is sent by someone who cares about your well being.

3.3 - Visitor Satisfaction with their digital property interaction upon exiting that property.

The difference between people's expectation of their near-future experience (Figure 3.2, page 119, a measure of their emotional-cognitive bias as they enter the website or use any interface in general) versus their satisfaction (Figure 3.3, page 121, a measure of their emotional-cognitive bias when they leave the website or stop using an interface) is startling.[577] Let me put this in terms of neuromathematics; subtract exit bias from entry bias and you have experience.

$$Bias_{(entry)} - Bias_{(exit)} = Experience$$

Figure 3.2's (page 119) longest bar is yellow, indicating 90% of visitors had mediocre expectations for their experience. Only

10% came with high expectations (the size of the green bar). Figure 3.3's (page 121) longest bar is green (40%), but not by much because the yellow, average bar is 38% and there's a recognizable chunk of people who left the site unsatisfied (red bar at 22%). This means the sum of visitors leaving the site with an average to poor experience is greater than the number of visitors leaving the site with a good experience. Note that ET is measuring emotional states, not cognitive states. Emotional states are chosen because externally masking emotional states is difficult for the majority of people. People externally mask cognitive states all the time. It's called *lying* and before you think lying is a negative, do remember that our social networks would collapse without those little white lies that hold things together ("You've lost weight, I can tell." "You look great in those slacks." "That car is you!" "Everything you say is important to me."). If someone's social lying is below 3% then people will wonder what's wrong with the individual. Social lying above 17% and people expect you'll let them in on the joke. As we offer in NextStage's BlueSky Meter[i]:

> Remember, everybody has a little BlueSky (3-17%) in their normal, everyday exchanges. Without that little bit of BlueSky human communications would break down, so less than 3% could be a concern (unless you're analyzing technical or research material) and greater than 17% should be a concern (unless you're analyzing fiction material).

These expectation-satisfaction charts are interesting and given added meaning when we appreciate an assumption hidden in them (and in most metrics offered about digital property traffic); the digital property and the digital property alone plays a significant role in visitors' experience and satisfaction levels.

This isn't the case. To demonstrate this, I'd like to begin by combining Figures 3.2 (page 119) and 3.3 (page 121) so that

---

[i] – NextStage's BlueSky Meter and most other NextStage tools are available to NextStage Members. See http://nlb.pub/4 for more information on NextStage Membership.

expectation and satisfaction are shown stacked to 100% as in Figure 3.4 (page 123).

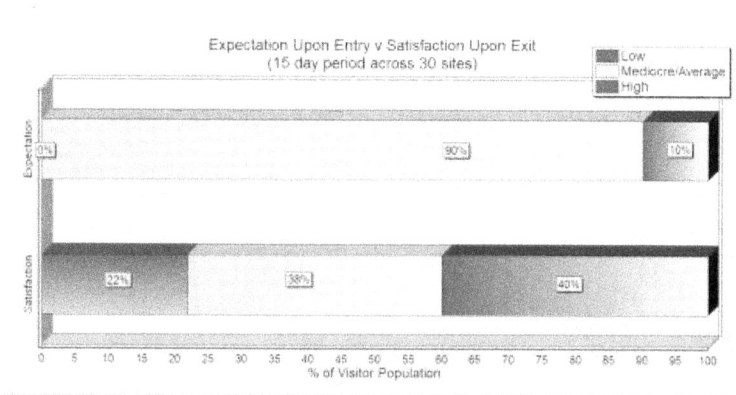

3.4 Expectation and Satisfaction combined into stacked bars
totalling 100% of the visitor population

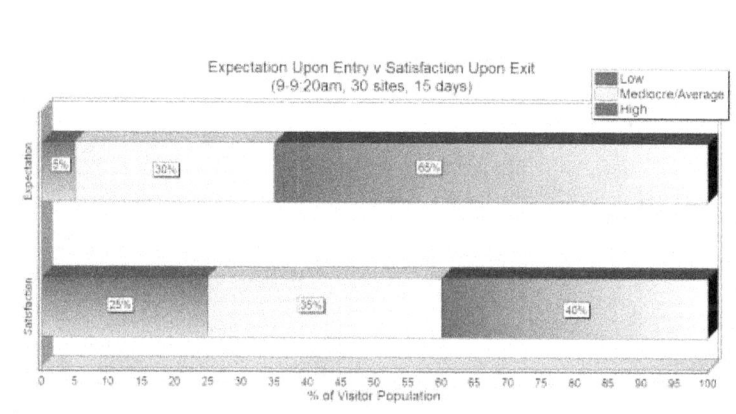

3.5 Expectation versus Satisfaction across 30 sites over a 15-day
period, 9:00-9:20am

Now compare Figure 3.4 on page 123 with Figures 3.5-7 on pages 123-124. Figure 3.4 (page 123) shows the average expectation and satisfaction results for a 15-day period. Figures 3.5-7 (pages 123-124) cover three different 20-minute time periods (Figure 3.5: 0900-0920h, Figure 3.6: 0920-0940h, Figure 3.7: 0940-1000h). It can be jokingly stated that the differences in expectation levels in Figures 3.5-7 are due more to the wearing off of the effects of morning coffee and having to sit down and get some work done, and you wouldn't be too far from the truth.

Expectation Upon Entry v Satisfaction Upon Exit
(9:20-9:40am, 30 sites, 15 days)

Low
Mediocre/Average
High

Expectation: 89% 4% 7%
Satisfaction: 29% 31% 40%

% of Visitor Population

3.6 Expectation versus Satisfaction across 30 sites over a 15-day period, 9:20-9:40am

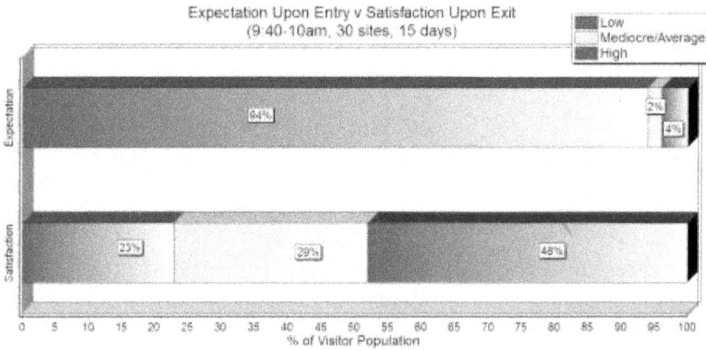

Expectation Upon Entry v Satisfaction Upon Exit
(9:40-10am, 30 sites, 15 days)

Low
Mediocre/Average
High

Expectation: 94% 2% 4%
Satisfaction: 23% 29% 48%

% of Visitor Population

3.7 Expectation versus Satisfaction across 30 sites over a 15-day period, 9:40-10am

Figures 3.2-7 are examples of expectations being met and not being met, and in many cases whether an expectation is met or not is only partially controllable by media design. New England based readers might remember how the 2004 Red Sox World Series and playoff standings affected people's excitement level online, regardless of the site they were visiting. This was detailed in *Reading Virtual Minds V1: Science and History* and the image is shared here in Figure 3.8 (page 125).

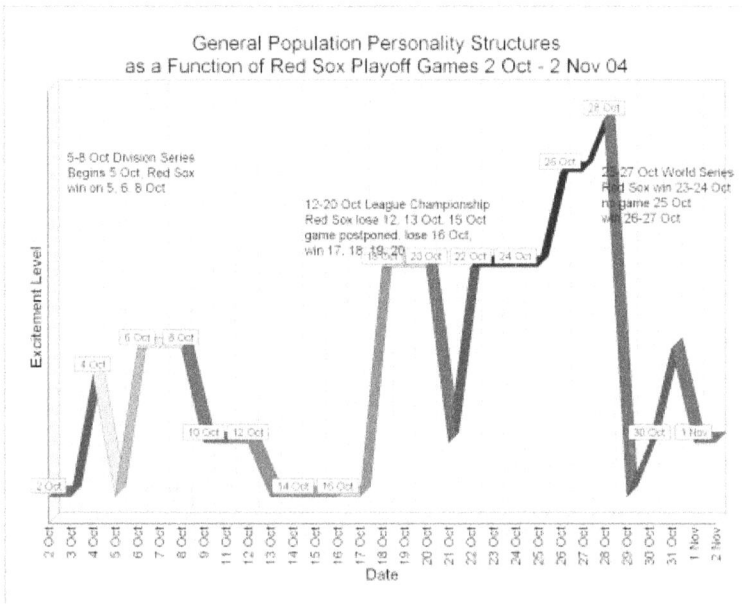

General Population Personality Structures
as a Function of Red Sox Playoff Games 2 Oct - 2 Nov 04

5-8 Oct Division Series
Begins 5 Oct. Red Sox
win on 5, 6, 8 Oct

12-20 Oct League Championship
Red Sox lose 12, 13 Oct, 15 Oct
game postponed, lose 16 Oct,
win 17, 18, 19, 20

25-27 Oct World Series
Red Sox win 23-24 Oct
no game 25 Oct
win 26-27 Oct

3.8 New Englanders' online experiences were goverened more by
how the Boston Red Sox were doing in the 2004 World Series than by
anything else

Figure 3.9 (page 126) is one of NextStage's favorite charts from our early days as a company. It shows that the best designs are subject to visitor behavioral sways well beyond the designs themselves and that people's expectation is based on far more than any thoughts of the website they're visiting. I've shared the chart at several conferences and, once explained, it always causes nods and smiles. Internally we've taken to calling this slide *Bad Day at Black Rock* (with all due respect to the Spencer Tracy movie of the same name) because we noticed that visitors to all websites in our system were experiencing out-of-whack anxiety patterns during this time period. The level of anxiety was so uniform as to be statistically invalid. Fortunately, Susan, my wife (and co-founder, -inventor and -developer of Evolution Technology) is a much better sociologist than I.

She took a look at the time interval involved and explained what we were observing. Readers with a detective bent are invited to see if they can figure out what Susan uncovered before continuing.

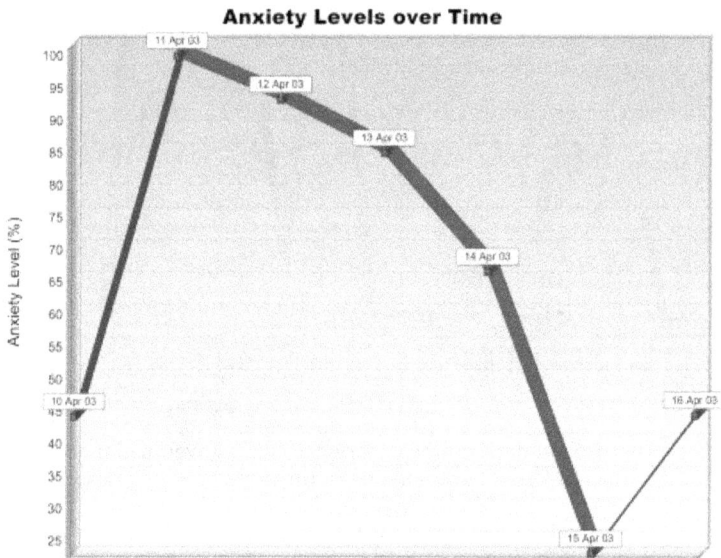

3.9 Bad Day at Black Rock. Why were so many US based visitors to site having such bad days?

Figure it out?

The *Bad Day at Black Rock* chart shows Anxiety Level over time. Snapshots were taken at 1500h on 10, 11, 12, 13, 14, 15 and 16 April 2003. US readers should be able to pick one day of particular interest out of that string of days.

The 10th through the 16th of April 2003 cover "Income Tax Weekend", from Thursday, 10 April 03 to Wednesday, 16 Apr 03. What we were witnessing (without realizing it until Susan explained) was the visitor populations' anxiety as they prepared their income taxes, starting Thursday, 1500h 10 Apr 03, spiking

Friday, 1500h 11 Apr 03 (our guess is that the visitor population wasn't looking forward to spending a weekend doing their taxes), slightly decreasing Saturday, 1500h 12 Apr 03, continuing to decrease on Sunday and Monday, bottoming out on Tuesday, 1500h 15 Apr 03, and then returning to the normal level on Wednesday, 1500h 16 Apr 03. Knowing how many visitors were coming to all sites in our system, we could make a good guess as to how many people in our visitor population had completed their tax returns and when.

Sometimes the best designs fall prey to influences beyond their control.

TakeAway #19 - Launch new designs when cultural and societal pressures are favorable (or at least neutral) to ensure high usability marks.

Bad Day at Black Rock is an example of a report which we use internally for research purposes. Our clients saw the same information slightly differently, as the "Visitor Experience" charts shown in Figures 3.10-13 starting on page 128. These figures show a good experience as green, a negative experience as red.

Figures 3.5-7 on pages 123-124 were from the prototype of what is now called NextStage Immediate Sentiment (NSIS), a tool that:

> ...provides a quick analysis of how a given campaign is doing on a given property by reading the attitudes of all visitors at a given point in time. Are the majority of visitors having a negative experience? Time to pull the plug. Are the majority of visitors having a positive experience? Celebrate! NSIS is a simple gauge representing negative (red), neutral (yellow) and positive (green) sentiment as percentages of a property's entire visitor population. Oh, wait a minute...isn't that almost kind of maybe a little like what all the other companies offer and call Sentiment Analysis? Gosh, you mean we're outperforming them again? Oh, darn...

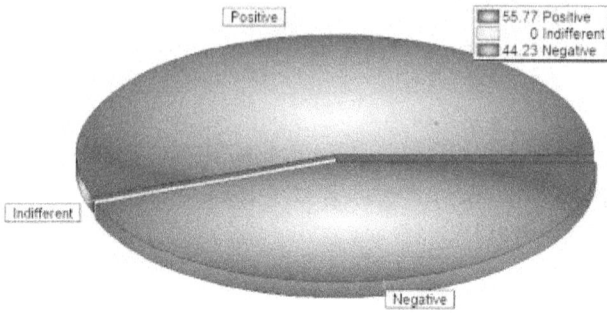

Visitor Experience 3:35pm, 9 Apr 2003 - 3:35pm, 10 Apr 2003

Positive

55.77 Positive
0 Indifferent
44.23 Negative

Indifferent

Negative

3.10 Visitor experience Thursday afternoon, 10 Apr 2003

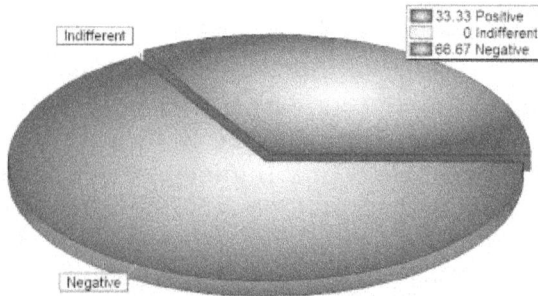

Visitor Experience 11:41am, 13 Apr 2003 - 11:41am, 14 Apr 2003

Indifferent

33.33 Positive
0 Indifferent
66.67 Negative

Negative

3.11 Visitor experience Monday morning, 14 Apr 2003

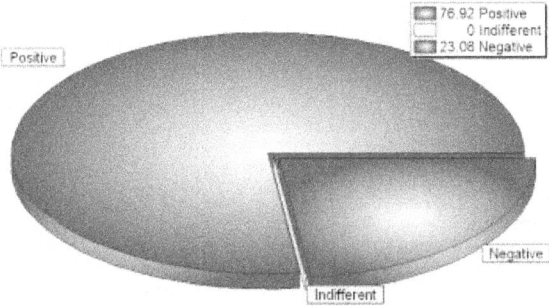

Visitor Experience 3:49pm, 14 Apr 2003 - 3:49pm, 15 Apr 2003

76.92 Positive
0 Indifferent
23.08 Negative

Positive

Negative

Indifferent

3.12 Visitor experience Tuesday afternoon, 15 Apr 2003

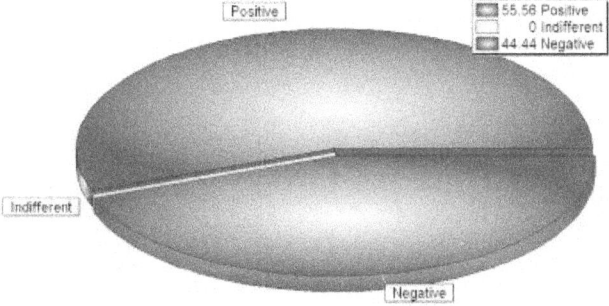

Visitor Experience 3:44pm, 15 Apr 2003 - 3:44pm, 16 Apr 2003

55.56 Positive
0 Indifferent
44.44 Negative

Positive

Indifferent

Negative

3.13 Visitor experience Wednesday afternoon, 16 Apr 2003

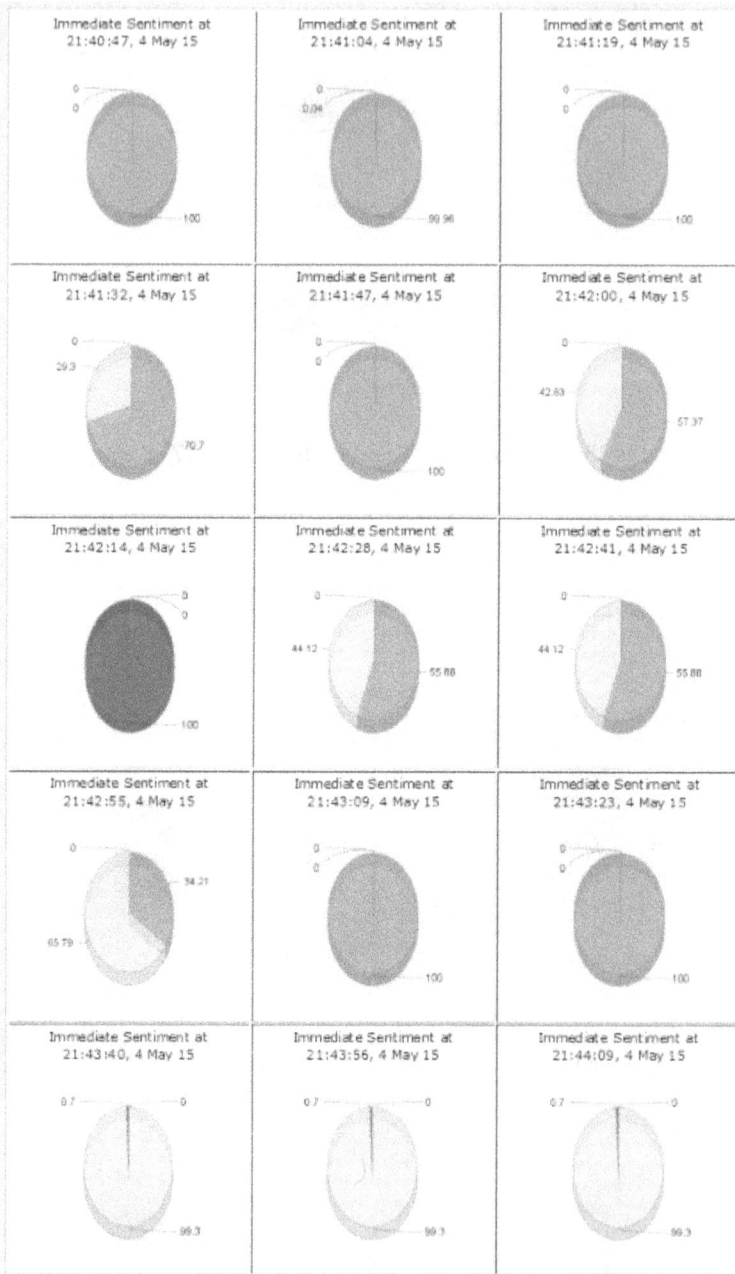

3.14 Monitoring campaigns too closely may be less useful than you think

This part of our discussion started by demonstrating the differences between expectation and satisfaction. What Figures 3.2-7 on pages 119-124 demonstrate is that you can't control expectation but you do have a good chance of influencing satisfaction. Note that the satisfaction levels in Figures 3.4-7 are fairly consistent. Maintaining a healthy satisfaction level is achieved by changing visitors' *expectation* after they've arrived at your website by making their *experience* on your website work to meet their goals first and yours second.

TakeAway #20 - Keep expectations low to keep satisfaction high.

There's nothing quite as wonderful as a pleasant surprise and nothing worse than discovering the Emperor's naked and you paid for the clothing.

But be advised, this is a dangerously slippery slope and the threat comes from social networks, social media, social marketing, social social social.

The lurking beast works this way: I came to your site, my experience was good, I left satisfied. I did that again. And again and again and again.

My experience of your site was so good and I left satisfied so often that I tell all my friends.

Some of them decide to go to your site.

But they've never experienced your site (which is intentionally mediocre in design but highly productive in output), they've only heard about my experiences, which have been great.

Their expectations, then, are quite high.

And their high expectation, transmitted through social networks and having nothing to do with direct contact with your property, can kill your business.

TakeAway #21 - The most effective social campaigns equate low expectation with high delivery.

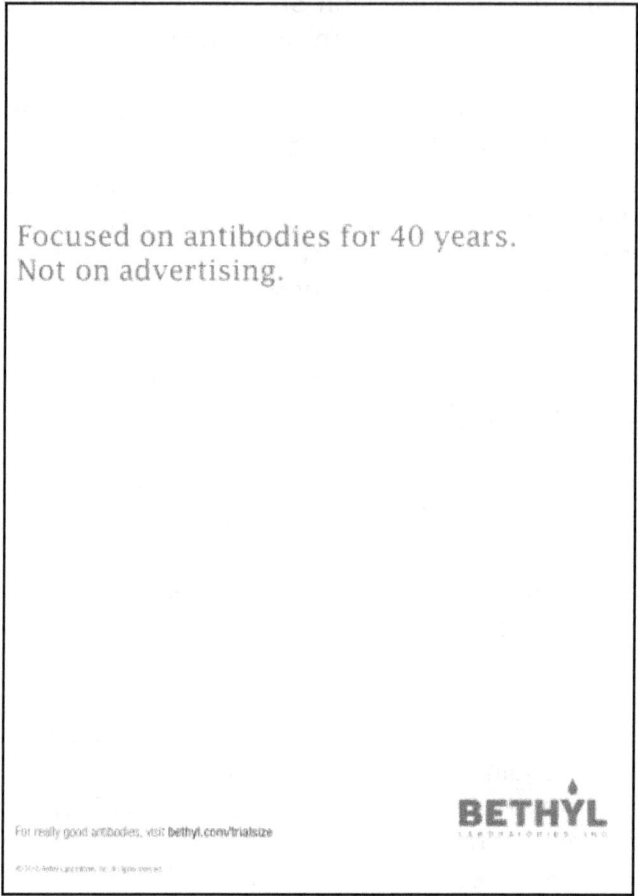

Figure 3.15 - This ad provides just enough
information to cause the user's experience
to kick in, driving expectation and insuring
satisfaction. Good work and nicely done.

An excellent example of the above in action is a recent series of ads from bioscience company Bethyl. The ads (see Figure 3.15, page 132 for an example) are full-page, white background with black text in a standard font that read "We make great .... Not great {ads}". At the bottom of the page is the company's contact information. The ad directs reader attention to the product, not the ad, and plainly states that the quality of their ad shouldn't be equated to the quality of their product. The series has been running in major science journals throughout 2015 (Bethyl's product offerings are extensive).

Nicely done, Bethyl. I always rejoice when I encounter a company that refuses to don the emperor's clothes.

But this gets us back to the fundamental question: How do you design such that people across all generations and income groups and education and ethno-cultural backgrounds will use your interface with equal ease, interest and especially, desired results?

Two things to remember: One, we're designing an exchange of information. It could be a business interface, a gaming interface, it doesn't matter. The ultimate interaction will be a give and a get[j]. Two, users and visitors will be bringing their own, vast, virtual experience to whatever you design.

Two first. The more experience you design into your property the more your experience will be compared to every other experience the user's had (see *2.A – The Ubiquity of Failed Expectations*, page 104). Or thinks they've had, going back to our previous recognition that the increase in digital technology has caused a decrease in the ability to differentiate real from virtual experience. Thanks to digital divisivity,[170,171,177k] and regardless of how brilliant your design is, it'll be found wanting. Users and visitors may never voice that opinion, they may not be aware that's what they're feeling, and still it'll be found wanting. This will especially be true among Millennials who are coming into their own with a sense of privilege and "right".[25,239,470,488,557]

Are you familiar with the Buddha story about him sitting in front of a blank, white wall for some period of time (I've heard it told as several days, sometimes a week, definitely more than a few hours)? He sat and stared and after a while of sitting and staring he rose and claimed, "Now I understand." Or perhaps you've heard the saying "Everyday awake a blank slate so that the day may write itself upon you?" Or how being a *tabula rasa*

---

[j] – we're anticipating *Reading Virtual Minds Volume III: Fair-Exchange and Social Networks* here.
[k] – covered in *Reading Virtual Minds Volume III: Fair-Exchange and Social Networks*.

opens one up to new and wonderful experiences? Or simple meditation where one empties one's self of all thoughts and preconceptions?

What all these and your best designs will have in common is that blank slate, empty, *tabula rasa* thing.

> **TakeAway #22 - The best, most effective designs offer the user/visitor minimal information.**

> **TakeAway #23 - Because the best, most effective designs offer minimal information, they must provide minimal functionality.**

For any interface to be successful, it must be extremely easy (i.e., psychonomically intuitive or "requires no training" based on a given cultural paradigm while recognizing that proper use may require a cultural shift) to use. The setup instructions included with most modern household electronics sold to international markets are brilliant examples of how production, packaging and information design come together to create a "one size fits all" setup guide using minimal written language and maximal experiential language (visual metaphor, and as noted on page 105).

But what are designers to do when they're creating an interface for a system that is complex?

Easy. Decomplexify the system. Design for only the immediate task, not the entire chain of events involved in the *über*-task's completion. People may think they can multitask and they can't, at least not in a way that leads to multiple task productivity unless the individual tasks are so minor that no task-directed cognitive effort is required to perform them.[182,189,267,288,336,399,424,488,569] What humans are remarkably good at is *serial tasking*. We may have several things going on around us and we're taking part in all of them but only one at a time.

Humans can't give all the information sources in their environment equal attention simultaneously without lots of training. We're not naturally designed for it. Technology may be encouraging it and we're still closer (in design) to the jungle than to the microchip. High-level musicians can listen to multiple simultaneous conversations and separate the voices into distinct speakers for two simple reasons: 1) Because it's the same aural-cognitive skill they use when they play with other musicians and 2) human aural-cognition developed so we could separate predator and prey sounds from all the background noise in our environment. Not many people require that skill today but the ability is still there, waiting to be used (usually via *exaptation*, "the process by which a feature evolved for one purpose gradually becomes used for another function"). And even then, to focus our auditory cognition on one sound source means we stop paying attention to the others. Our evolutionary history was such that we weren't the only hunters out there. Learning to pay attention to several sounds simultaneously and rapidly cycle thorough them to isolate sources meant getting back home whether our hunt was successful or not. The modern version of this ability causes some people to become annoyed when they're listening to something they want to hear (a game, a song, a speech, basically anything with words) and someone interrupts that activity by talking to them. They may ask the interrupter, "Can you wait until this is over?" or "Can you give me a few minutes?" or "Can we talk about this later?" all the way down to "Will you please shut up so I can listen to this?". What's happening is auditory cognition – our ability to understand and respond to sounds – has to focus on two high-demand information sources (decoding language, spoken or otherwise, requires amazing neural activity) and sends out a distress signal to the rest of the brain.[258] The response can be either emotional ("shut up!") or logical ("Can this wait a minute?") depending on training, culture, education, how important the game is, ...

Let me give you an overused example of different sensory systems working together and not; driving a car. Simple, isn't it? Usually, the more you do it, the better you become at it. We're going to add in another thing you do very well because you do it so often: talking on the phone.

Do the two things simultaneously and you believe you're multitasking and you're really serial tasking, rapidly switching from driving to talking back to driving back to talking back to...

The part of your mind that manages this switching back and forth is called *executive function* (some researchers call it *modeler*) and it's going to consume more neural resources than either driving or talking ever could.[40,52,336,550] The only real problem is that you'll be completely unaware of it until your reasoning and decision-making abilities collapse and you've had an accident.

Yet people believe they can perform this kind of multitasking routinely[l] That *ka-ching* you heard is your insurance rate going up. There is research indicating that people are developing the ability to pay attention to more things simultaneously. I completely accept that. What few researchers add is that our ability to pay attention to anything is based on our biology and is therefore a finite resource. We can learn to pay attention to more things at once until cognitive exhaustion and mental fatigue come a'knockin', then watch out.

Driving and using a mobile demonstrate an interesting intersection of how our brains deal with information in the environment (a part of what NextStage studies, i.e. "how people interact with information in their environment") and is a wonderful demonstration of exafference and reafference.[61,62,106,107,135,138,529,604]

Many US states are enacting laws to stop people from using mobile devices while driving cars (all Australian states have this law in place as do other principalities, no doubt). Automobile manufacturers, knowing such laws were coming, performed a quick turnaround to restricting the use of mobile devices while driving by making the mobile device part of the car, i.e. including

---

[l] – Ask information workers who claim to multitask routinely how competent they feel regarding their ability to complete each task successfully and they usually rate themselves high, probably because people tend to overestimate their abilities when asked.[211,363,377,615] Follow up with questions to determine when they're most likely to multitask intentionally and it's usually during the periods of the day when the body is most likely to be either slightly dehydrated or slightly hypoglycemic, meaning when the brain is least likely to function optimally.

them as a dashboard unit. More and more cars are 'net enabled. Google and others will offer self-driving (and highly hackable, as noted on page 56. Wonder what laws will be in place to deal with that) cars in the near future.

The pushback to laws restricting the use of mobile devices while driving is "if talking on a cell phone is a distraction then so should be listening to radios. We'll have to outlaw listening to radios while people drive, too" and this logic is about as insane as it gets. It demonstrates the same lack of comprehension of the nature of the solution as does the question "Which came first, the chicken or the egg?"[m] Mobile devices are highly reafferent, meaning they require our interaction, meaning they require our attention. Radios are highly exafferent, meaning they do not require any interaction (unless we're changing stations) and do not require our attention. Indeed, several people have their radios turned on while they drive simply to suppress road noise.

Let's take a moment to consider mobile devices as chickens.

Many people have spent a great deal of time and money explaining why people shouldn't use mobiles while driving, not even handsfree sets should be allowed. This will be true for perhaps a few more years and I will be shocked if any such prohibition continues past 2025, 2030 at the latest.

This prediction is based on semiotics and neurophysiology, and is based on the simple fact that most people aren't ready to drive while talking or TXTing on a mobile but are perfectly able to drive while listening to a radio – driving a car and talking/TXTing on a mobile cause competing information exchanges along the same primary modality channels.

Well, thank you for explaining that, Joseph.

What I'm suggesting is that people haven't had phones and cars in the same immediate environment long enough to have learned how to adequately and quickly non-consciously direct their attention to whatever information source requires the most

---

[m] – The egg had to come first. Whatever laid the egg was not a chicken until the first time someone pointed at what hatched and said, "Look! A chicken!" Until the first time someone pointed at some creature and defined it as a "chicken" there were no chickens to lay eggs, hence whatever laid the egg that hatched a chicken wasn't a chicken, hence the egg came first.

immediate response. Their executive function hasn't been environmentally trained.

Aren't you glad I explained that?

Fair enough. One more try.

People haven't learned how to switch their attention from driving to mobile, back and forth and quickly enough, to be able to respond to both the road and whomever they're talking with without some kind of collision – usually between neural channels and sometimes between cars – occurring.

Phones have been with us for quite some time and as such we are culturally immune to them. We have been societalized to respond to a ringing phone in certain ways and those behaviors are trained in us from an early age. As such, we can walk and talk, take notes and talk, watch TV and talk, and so on.[n]

Likewise, cars have been with us for quite some time and we are culturally immune to them, as well. We have been societalized to respond in certain ways when we are inside a car versus outside a car, when we are driving versus when we're being a passenger, front seat, rear seat and if you kids don't quiet down there'll be no stopping for ice cream on this trip.[o]

The primary modality channel for phones is auditory, for TXTs it's visual. In fact, it is extremely auditory or extremely visual. Talking on a phone (for most people) usually requires a relaxation of the other primary modality channels to the extent that we defocus our eyes or look out a window or allow our gaze to migrate through our surroundings. Should something catch our eye we often require the person we're conversing with to repeat themselves. If we're required to visually focus on something, say a piece of work or a TXT, we often require the other person to

---

[n] – And yes, this is rapidly changing with the net-aware generation, those who never knew a time without internet access.

[o] – It is fascinating to travel in countries where technologies are arriving *en masse*: mobiles with TVs with 'net with cars with home satellite dishes. People are learning what is important and again, language- and culture-dependent concepts of time and space come into play. A friend related a story of traveling to a sub-Saharan village where people could not read yet everyone had a mobile device. His team's function was to provide health education. His team brought flyers, handouts, whiteboards, ... typical educational materials in the West. They were ignored until one team member suggested they send out automated TXTs to distribute the information. Not only did everyone's health improve, requests for literacy classes increased.

change the rate at which they're sharing information with us. They have to either repeat what they're saying, stop talking while we perform our visual search for the required information, or speak slower so we can switch between visual and auditory modalities more easily.

The primary modality channels for driving are visual and auditory. We are taught to look and listen when we drive. Talk on the phone and we have to slow down so our visual cognition systems can keep up with environmental (traffic) clues. Have you ever been going down the highway and somebody in front of you suddenly slows down ten, maybe fifteen miles per hour? Go past them and nine times out of ten it's because they're on their mobile.

The problem lies in the fact that we haven't had a chance to build a cultural immunity to driving while talking on a phone and the old trainings apply. Thus, when we drive a car and we talk on the phone, our cultural training is to defocus our vision to pay attention to what is being said.

Yes, indeedy, folks. We're going down the highway at 70mph, the mobile rings, and our brain tells the occipital cortex (eyes) to go on vacation for a while so the auditory cortex (ears) can tune itself up. Or worse, we receive a TXT and tell the occipital cortex to signal the higher cortex that a small, stationary object in our hand requires more attention than the world whizzing past us at 70mph.

And then it gets still worse. TXTing demands near exclusive use of the brain's visual centers, first to read the incoming TXT message and second to coordinate a secondary visual-kinesthetic channel (your eyes have to guide your fingers while checking that your TXT is correct) to TXT back a response. Think talking your TXT is better? Maybe, maybe not. Do you ever read what you spoke into your mobile before sending your TXT off?

Ouch and Congratulations! The primary channel used for driving is now completely compromised. Yahoo and yippee, is it any wonder the number of accidents of people using mobiles while driving compared to people just driving is so high?[p]

So your user is active on your interface while being distracted by everything from downtown or highway traffic to pets needing to go outside to children being children to partners being partners. How dare you give the user anything more than a single-step, immediately useful and most necessary functionality! Two things make using new interfaces easy from the get-go.

> **TakeAway #24 - Place text-based instructions to the left of the visual field to utilize the brain's natural language parsing abilities.**

> **TakeAway #25 - Place image-based instructions to the right of the visual field to utilize the brain's natural spatial parsing abilities.[q]**

And then be sure to let them know they successfully accomplished that single, immediate, most necessary function so they don't have to devote any cycles to determining if they were successful or not, and then get them to the next single, immediate, most necessary function so smoothly that they know they were successful already, hence have a faith that they'll be successful again.

> **TakeAway #26 - Interfaces must provide a series of minor successes if the user is to achieve overall success.**

---

[p] – I attended an insurance industry meeting in Boston, MA, in May 2010. One of the statistics offered was that each year 6,000 people are killed, 500,000 people injured as direct results from using mobiles while driving.
[q] – Observe relaxed people (under no performance pressure) following instructions. Right-handed people, as an example, place text based instructions to their left and work on whatever to their right, visual-based instructions to their right and work on whatever to their left. One of the tricks to induce cognitive load, transference and interference is to switch these things around and determine how well the individual performs.

TakeAway #27 - An end-user tool should result in an immediately successful experience for the tool user.

TakeAway #28 - An end-user tool must never ever ever run through the end-user's resources.

TakeAway #29 - An end-user tool must provide more detail/explanation only when specifically asked.

The basic premise in the above is that a tool is not a solution. A tool is a means to a solution.

Your interface must lead them from non-conscious success to non-conscious success along their conscious goal-path. Anything less and you risk losing them. There may be several steps involved in the visitor/user achieving their goal and they're only going to perform one task at a time.[103,104,123,126,127]

The best usability designs let the user draw on their own experience to flesh out the interface itself. Cause a user/visitor/audience to extend beyond known experience and, unless some surrogate is there to intervene when problems occur, you run the risk of *resource depletion*. In this case the resource being depleted is the brain. Having to figure out a new interface when you need to get something done will make the brain run through batteries (exhaust its fuel sources) faster than you can imagine.

The only way to guarantee a maximum number of users with a maximum number of different experiential backgrounds having a maximum number of successes on any interface is to design the interface as minimally as possible to achieve the user's immediate goal.

TakeAway #30 - Unless you're able to throw all your experience out and let only the user's experience in, get out of the usability and design business.

Because the user will be drawing on their own experience to reach their goal, and because their experience is increasingly virtual and mediocre, and because you're doing nothing to cause a mediocre experience, you're genuinely and ultimately procreating (hopefully desired) experiences with them.

TakeAway #31 - The best interfaces provide the least resistance to the user achieving their goal.

TakeAway #32 - The best interfaces provide the shortest distance between the user and their goal.

TakeAway #33 - The best interfaces are information exchanges between the user and the interface environment.

Now let's toss in social interaction and the enormous amount of wetware that's consumed when we're being "social" online and off. People are rarely completely relaxed in social settings and the degree to which they relax is a measure of their trust of their safety in the social setting. Rules of social exchange are changing due to increased virtual mobility; millennials and those following are less sexually active than they used to be,[381] have weaker verbal skills (perhaps this is why we need to teach that "no" means "NO!"?) and stronger non-verbal skills,[425,463] all of which means we're losing our *social referencing*[268] ability. When the majority of our social interactions are with a device then we learn how to behave socially with the device, not with those on the other end of the device, and our emotional development suffers, i.e., we lose the ability to interact with people as people because they are no longer our primary social reference.

Sad, don't you think?

Youth's greatest goal these days is to make money[425] tempered by *digital divisivity*[r]. Are we to be surprised when the desire for financial gain – something promoted 365x24x7 on all media without having to look – is the outgrowth of our highly networked world? Our biology makes us competitive creatures and our most competitive period is our teens through early 30s, when we're attempting to establish ourselves, our territories, etc., in the world? Marketers complain that it's tough to reach youth because they don't leave their rooms anymore, instead focusing on YouTube, Netflix and related channels. Hey, you created the little monsters, live with the outcome.

But I'm essentially asking marketers to think before they publish. *Sono pazzo!*[s] What am I thinking?

Ready to call it quits? Hang in there. So far we've covered only item two of the two things to remember: users and visitors will be bringing their own, vast, virtual experience to whatever you design.

Now one: we're designing an exchange of information. It could be a business interface, a gaming interface, it doesn't matter. The ultimate interaction will be a give and a get.[t]

---

[r] – covered in *Reading Virtual Minds Volume III: Fair-Exchange and Social Networks.*
[s] – Italian for "I'm crazy! When said with the proper inflection, there can be no doubt.
[t] – We cover some of this here and the concept of "a give and a get" is covered in detail in *Reading Virtual Minds Volume III: Fair-Exchange and Social Networks.*

Everything in life has a price tag on it. You have to decide if you're willing to pay the price.

4 - Privacy is the Price Tag of Experience

Readers may remember the early to mid 2000s as a time of great concern in the online marketing world. Privacy issues were the talk of the day and every news outlet was running stories on how to ensure privacy, how to deal with cookies, online tracking technology, who knew what about you and so on. People were privacy conscious because "privacy" – at least what they'd come to think of as "privacy" – no longer existed.

The truth is, privacy as they thought of privacy never had existed. There's information we don't want others to know, hence we wish to keep it "private", and then the question becomes "Private from whom?" Class, culture and social distinctions come into play. Middle-income Americans consider it bad manners to ask how much each other earn and upper-income Americans consider knowing each other's incomes a necessity for self- and social-measurement. The global middle-class may ask what someone does for a living and, once told, the mental calculations take over and we're measuring each other by all kinds of standards. We look at people's homes, vehicles, clothing, ornamentation and make judgments that relate back to "private" matters.

> **TakeAway #34 - The smaller the community, the less the experience of, hence the less the expectation of, privacy.**

What do we share and under what circumstances? Again going back to the earliest days of online commerce, people learned they had to give a little to get a little. Ever been asked to provide contact information in order to download some content? Figure 7.17 (page 210) is a representative example.

It's also one of the first online examples of experience and expectation getting into conflict. Online activity prior to the mid-1980s was on BBSes (bulletin board services) and only "geeks and nerds" used them because only geeks and nerds knew about them.[a] Mass culture didn't experience online anything until BBS variations such as CompuServe, GENIE and AOL dominated the world, provided user experiences and defined user expectations.

To date marketing methods and systems rely on such methods as bayesian analysis, syntactic analysis, "Big Data" (which could not exist as recognized today without the algorithms developed by forensic linguists, geneticists, space scientists and geophysicists), "open profiling" (which is variations on ELIZA and HOMR[b] analytic methods) and similar tools to generate usage characteristics over time. All of these systems make use of questionnaires, response analysis surveys, site surveys, multi-platform and cross-property analysis and so on to create their demographic profiles, and each is heavily dependent on "what" happens when someone interacts with a brochure, collateral material, an email or a website. Somehow or other these "what"'s got termed "behaviors" as in "Behavioral Analytics" and the use of the term "Behavioral" in this context has always confused me.

I started research both in books and online to find a definition of "behavioral analytics" in 2005 and repeat the process every few years. One would think finding a definition of "behavioral analytics" would be easy to do, considering how many companies and individuals claim they do it, wouldn't you?[c]

What I've found so far is that "behavioral analytics" involves "human behavioral models". That's about as close as you can get to looking up "circular definition" and seeing "see 'circular definition'".

I also found "Traditional customer tracking software or clickstream analysis...". Sorry, uh-uh. In my world, customer tracking and clickstream analysis only tell you about the browser, not the person using the browser. Behavior doesn't automatically

---

[a] – If you ever played *Adventure*, also known as *Colossal Cave Adventure* and *Advent*, welcome!

[b] – ELIZA is most often thought of as a therapist emulator, although the system has been around since 1966 (http://i5.nyu.edu/~mm64/x52.9265/january1966.html). HOMR was the MIT MediaLab's Helpful Online Music Recommendation service, which became the FireFly product.

[c] – You'd think I'd learned after researching such things as "engagement" and "sentiment analysis", but I started this research in 2005 before people were driving their stakes into the ground by claiming terms already in usage elsewhere. I was naive back then.

reveal its cause and can be misleading. You are witnessing the effect of the behavior, not the behavior itself. For example, I looked at a lot of sites that came up in my search for "behavioral analytics". If the behavioral analytics systems which I was reading about were tracking me, I doubt that they identified my interest in getting a definition of "behavioral analytics" so much as they guessed I was interested in network security, ad publishing and delivery, co-branding opportunities, content delivery systems, custom tagging, ...

None of those sites came back with, "Hey, Joe, you looking for info on 'behavioral analytics'? Then just looky here..."

No wonder searching for information on the Internet can be so frustrating. The evidence that search engine use has shaped our expectations of results is staggering or amusing, depending on your...umm...expectations of such things.[85,232,299,338, 401,469,509,555] Search behavior relies on instincts developed when humans were hunter-gatherers. Search engines, to make use of how humans function best, must satisfy our foraging skills and they don't. Not if they want to satisfy their current income models.

Anyway, these sites were seeing the effects of the behavior and not the behavior itself. *Behavioral Analytics* is, to me, "A determination of an individual's internal state based on what they're externally demonstrating." In other words, the *behavior* is the way they stand, the way they walk, the way they talk, ..., and by analyzing those behaviors in sequence we learn what's motivating those behaviors[d] Perhaps we should use the term "motivational analysis"? My behavior was looking at a bunch of web pages. The analysis of that behavior is performed by asking "What is causing that behavior?" and the answer to that question is "He's researching 'behavioral analytics'."

There is a technique used by psych professionals (this covers lots of fields from interrogation to therapists) to find the base behind someone's behavior. They ask a question, then ask a question about the answer to that question, then ask a question

---

[d] – That's straight out of *Reading Virtual Minds Volume I: Science and History*. I told you it'd help to read it.

about the answer to that answer and so on. Eventually the person being questioned starts repeating their answers and the professional knows they've reached the base reason for the behavior. If the person being questioned starts repeating the same answer to each question, the questioner has struck gold. Consider the following example based on the preceding discussion:

> Q: Why is Joseph doing a search on behavioral analytics?
> A: He wants to provide the most accurate information to his readers.
> Q: Why does he want to provide the most accurate information to his readers?
> A: He feels an obligation to be as correct as possible in what he writes about.
> Q: Why does he feel an obligation to be as correct as possible in what he writes about?
> A: Because he feels there are a lot of charlatans out there, claiming knowledge or expertise while not possessing either, and believes that by providing the most accurate, correct information possible he won't be lumped with those who make claims without ability.

There's a lot going on here. Once the person being questioned shifts from cognitive to emotional terms, the questioner knows they are getting closer to finding the gold, base, rich ore of motivation.

My last response above would be a field day for a well-schooled interrogator (I'm using the term 'interrogator' in a general sense); why does Joseph feel there are a lot of charlatans out there? (and note that "charlatan" is an emotional word, not a logically evaluative expression such as "not well-schooled", "poorly educated", "lacking an in-depth understanding of the subject matter", ... Also, the use of "possessing" is telling of how Joseph recognizes "expertise" and "knowledge"). How does Joseph determine that information is accurate/correct? Why is it important not to be lumped with those who make claims without ability?

In my opinion, a good motivational analysis engine should be able to at least get to the rich ore if not mine the gold completely.

That being the answer, the role of behavioral analytics is to deliver desired information to the questioner while cataloging the answerer's motivations so that the interrogator can exploit the answerer further down the road, not to tag me as someone looking for network security solutions, ad publishing and delivery systems, offer me co-branding opportunities, content delivery systems or custom tagging solutions.

All that offered, I'm not going to disparage behavioral analytics as it exists in the lingua franca or those who profess to practice it. What I will offer is that there is, to me, a flaw in the logic under which the lingua franca understanding exists.

The flaw in the logic comes from the methods used to create the "human behavior models". These models infer that the stated tastes of the individual in question are based on that individual intentionally or unintentionally submitting information and matching that information against pre-existing, mass-market defined visitor profiles which are in turn based on amalgams of millions of visitor profiles. This method of models based on amalgams of hundreds of thousands if not millions of visitors goes along with "Hey, three billion people can't be wrong."

That's accurate although not true. It depends on what you're asking and needs to be balanced with Anatole France's "If a million people say a foolish thing, it is still a foolish thing."

Everybody knows that Florida is west of Ohio, correct (page 65 and also covered in *Reading Virtual Minds Volume I: Science and History*)? It is if that's what your market, audience or users think.[e]

Pay attention to the movement of great bodies. You'll know when earthquakes, hurricanes and volcanoes are happening. You won't know what's causing them, how to prevent them, how to predict them, and most importantly, *how to use them to achieve your own goals when they happen*.

---

[e] – This is covered in *Reading Virtual Minds Volume I: Science and History, Chapter V.2 – Subjective versus Objective Experience and Why it Matters*.

And of course, now that everyone is doing behavioral analytics, we need to come up with new words to differentiate ourselves in the market. We're no longer doing behavioral *analytics*, now we're doing behavioral *targeting*. No, wait...there are too many companies doing behavioral targeting. Okay, now we're doing behavioral *marketing*. Oops, too many using that moniker. What else what else what else? I've got it! Now we're doing *ToeJam Sponge Manifold Recruitment*! Yeah, let's see somebody else claim they're doing that!

Many "behavioral analytics", "behavioral marketing" and "behavioral targeting" companies acquire their information via people's responses to questionnaires or "buy-ins" on websites. A common buy-in on a website takes the form of a conversion page, which brings us back to Figure 7.17 on page 210.

Conversion pages and their kin require the individual to buy-in to something and usually to perform the buy-in before the individual is sure of the value of what's being bought. The buy-in often takes the form of giving over some contact information, which means increasing the company's ability to contact you at some future point in time. Giving a company the ability to contact you when you might not want to be contacted has to do with *identity management* and is discussed in **7.A – Turning Tourists into Locals** (page 183).

The flaw here is that people will only share truthful information if:

1) They trust who they're sharing that information with and
2) They believe what they'll get in return for that truthful information is equal in value to the *long-term value* of that information[f].

One individual shared with me that he routinely lies about several key questions when filling out questionnaires just so no one will bother him. Just think, if he was lying to me when he told

---

[f] – a basis of *fair-exchange* and covered in detail in *Reading Virtual Minds Volume III: Fair-Exchange and Social Networks.*

me he lied to others...? And this doesn't count marketing panels, many participants of which don't respond accurately simply because they don't read the questions correctly.[159,160,403]

Experience, at least in business, is an interesting thing. We want potential and existing clients, customers and site visitors to be comfortable...so long as we can get what we want from them. Two businesspeople talking to each other can be as arcane as two lawyers, two politicians, two doctors, two microbiologists, two economists, two...it doesn't matter the culture, each of them have a language unique unto themselves and the function of that language is to quickly and easily establish identity and trust. Thus marketers must communicate in the client's, consumer's, customer's and site visitor's language as quickly and easily as possible. Doing so is the key to providing a mutually profitable experience (despite Dogbert's thoughts otherwise, as in Figure 4.1 on page 151).

The psych game mentioned on page 147 is also useful in creating mutually profitable experiences between target markets and the businesses hoping to serve them. But beware, it's not a popular game unless both therapist and client are ready and willing to go through it. Similarly, the business person who asks their in-house peers "Why are we doing this?" tends to sit alone during lunch more often than not.

© Scott Adams, Inc./Dist. by UFS, Inc.

4.1 - Dogbert uses *business-speak* to great advantage

But it is this "why", this "why did we choose that color for our brochure?", this "why did we use that model for this layout?" and so on which needs to be asked in order to ensure that the experience we create is one in which our target market will flourish rather than fail to thrive.

For example, go to a website or look at a piece of collateral material you had a direct hand in creating and strip it down to its component elements of font size, color, background color, background images, image placement, text use, highlights, shading, ... and for each element ask "why was that used there?" The in toto question to this "whying" is "What was the goal?" Start with the collateral material as a whole. That question is usually easy to answer – "We wanted to motivate people to buy from us" or "We wanted to get people to work with us" or basically, "We wanted to {x} people to {y} {z} us."[g]

Recognition deals with invariant features (things that don't change, something familiar to topologists and colloquially as "the things that make a cup 'a cup' regardless of how you're seeing the cup"). Action doesn't require recognition, only intent. Polarity action items need to be *kiki* and *bouba* (Figure 4.2, page 152) in shape and users need to be taught what to expect as an outcome.

KIKI   BOUBA

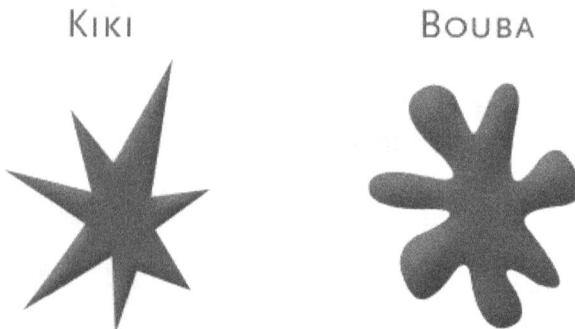

4.2 - People thought the left image was "Kiki" because the word sounds sharp and pointy, the right image was "Bouba" because the word sounds soft and puffy

You've not heard of *kiki* and *bouba*?[460] Then you're probably not aware that your choice of Nook™ or Kindle™ (if you'd selected

---

[g] – Or, more eloquently, G(z) = F(y,x). Yes. An equation forms. You're surprised?

one over the other) may have more to do with bouba and kiki than the actual Nook™ or Kindle™ you purchased. NextStage studied a random selection of Nook™ and Kindle™ users in Canada and the US. The only selection criteria was that they used their device in public, hence our investigators could approach them conversationally with something like "Hi, that's a ..., isn't it? I'm thinking of getting one for my... . Would you mind telling me if that's a good idea or if I should go with {other device}?"[h]

The first division was generational. People less than 40 years old preferred the Kindle™, people more than 40 years old preferred the Nook™. The second division was gender based. Women preferred the Nook™, men preferred the Kindle™.

We discovered through conversation that the word "nook" signaled an easier to use, easier to manage, generally "softer" device that they could be comfortable with. The word "kindle" signaled edgy, on the go, interactive, on top of things, etc..

So if you chose one or the other, say thanks to psycholinguists everywhere.

Often product designers, collateral designers and site owners have an incorrect goal in place for their material. When asked, some will give an answer that boils down to "we want to make money". That's a worthwhile but incorrect goal unless you ensure that site visitors receive something worthwhile in exchange for the money they give you. Perhaps you're a product or collateral designer or site owner who doesn't want to make money. Perhaps all you want is for people to give you information (YouTube™ is an example). What do you plan on doing with that information? If you want it, it has value to you and whatever has value can be assigned a monetary value in the end. Perhaps all you want is social recognition? Let me share some personal philosophy with you: Everything, everything, everything in life comes with a price tag on it. That price tag may be time, money, energy, family, friends, honor, respect, love, recognition, life, even death. Whatever the price tag, you have to decide if you're willing to pay

---

[h] – Linguists, survey and research designers take note; we avoided acquiesce bias via the induction's phrasing.

the price for what you want in life. Once you're willing to pay that price, whatever you want is yours.

In marketing, the trick has nothing to do with the existence of the price tag, it has to do with knowing what value to list as the price and what psychological dimension the price exists in. Someone seeking praise will work hard and long hours just to be told they're incredible workers, someone seeking money won't. Give the praise seeker gobs of cash for their efforts and they'll feel unfulfilled and quit, ditto the money seeker who's told they're an incredible worker but receives no cash. Knowing what value to list as the price and what dimension the value exists in means you've discovered what price people will pay for what you offer and what you need to offer in order to have them accept your price. Again, fair-exchange. If the price tag of your offer is an aspect of the individual's privacy then the offered experience goes on a sliding scale as follows:

1) Personality level privacy - better or worse than average daily experience (excellent or terrible dining experience, excellent or terrible vacation experience, being recognized at work by management and/or peers, ...)
2) Identity level privacy - self-recognition changing experience (marriage, divorce, birth of a child, loss of a parent or sibling, being hired or fired from a prestigious position, ...
3) Core level privacy - life-changing experience (near death, loss of a significant other, surviving natural or man-made holocaust, surviving life-threatening illness, ...)

This sliding scale becomes increasingly dangerous the digital versus sensory (real-world) experiences the audience has. An audience whose majority experiential frame is based on their sitting in their room, being online rather than socio-physical interpersonal interactions doesn't have much Core or even Identity that's separate from their Personality. Make one mistake with these audiences and you're out of the game forever. A recent example is how 20-somethings are responding to *Star Wars: The Force Awakens*™. A random interview of those leaving theaters was that it was an okay movie but it had "too many hipster references", the latter spoken with dismissive tone and minimizing gestures. Nothing about the acting, the effects, the visuals. My generation still talks about what a mind-expanding experience the original *Star Wars*™ movie was. This generation's response is a collective *Meh* and the movie will be forgotten when the next big screen adventure comes out.

People must be willing to pay your price and you, in return, must be willing to pay their price. Their price – at least in the beginning – is their time and their attention. Unfortunately, these are the most expensive things they have to give you. To get someone's attention and possibly forfeit their privacy you have to:

TakeAway #35 - Promise and then provide an experience in the user/visitor/audience's chosen psychological value dimension that is better than the experience they're already engaged in in that dimension and...

TakeAway #36 - Make sure the experience you provide in the user/visitor/audience's chosen psychological dimension is better than any other experience in that dimension that they're likely to have elsewhere.

These, like the over-largely lettered signs and placards of the street, escape observation by dint of being excessively obvious; and here the physical oversight is precisely analogous with the moral inapprehension by which the intellect suffers to pass unnoticed those considerations which are too obtrusively and too palpably self-evident. - Edgar Allan Poe, The Purloined Letter

5 - False Attractors, Meaningful Noise, Experience and Expectation

Business readers will recognize the TakeAway at the end of the last chapter as a simple market concept; you're providing a product or service and you hope the client will purchase your product or service rather than your competitors'. Here the product or service is an experience you're providing and the competition is everything else vying for the client's attention (and dollars). Here I'll also add something said to me by John O'Leary, then Western Regional Sales Manager for Progress Software, "If you don't have competition, you don't have a market."

I remember Mr. O'Leary telling me that at a seminar and, for me, learning that one thing was worth the price of admission. Mr. O'Leary's statement is an excellent reframing of something neuroscientists, cognitive psychologists and psycholinguists have known for quite some time: "If you can't be distracted, you can't lose your focus."

Science calls what Mr. O'Leary was describing as *meaningful noise*. Meaningful noise is something which would normally be considered an interference or distraction but can't be truly an interference or distraction because the noise was selected as something worthy of notice. If it gets our attention, it's not interfering because our attention is now directed at the noise. What this does, though, is beg the question of how our selection mechanism gets in place.

An example of meaningful noise was the discussion about driving a car while talking on a mobile in **Chapter 3 – Expectation versus Satisfaction** (page 138). Mobiles can distract most people while they're driving because most people drive non-consciously; driving is mostly automatic and reflex. Few people focus on their driving, hence they can be distracted – be it the dog jumping up and down, the kids in the back seat, something on the radio, someone they pass on the street, ...

The key to keeping people focused on what you want where you want is to recognize that meaningful noise is going to exist and to use both it and the concepts behind it to your advantage.

What are you offering people who pick up your collateral material or browse your website? Is it some "product" or "service"? If so you're being lured by *false attractors* in your design methodology and are probably not designing highly effective material. Designing for false attractors is fairly common and easily avoided once you're aware of it.

A typical false attractor scenario goes like this:

> 1 - A company wants to market its time accounting
>   products to a given audience.
> 2 - A survey is done which determines that a concern for
>   this audience is time management.
> 3 - A campaign is designed, produced and published which
>   emphasizes the company's products' time
>   management benefits.

All of the above is good information and useful, and also points to a confusion of levels and the motivations for behaviors. Psych and behavioral science clinicians know this as "What good is a diagnostic if there isn't a therapeutic?" meaning "Glad you recognize some problem exists but the problem you're treating isn't the problem I'm having."

The first question to be asked in the above is "What do you mean by time management?" Let's say the answer is "I never seem to have enough time to complete the tasks I'm given."

A general follow-up question – indeed the more important question – comes out of the first, "What does having more time give you?" Using the psych example described on page 147, a more directed question would be "What is stopping you from completing the tasks you're given?"

Let's say the answer to the follow-up is something like "I'm always waiting for people to get back to me with the answers/information I need, and they're never on time." Ah, now you have something that should be designed into your marketing material. The problem isn't time management, it's communication and access to specific individuals. Designing collateral which emphasizes time management capabilities is designing for a false attractor; you've essentially communicated that your product knows the user's problem exists and does nothing to solve the reason the problem exists. Acknowledging a problem exists may work for audiences who want to know everybody's going down on the same ship together, however most audiences want solutions to their problems in addition to a recognition that their broadly shared problem exists.

TakeAway #37 - Design the material around the reason a problem exists and you'll get results.

This "designing for a false attractor" is a golden egg in many circles and raises two questions: How do you know if what you're designing for is a false attractor and how do you get to the real problem?

The answers tend to be obvious after the fact and recognizing them before the fact takes a little practice.

You recognize you're designing for a false attractor if the *raison d'etre* for your design gets little repeated use during any given work session, or little repeated use through time. In the example above, the well designed time management features are used but not regularly and without enthusiasm (because nobody gets back to the user, hence using the well designed time management features are a frustration *anchor*. Non-consciously the user knows that using the time management features will lead to frustration hence avoids using them).

You get to the real problem by observing where the user spends time but does little. Again using the above example, it would be the part of the tool or environment where the user gets and catalogues responses. People never get back to the user, the user needs that information, hence the user checks communication channels (IMs, Skype, FaceTime, email, TXT, their phone, ...) for missed responses and confirms their fate by checking their catalog.

When a man sits with a pretty girl for an hour, it seems like a minute. But let him sit on a hot stove for a minute and it's longer than any hour.
— Albert Einstein

6 – Using Time to Mitigate Experience and Expectation

At their root, experience and expectation are based on our perception of time and the Einstein quote prefacing this chapter is an indication of that. How humans perceive time is greatly based on their culture and language, and nowhere does the human perception of time come into play more than in communication, digital, virtual, online or otherwise. Know how long someone will wait for information from you (a response to a question, for example) and how long it takes them to respond to a question and you know their history, their immediate situation, how much they value the information and quite specifically, how much they value you. In the digital world, you can give someone what they want quickly and they're ecstatic...until they realize what they wanted won't do what they need; the immediate expectation was fulfilled but the motivating experience that created that expectation was not addressed and you've lost a client, prospect, consumer, friend, lover, ...

Human concepts of experience and expectation are demonstrated most strongly in communications (verbal and non-verbal language, visual arts, music, somatosensory systems, etc). How we lingualize our environment (how we describe things to others and ourselves), for example, is rife with time-based experiential and expectational metaphor and simile. When we say "It's half *past* the hour" we're speaking of experience, when we say "It's quarter *to* the hour" we're speaking of expectation.

It is interesting and understandable that experience's and expectation's relation to language is stronger in modern languages than in aboriginal languages; when experience is that the sun rises in the morning and the expectation is that the sun will set in the evening, there's little changing in an individual's day to strongly tie "this did happen" (experience) to "this will happen" (expectation). And if you haven't heard, our native language, languages we learn and how we lingualize our environment shape us greatly.[245,289,397,414,437,449,563]

Societies that came into economic power in the past six hundred or so years, especially since the industrial revolution coupled with the advent of town clocks in medieval villages, have had those six hundred years of tick-tock-ticking to indoctrinate them to the slavery of the hour. Originally, people feared that the clocks appearing in town halls and such were stealing time, not reporting it. After all, why is it so important that 6am be 6am or 4:30pm be 4:30pm or...?

Because industry required a reliable workforce. People had to be at their position at their appointed time or production stopped. Before towns industrialized, the church kept track of time; monks were required to offer specific prayers at specific times. The god who moved the stars through the heavens did so with a watch.

The concepts of experience and expectation are changing and it's taking far less than six hundred years. The advent of digital watches in the mid-1970s changed how people relate to and report time. The concepts of *clockwise* and *counter-clockwise* are fading from cultural meaning. Experience was built into language with such phrases as "It's quarter past" or "It's ten past" or "It's half past". We were reporting a present time, this minute, based on past experience, that hour. Expectation was built into language with phrases such as "It's quarter to" or "It's ten to" or "It's five of". We expected the next hour to come into being in some number of minutes.

Past, *on*, *at* and *to(wards)* or *of(f)*. "On", "at" and "off" were killers because they also incorporated exactness. The seeds of Digital Divisivity[170,171] were sown in our great-great-great-great grandfather's (ahem) time.

If analog clocks started us down the digital divisivity road, digital watches fueled our ride. "What time is it?" "It's 10:23 *exactly*." We no longer have to approximate time. The result is that we're losing our ability to create expectations based on past experiences because those concepts don't exist in language as they use to. Younger people have trouble making and keeping plans.[268,613]

Traditional watches are still worn and mostly as ornamentation, not timepieces. Ask someone for the time and they'll more likely show you their mobile's screen than show you their watch.[156]

All of which affects how people interact with their environment, how they make decisions, what decisions they'll make and more. It is a challenge to make a decision about a future event (expectation) if my language limits me to the digital *now*. It is a challenge to decide if I liked or disliked some past event (experience) if my language likewise ties me to the digital *now*.

But humans are biorhythmic creatures. Our evolutionary history ties us to the movements of the sun, moon, stars, oceans, tides, waves and winds at a cellular level. It's in our DNA. The neural circuitry is there, in the balance, keeping us tied to a circadian clock that has served us far longer than gears have turned hands on walls or quartz crystals have kept silicon pulses steady. Our internal circadian clock is working whether we want it to or not. We can choose to ignore it but we deny it at our individual peril.[1,33,34,216,228,248,261,266,287,353,373,402,405,435,452,491,498-500,559,564,567,570,616]

Let's use it to our advantage, okay? Tapping toes, clocks and pots that won't boil are ours for the using but only if we know how and are willing.

I mentioned that most modern language speakers think of time as formulated by Minkowski and as shown by Minkowski's Cones (see page 43). There's a difference between how people *think* of something and how people *demonstrate their experience* of that thing. The latter, the demonstration of an experience, is much closer to their Core because it's (often) non-conscious.[268] The former, how someone thinks, requires two important factors: education and self-awareness. Without the education and self-awareness, thinking will never influence the Core. However, the Core will always influence how we think.[a]

---

[a] – Recent studies indicate that Core to cognition pathways take as much as 0.25 seconds for signals to travel while Core to emotion pathways take as little as 0.15 seconds to travel. No wonder most people's first response to unexpected stimuli is emotional rather than logical.

TakeAway #38 – Design marketing material for emotional impact first, for logic second and use the logic to explain/defend the emotional response[b].

People may think of time as some kind of Minkowskiism and they demonstrate time via experiential timelines that go from their left to their right, from past to present to future with their personal present placed directly in front of them. Ask someone to demonstrate a sequence of events and they'll place the most past event furthest to their left, the most future event furthest to their right.[c]

TakeAway #39 – Move action items into users'/visitors' "Now" space to get immediate actions.

I have often wondered why most action items are off to the sides of the visual field. I've often told clients to place action items closer to the visual center of their digital properties and chuckled quietly when they report that such a simple change lifts visitor/user activity by double and triple digits.

Place an action item to the right of a property and you've sent a non-conscious signal to the visitor/user that the action need not be performed "now" because it'll be performed at some indeterminate "future" time. Place an action item to the left of a property and you've sent a non-conscious signal that the action's already been performed in some indeterminate "past". Users/Visitors who act on action items so placed are doing so only after overcoming lots of non-conscious inertia (and should be congratulated for their efforts! Give them a discount!).

---

[b] – This TakeAway requires some subtlety. The Audi audience, for example, has been a logic driven audience from much of the early 2000s, thus the language must be logic based, everything else emotion based, and then more logic to tap into the buyers' decision and convincer strategies (see page 175).
[c] – People who are process-challenged or have a poor sense of time involvement and commitment often demonstrate non-linear, convoluted timelines.

Now let's make use of the other side of this.

TakeAway #40 –Move traditional "drop off" items into users'/visitors' "Past" or "Future" spaces to continue engagement.

Are users/visitors abandoning their shopping carts or worse, going only so far in the online experience you've designed for them then dropping off your property completely?

Simple solution. Look at the point where users/visitors are dropping off/abandoning and check for action item placement. What's tricky here is that the action item may only be an engagement check, something like "View Cart". Placing evaluation or conclusion items in users'/visitors' "Now" space causes them to perform an immediate and non-conscious evaluation of whether what's being evaluated is worth whatever's required to complete the transaction.[d]

You've essentially caused users/visitors to decide if what you're giving them is worth what they're giving you, if the exchange is fair, and in our digital age most users'/visitors' default response is "No, it's not."

Make sure evaluation and especially "check out" action items are placed to the right of the visual field. This sends the non-conscious signal that any exchange will be in the future and does not need to be evaluated "now". Most people buy online via credit cards so this placement validates their existing experience of having to "future" pay and you've provided a non-conscious confirmation and pat-on-the-back that yes, the user/visitor knows what they're doing and is doing the right thing.

---

[d] – these concepts are discussed in great detail in *Reading Virtual Minds Volume III: Fair-Exchange and Social Networks.*

6.A – Linguistic Constructs We Use for Degrees of Communication

TakeAway #41 - The time it takes for a tool to become societally ubiquitous is inversely proportional to the amount that tool decreases the spatial and temporal distance between people.

Don't worry. I'm going to explain that and without using equations. It deals with two very closely related concepts that most people wouldn't think to group together. The first concept deals with the fact that our brains still equate physical distance with the length of time required to send a message and receive a reply, a phenomenon known as *psycho-social distance*[161] (which also plays a role in whether or not we consider someone a strong or weak connection in a social network).

The second concept deals with the fact that the history of technology is a study of putting the greatest amount of power into the most hands as economically as possible.[16,105,134,141,143, 149,154,163,417]

It is an odd thing, the linguistic constructs we use for the degrees of communication.

Basically, western culture's sense of communication is closely tied to western culture's sense of distance. We've all heard about "not violating someone's personal space." Ask a professional boxer about their concept of personal space and you'll learn very clearly that personal space is based on threat concepts. This comes out in language as "I see", "I hear" and "I touch".

Is someone very special to us? A close personal friend (a "close" personal friend)? Do they touch us in a special way (they can't "touch" us unless they're physically close to us, correct?)?

We only allow direct touch with great trust. Touching the skin, either by someone else or by ourselves, is to make contact with our Identity. Remember the difference between Core, Identity and Personality?[79] Personality is what the Identity extends into the world. In other words, the Personality is our "aura", if you will, and our Identity is our sense of self. That sense of self occurs at the surface of the skin. When people touch themselves they're doing an *Identity Check*, basically asking "Am I okay? Am I who I think I am?" People who go through some life change or who wake up from coma often want to see themselves in a mirror and touch the face they see, first in the mirror then their face itself, perhaps asking "Am I the person I remember? Am I the person I was?"

Direct touch also occurs with personal threat. Someone strikes us, violates us, hurts us or those so close to us (there's "close" again) that to harm them is to harm us. Personal distance, people's comfort zone, equals how comfortable people are with who they think they are. Boxers tend to have a strong sense of comfort with themselves (as well they should). They've both taken and given pain, so are well aware how far they're willing to go when in contact with people in their immediate physical vicinity.

Take a moment to break down that last sentence:

- "how far" – a distance metaphor
- "to go" – a travel metaphor integrating both time and distance
- "contact" – a physical metaphor
- "immediate physical vicinity" - a time metaphor, "immediate", is mixed with physical and spatial metaphors, "immediate physical vicinity" is literally "now touch me".

Is someone only comfortable when another person is greater than arm's length away? A weak sense of self or personal identity could be the cause. Is someone only comfortable when someone else is right on top of them, constantly bumping into them? Same problem, simply a *polarity response* of the previous manifestation[e]. Does someone allow different people close and

---

[e] – Polarity Responses are opposite psycho-physical responses to the same stimuli. People who have to be right on top of someone are manifesting the same response to close contact as people who work to keep people at a physical distance from them, the former are merely

others not so close to them? Family and children are held and touched often? Friends are hugged and kissed but not as often as family? Newly met people receive a handshake and then very subtly the two people pull slightly back, perhaps standing slightly off center of each other? These are two sword-fighters waiting to learn if the other person can be trusted to lower their sword, who will make themselves vulnerable first, in other words, "Can I trust you enough to lower my defenses and let you in?", the Ten Must Marketing Messages' "I Trust You/You Can Trust Me" demonstrated in real life in real time.[81,f]

After touch our next spatial metaphor deals with hearing. "I hear you", "I hear what you're saying," followed by sight, "I see that", "I see what's coming", "I see where you're going." Without going into more painstaking detail, we touch what is happening right now, we hear what's a little further away in time and space, and we see those things which are distant in these same dimensions, and remember, these are general in western culture. Other cultures and language groups demonstrate sensory metaphors with such phrases as "Give me a little taste" ("I want to benefit, too"), "Something doesn't smell right" ("I'm uncomfortable with this situation"), "Have you eaten today?" ("Hello/How are you?") and so on. Individuals will communicate differently based on their education, history, culture and up-bringing. The fact that our language defines who we are demands that we create language for new information and informational metaphors as they enter our environment. For example, how many of you still *tape* a tv show for later watching? Or do you *tivo* it? Do any of you *burn* it? Why did we *tape* a show and why do we

=====

demonstrating their response differently. Both fear physical contact. The former avoids it by being able to directly manipulate and control the level of contact by initiating contact. The latter avoids it by simply getting away from the possibility of it.

f – Tacticians have strong, firm handshakes, visionaries weak ones. Strategists, both those who strategize good and those who strategize ill, may have a strong handshake while they look you in the eyes, searching for weakness, noting for future interactions, possibly for manipulation. A strong handshake without meeting your gaze is a demonstration of domination, or a desire to. A weak handshake while meeting your gaze is a demonstration of submission, a desire not to be hurt or harmed. Thus before the meeting begins, with a simple shaking of the hands, you know who you're dealing with, how they think, what to expect and what they'll expect from you.

now *burn* one? Because before we used a tape cartridge and the metaphor of tape had been with us for some 40 years. How many of you were using DVDs and were still "taping" movies? Why do we "burn" a CD or DVD? Because CDs and DVDs are created by lasers and lasers burn. How many of you have personal MP3 or WAV players? Why do you *rip* music?[g]

6.A.i - Why We Can't Stay In Touch Any More

Business often demands that we "stay in touch" or "be in touch" 365x24x7. At the same time, they implicitly demand that we stay in touch or be in touch by not touching or interacting with a human at all.[h] How often are you invited to go to a company's website while you're waiting for a human to respond to your support call? How many of you have direct deposit and do most if not all of your banking on line? How many of you would be upset if ATMs vanished and you – Gasp! – had to wait for a human teller to handle your transactions? How many of you spend your day listening to your personal music player regardless of whether you're in an office surrounded by co-workers or one of many people walking a crowded street (as demonstrated by the Paul Gillin anecdote on page 45)? And how many of you would be upset if someone told you you couldn't listen, that it was distracting you from something they deemed more important, like work, or that truck rushing down upon you which you can't hear because your earphones cancel out all other noise?

The truth is we as a society in this "modern" world are allowed the solace of others less and less even though the increased pressure this same society and modern world places upon us demands it more and more.

---

[g] – The answer comes from a fascinating bit of linguistic etiology. Remember that language evolves to communicate the greatest amount of information in the least amount of time? Thus in slang and jargon, a single word can serve for several not in that slang or jargon. In this case, we would not have ripped music (regardless of technologies involved) before 2001. Enough clues. Write me if you know the answer.
[h] – The seeds of Millennials' demand for "authenticity" is written here.

And be aware of how language was used in that last paragraph to make you feel something you might not have otherwise; *modern* is in quotes, separating it from the rest of the sentence, *allowed*, *solace*, *increased pressure* and *places upon* are all metaphors of physical contact and distance. The message hidden yet strongly suggested in the above? "Oh, these devices, we use them at our peril! Be Aware! Watch the Skies!" and all that.[170,171,177,381]

> **TakeAway #42 - Use tactile metaphors and images of people in physical contact when you want visitors/users to do or experience something now.**
>
> **TakeAway #43 - Use visual metaphors and images of people looking at something/each other when you want visitors/users to consider or evaluate something to induce a response at a later time.**

We respond in the moment with a lifetime of experience.

7 – Experience and Expectation in Communication

The first goal in designing any communication is to ensure that whoever receives the communication has a (definitely) valued, (and preferably) pleasurable *internal experience*[67] and then conceptually attach that pleasurable internal experience to a favorable *external outcome*.[73] An example would be completing something in twenty minutes that you thought would take you all day and enjoying the experience to boot. Psychologically and socially, people tend to repeat activities which they find pleasurable and favorable.

The question becomes "How does one satisfactorily answer the *why* via the *what*?" This "why via the what" is demonstrated in the reframe of the time management marketing campaign on page 158: "Why don't you have enough time in the day? Because you're always waiting for someone to get back to you. Wait no more!"

This "why via the what" question is also where most focus group and interview paradigms demonstrate their weakness. Respondents can easily answer "what" happened and are often at a loss as to "why" something happened. In Western cultures, "why?" is a *defensible* question, meaning most people respond to a "why" style question by getting defensive, probably because so many of us grew up hearing "Why did you do that?" and knowing we were in trouble when a *Why...?* question was asked. The result of that cultural cuing is that we don't like to be asked *why* in direct address. It's fine to be asked *why* in the first or third person ("Why did *I* do that?" or "Why did *he/she/it/they* do that?") but rarely in the second person ("Why did *you* do that?")[a].

---

[a] – As a tool for your own studies, the next time you want to ask somebody "why" and would like a better chance of getting a non-defensive answer, phrase your question as "*That happened because...?*" You've removed the agent (the person) from the act ("that") and framed the question as causal ("because") rather than inferential ("why"). This allows whoever's answering the question to focus on the event rather than defending their participation in the event, and 99% of the time they'll answer in the first person because the pressure is off. People who can comfortably respond to "Why" style questions tend to be more self-aware than the average person and the more self-aware people are, the more they

This is where research and methods based on psychomotor behavioral cuing[24,66,80,83,152,167,169,176,217,334,339,377,464,475,490,517,565,612] become a better tool[b], me thinks. In other words, it's not important that someone bought a bottle of wine online, it is more important to know the *whys* behind the *whats*. For example, why did the individual purchase that particular wine from that particular site at that particular point in time (see ***Appendix C – eCommerce Wine Store Example***, page 248, for an example of this)?

Thus "why" purchases or decisions are made become a series of catalogueable and repeatable "whats". By repeating a known sequence of "whats" it is possible to recreate the *why* something happened. In *Reading Virtual Minds Volume I: Science and History,* **Chapter 3 – Behaviors, Offline to On**, we talked about seeing someone walk or hearing a few words and instantly knowing who the person was. Technically this is called *anchoring* and it means that you've created a non-conscious connection or "anchor" to a person, place or thing. You've become one of Pavlov's dogs, only instead of hearing a bell and drooling at the thought of food you smell something or hear something or taste something or see something or feel something and a deep memory is invoked which is related to the original sensory experience.

Here we have a case where the collected and repeatable "whats" are the anchors to the "why" of the experience. It doesn't matter what that experience was, if you know the anchors – the "whats" – that surround that experience it can be recreated at will. The "why" can be purchasing wine, filling out a form, listening to a favorite piece of music, simple enjoyment or something else.

The "whats" are the external outcomes, the "whys" are the internal experience. It's not necessary to know the "whys" in

=====

become anthemic to tool and interface designers, marketers, salespeople, basically anyone wanting to get them to do something they would not normally do. Self-aware people usually counter, internally or externally, with something like "Why do I need...?" and often the result is "I don't need...".
[b] – A client sent me a pointer to research similar to NextStage's, and indicating results similar to NextStage's: http://www.technologyreview.com/articles/05/08/wo/wo_081505chabria.asp.

detail, only to ensure that the internal experience is a favorable one. How does one do that? By ensuring that the external outcomes – the "whats" – are consistent. You're using something everyone does automatically and without realizing it – creating anchors from internal experience to external outcomes – to make experience as favorable as possible.

The (perhaps) more interesting aspect of mapping internal experience to external outcomes is that, once a favorable result is achieved, you can tell your automated system to watch for the external events which led to that favorable result with other people. Whenever the automated system finds closely matching external events it's also found a closely matching internal experience. Recreating the non-conscious *why* of a favorable event encourages more favorable events. This recreating of a *why* can be likened to hearing a song on the radio you haven't heard in years and immediately being transported to what you were doing when you first heard it, or tasting a confection you haven't had since childhood and being magically transported back to sitting on your grandfather's knee as he unwrapped the delight.[c]

Ensuring a pleasurable internal experience can be a challenge – current studies show that electronic media has between 1-10 seconds (depending on device and format) and non-electronic media between 7-30 seconds (again, depending on format) to capture an audience's interest before that audience wanders elsewhere. That stated, designers, owners and publishers need to create a rewarding, fulfilling, compelling and uniquely individualized experience, one that so engages each member of the target audience's community that it all but guarantees each member of the target audience will stay engaged until that individual has completed the originally desired action.

The double entendré in that last sentence is purely intentional. The "desired action" has the two-fold meaning of

------

[c] – Such was my experience, and there are the tastes of some Italian candies that, many years after my first taste, still cause me to hear my grandfather's gentle, sonorous voice and deep laugh, to smell his clove-based cologne, to feel the roughness of his beard when he kissed my face or hands (even though he'd shaved only hours before), to feel the power in his breathing as he held me close, the strong pulsing of his heart when he hugged me (can you tell I'm crying from the joy of the remembered experience?).

"what the individual desires to complete" and "what the property owner desires that individual to complete." If an individual comes to a digital property wishing to purchase something and the property owner wishes to sell something, the two goals can be mutually inclusive. If the visitor wishes to do research and the owner wishes to sell something, the owner needs to determine the visitor's *convincer strategy* and *decision strategy*[223,278] in order to turn their desire to research into a desire to purchase. Convincer strategies are the internal processes people go through in order to convince themselves they should or should not do something. Decision strategies evaluate the merits of the convincer strategy to make the final decision. Both are non-conscious processes.

TakeAway #44 - Understand your audience's "why"s and you'll design near perfect "what"s.

Again, creating this satisfying internal experience is easily done. All designers need to do is understand how their target audience thinks, then design their material to address the thought patterns (the decision patterns, the learning patterns, the belief patterns, etc.) of that audience. This is called being *socially aware* of your audience.

It's a given that you won't be able to get 100% of the audience but you should be able to capture 100% of the target audience. The difference between the two is the recognition that the entire audience of a property is a superset which includes the target audience as a subset, much as the US population is a set which includes seniors, Boomers, GenYs, GenXs, and so on (this was the purpose of the culling mentioned in *Reading Virtual Minds Volume I: Science and History,* **Chapter 3 – Behaviors, Offline to On**). Your material's target audience may be baby boomers and, unless you can ensure perfect placement, the entire audience of the material will include other groups not in your target[d].

---

[d] – The degree to which a given target audience will influence the design of a website to

But let's make sure you read what was written above; *Social awareness is a necessary part of design.*

Really, Joseph? I'm not sure I know what social awareness is when it comes to design.

Not a problem. Let me explain how social awareness is a necessary part of design...

I took part in a panel discussion at a local college in the early 2000s and witnessed something fascinating. There were five of us on the panel and each of us had about seven minutes to cover our aspect of the topic. The auditorium was equipped with a projector hooked to a laptop and the moderator asked for our PowerPoints so he could load them onto the laptop. One fellow pulled out a mini CD-RW. "Here you go," he said. "Everybody can burn their presentations on this. You won't need to fumble with lots of disks." He was thanked and the CD was passed around.

One panelist had a very flashy little lap... noteb... palm... something. No CD drives, no floppy drives. Incredibly fast little machine which could find any wireless network from ground level to the International Space Station and with enough USB ports to pilot the aircraft carrier USS John F. Kennedy through heavy seas. This fellow pulled out a USB drive on a keychain, copied his presentation to it, pointed to those of us passing around the CD and said, "That's obsolete."

The laptop attached to the projector, however, was a Compaq Armada 7200 (266MHz, 256M shared RAM, 4GHD running W98se and I did write above that this anecdote is from a while back, remember?). It was attached to the projector because it was not being used for anything else, worked perfectly as the "driver" for the projector each and every time, and nobody wanted it (think *Mike Mulligan and His Steam Shovel*). The Compaq Armada 7200 had a built-in CD reader (not a burner) and nothing else. No PCMCIA cards, no wireless capabilities, wasn't internet ready, nothing, nada, zip.

=====

suit the target audience's own needs is given by Richard Lewontin's evolutionary biology equations, $O' = f(O, E)$ and $E' = g(O, E)$. Digital property design changes, like habitat niche construction, should be influenced by the impact of visitors to the site and these equations set the order and rule. Unfortunately and much like Lewontin's experience in the field of biology in the 1980s, this important and vital work is having little immediate impact on the web.

Did I mention that the Compaq Armada 7200 didn't have any USB ports? I walked over to the fellow who had offered everyone the use of his CD. "You've been here before," I said. He smiled one of those "Oops. You caught me" smiles and said, "Yeah, but can you guess how many times?"

Mr. CD knew his audience, both technologically and psychologically. He knew what to expect from them so he came prepared for them. His tools may have been obsolete to Mr. USB, but to the people in his audience and hosts he was dead center on the curve. Mr. USB, meanwhile, was from another planet as far as his audience and hosts were concerned.

Knowing your audience, knowing what they're prepared to do, what they definitely won't do, where they're willing to go and how they're willing to get there, are crucial to design of new material and redesign of old material, and this is especially true of digital properties. We call it *Audience Knowledgeable Design* and like Hecate, it sits at the intersection of branding and debranding dictating which road your users/visitors/audience will follow.

Here is the secret of the "Audience Knowledgeable Design" and, for those patient readers who made it this far, here is where we tie up understanding the "why" of an experience to correctly design the "whats": Gather information about your audience before you design for them, and I don't mean hiring research firms or doing some focus groups. The information gathering I'm talking about is what anthropologists call *participant observation*.[47,455,613] You want to know how people will respond to a new product? Follow American automobile executive Lee Iacocca's example of driving a convertible around and counting the number of people who looked and pointed. That told him more about how convertibles would do in the market after having been absent for several years than any focus group or research firm could. Mr. Iacocca went among the people he wanted to know about and got their responses and reactions. He observed them while participating in their lives.

Companies tend to stay companies by mixing two polar opposites: risk aversion and innovation. This comes through in their marketing efforts more than anywhere else. Here, then, is the key to creating marketing materials, devices and interface designs that work –

> **TakeAway #45 - Learn how the target audience is doing things now and you'll have a much easier time navigating them to something new later.**

> **TakeAway #46 - Make sure the target audience can access their historic methods of what you're usurping while you're getting them to use the new material, interface or product.**

> **TakeAway #47 - When the effort is around a new design, material or interface, make sure it is implemented in small, easily negotiable steps.**

> **TakeAway #48 - When the effort is around a new product, make sure you have a highly vocal and well respected group of beta users who'll act as evangelists.**

> **TakeAway #49 - When the effort is around a new product, make sure the cost-to-benefit meets the fair-exchange criteria.[e]**

> **TakeAway #50 - Regarding new design, material or interface, make sure your suggestions provide a clear path to the past (thus being risk averse while providing marketable innovation).**

---

[e] – *Reading Virtual Minds Volume III: Fair-Exchange and Social Networks* has a full discussion of fair-exchange criteria.

In the case of device and interface design, the fair-exchange criteria dictate that the benefits of the new product are greater than the sum of the psychological cost of adopting the new product plus the satisfaction lost due to the inability to achieve some goals because the user doesn't care about the new product's benefits, only about not being able to perform the old product's desired actions hence not achieving a desired outcome.

Providing a clear path to the past doesn't mean giving the client an easy out. People won't change without a clear incentive. The new interface or design must provide the client with two things. First and most important, make sure client-requested features are easy to use and prominent in the new design. Give people what they wanted and they'll come back for more. The features the designers and engineers wanted to put in is a shadowy secondary concern and much less important to clients than one might think.

> **TakeAway #51 - Consumers/Users/Visitors equate "ease of use" with "time to achieve a recognizable goal".**

> **TakeAway #52 - Consumers/Users/Visitors equate "easier to use" with "it takes less time now than before to do something I do a lot".**

Releasing a new interface or product without knowing if the new "ease of use" is equal to or less than the preceding interface or product's "time to achieve a recognizable goal" is a fool's errand.

Creating a look and feel – be it a digital property, marketing material, a software interface, leave-behinds, assorted collateral – involves making sure people can:

- achieve their goals
- get their work done
- do what they want to do

- communicate their message effectively

You might have the flashiest, pizzazziest material in the world but if the client doesn't want it or isn't psychologically ready for it, you're obsolete, not them. There is no mystery to creating winning material. It is a 3-step process and it works every time:

1 - Take the time to learn from your audience what they want and more importantly, what they're doing now.
2 - Learn as much as you can about yourself, your own likes and dislikes, your prejudices, what frustrates you and engages you in a design, interface or material.
3 - Whenever what you've learned in #2 gets in the way of fulfilling the requests of #1, stop. You've stopped creating Audience Knowledgeable Design. You've started designing for yourself, not the audience. Get yourself out of the way and you'll be designing for your audience again.[f]

The secret to Audience Knowledgeable Design is simple; save your cutting-edge work for the awards show. Your material needs to get a job done. It has been said that cooler is not better; *better* is better. Nobody knows what is "better" better than your audience. Your audience can be website visitors, people reading a business email, someone stopping at a mall kiosk to get information, attendees to a trade show walking the product floor killing time before they go to the bar where the real meetings will occur.

It doesn't matter who you're designing for, and it doesn't matter if you are in your target audience's demographic. Remove yourself from the design process by asking *why* at each step until all that remains is a clear series of *whats* that achieve the audience's goals, not yours. Help them achieve their goals and then show them a way to achieve yours. Their original

---

[f] — It is worth quoting one of our First Readers here: "This is SO important. I'm curious if people get this or if they are oblivious of how much their own preferences drive their choices."

pleasurable experience – achieving their goals – will now be translated into achieving your goals pleasurably.

But in all things, creating and ensuring a pleasurable internal and external experience is the key.

Now that we've gone through all that agony, let's get down to some concrete examples of simple ways to improve someone's experience of information using digital properties and marketing collateral as examples. We're going to explore seven elements:

1 - Turning Tourists into Locals
2 - Removing Outs from Conversion Pages
3 - Removing Barriers to Entry
4 - Visitor-Designed Navigation
5 - Reciprocal Evaluation and
6 - Improving Visual Search Results
7 - Always Tell a Story

These seven items were determined by ET as methods for improving experience and have been put into practice on a variety of digital properties many times. What follows are examples of social awareness of general B2x audiences specific to digital properties, mobile through desktop. With slight modifications, the techniques can become usable for any marketing material on any platform. Each section's heading includes the gains each method generated based on initial states. The measures are from some 30 sites chosen at random from those NextStage monitors. The metrics used for each section are the same: Time-On-site (TOS), Site-Penetration (SP), Site Comprehension and Retention (SCR) and Conversion Rate (CR). First let's clarify what these terms mean so we're all measuring the same thing.[9]

- Time-On-Site (TOS) - also known as "Average Time Spent on Site" and "Minutes per Visitor". This is a measure of the average number of minutes each

---

[9] – Many thanks to Angie Brown who helped me with these definitions long, long ago..

visitor spends on the site over a certain timeframe. It's used as a rough measure of interaction with the site, although the numbers are not precise. It's not a given that increasing this metric is good: for a customer support site or intranet we might actually prefer a decrease (get them the information they need in as little time as possible).

- Site-Penetration (SP) - the number of unique pages viewed before a visitor leaves a site. If nine unique pages of a 10-page site are navigated before the visitor leaves the site and those are the only pages navigated, SP is 90%. If 12 pages of a 10-page site are navigated but only nine of the pages are unique, the SO is still 90%.

- Page Comprehension and Retention (PCR) - a metric unique to ET and a measure of how well visitors remember and can act upon what they've seen on a page. Factors involved include number of unique pages navigated divided by the total number of pages navigated balanced against a time-to-action factor.

- Conversion Rate (CR) - a very broad term that means "when somebody does something of high value on your site" (high value from a business perspective, or high value from the customer's perspective... if those perspectives are not one and the same then that's probably not good for business). These high-value tasks can be almost anything under the sun, so although people can be somewhat retail-centric when they talk about conversions (meaning purchases), purchasing something is only one of a gazillion possible conversions. We're going to use CR broadly in what follows to mean "the visitor and the site owner exchanged something both valued highly and both went away happy" (fair-exchange is everywhere when you know how to look for it).

7.A - Turning Tourists into Locals:
Anonymous, Self-Expressive and Anonymous-Expressive Identity
(Improvements - TOS: 2m42s, SP: 38%, PCR: 90%, CR: 43%)

There are five stages of identity in any kind of social exchange, including and most prevalent in commerce. These five stages go from situations where an individual is unknown and unknowable, or anonymous, to where the individual is engaged enough to create a unique, self-expressive identity for themselves.

The first identity commerce assigns people is the *Anonymous Identity*. Anonymous Identity is defined by the fact that the only time the seller can touch the buyer is during the transaction. You're visiting friends who live in a different part of the country than you do. They've run out a few things they need for dinner – milk, bread, coffee, ice, patience. You offer to go to the corner store and pick things up. You pay in cash. You're anonymous. The proprietor doesn't know you and probably doesn't want to know you. According to Professor John Deighton of the Harvard Business School, "Anonymity means 'to be unrecognized on the second visit'".

Anyone familiar with the state of ecommerce in the mid-2000s knows that privacy and identity were the topics *du jour* and haven't let up since. People tend to think of privacy and identity as polar opposites on some scale and they're not (at least in a social commerce setting). You can have complete personal privacy yet have a very public identity and you can have zero personal privacy yet be someone completely unknown to others, just a face in the crowd. The reason for this is that "privacy" isn't what most people think it is. Privacy, as recognized at the start of the 21st century, is a relatively new historical phenomenon.

The social commerce scale which has existed as long as humans walked the Earth actually has Anonymity and Identity as polar extremes and the slider is Privacy. To be either known or unknown depends on how much of yourself you're willing to share and with whom you're willing to share it.

People browse your properties, they pick up your brochure at a kiosk or in a store, they walk past your booth at a tradeshow – all of these people have at least one thing in common: They all want to be left alone until they're ready to not be left alone. In other words, they want to remain anonymous in a social commerce setting, and specifically, they want to remain anonymous until they no longer want to remain anonymous. Anonymity occurs when someone decides they want to be unknown.

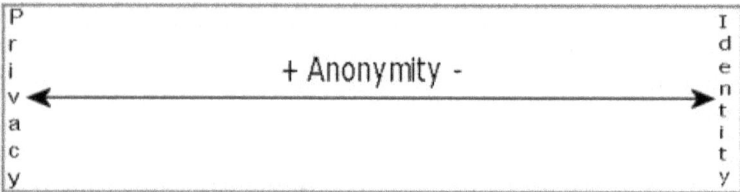

7.1 - Most people have the mistaken belief that Anonymity is the slider on the scale of Privacy to Identity

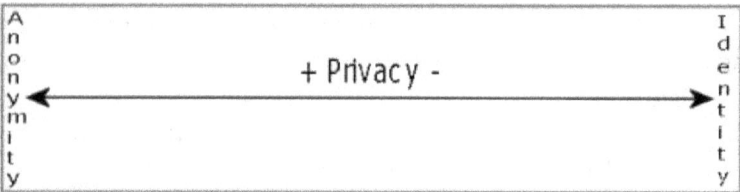

7.2 - An accurate belief is that Privacy is the slider on the scale of Anonymity to Identity

Let's explore "being unknown" in the context of *Reading Virtual Minds*.

To be unknown means to not have any community, no social connections, and ultimately to have no identity. Identities are formed within a social context, and to be anonymous (or "unknown") means to present an identity which is unknown...within the current social context. Only amnesiacs are unknown to themselves. Individuals wishing to remain anonymous and therefore unknown *to others* are doing so for a reason and within their current social context. For example, on the first day of teaching a new class, I'll often be the third or fourth person entering the room, smiling and nodding as I enter the room and take a seat in the back, as if I were a student. This gives me a chance to engage the students as their peer, to learn their goals and motivations, and to plan and adjust the course accordingly. An historic, literary example of anonymity is King Richard returning to England in the Robin Hood legends. King Richard needed to reclaim his throne but without alerting his brother, John, who'd usurped the throne while Richard was at the Crusades. Richard's only option was to travel anonymously, to hide his identity, until he could be guaranteed success.

So anonymity allows an individual to create a new social context in which they can define or assign a role to themselves which is independent of other roles other social contexts have assigned to them. It allows them to reveal only the information they wish to reveal in the current social setting. In other words, it allows them to keep certain things *private* and make other things public.

Now let's bring this back to people browsing a digital property, picking up a brochure, walking through a showroom or strolling a convention floor. Here anonymity morphs into "I see you, you see me, and you'll forget me as soon as I turn away."

Anonymity joined with privacy is relatively new in human history, having only been around since the advent of mass transportation. Prior to trains and boats and passenger planes, people never got very far from their village. If they did, they carried papers on them (the Cold War era movie question, "Your papers, please?" didn't happen because of the Cold War and wasn't limited to Communist countries. It was standard practice for people traveling in their own country – including the USA – up until the early 20th century) or some sign which clearly indicated their business and why they were about. The sign might have been a Cross, a leper's bell, a monk's robe, a king's banner or a robber's mask. All of these things and more were signs which clearly and quickly gave others the necessary information, "this is why I'm here."

Think about it and you'll understand why the lack of privacy and anonymity was not only the norm, it was required. Prior to recent times literacy wasn't the norm, and literacy plays a key role in the need for well-defined and recognized social roles. Person A wasn't likely to engage in commerce with Person B unless A knew B personally, hence knew they could trust and were trusted. Likewise for Person B. Remember "I trust you", "You Can Trust Me" and so on?[87] The faster these questions were answered the longer people lived, and living in small social circles where identity was defined by such things as:

- everyone around you knowing who you were,
- who you were related to, what you did,
- your shoe size,
- whether you limped,
- how you dressed and
- if your wife liked the way you kissed[202,247]

provided answers that cut through many of those questions quickly, cleanly and easily. The cohesiveness of the society you lived in answered those questions for you, and when you were setting up shop on your own the blessing or curse of that social network dictated your success or lack thereof.

Two hundred years ago people didn't carry identification with them (if anyone can tell me the real difference between "Your papers, please?" and being asked to show a photo ID when you use a credit card or cash a check, I'd love to hear it) and there was no national citizenship registry until the turn of the 18th century. At this point in time, European countries began enforcing the concept of "One person, one name". Prior to that any given person could have several of what we now call "aliases" and nobody cared because most of the aliases were nicknames given to an individual by people in that individual's social circle ("Morgan the Goat", "Johnnie One-Eye", "Velmuth the Butcher") or by society assigning a role to the individual ("Typhoid Mary", "George 'Longhair' Custer", "Atilla the Chiropodist").

Up until mass transportation and the industrial age, people worked from their homes. They lived above their smithy, next to their fields, on their farm, beside their granary, with their animals, ... Anonymity and privacy didn't exist and where it did, it was a cause for suspicion and distrust: if someone had something to hide, it was for a reason, and the xenophobic natures which benefited us when we descended from the trees still served us well during these times.

And now, once again, people are browsing your website, picking up your flyer at a kiosk, glancing at your brochure as they walk a showroom or convention floor. They have this belief that they are anonymous and want to remain so.

You want and need them to share information about themselves with you, your property/website, your salespeople.

Most people and especially website visitors believe they are anonymous and actually fall into the next identity level, which is *Transitory Identity*. Transitory Identity occurs when an individual can be reached through some non-permanent address or tag. A temporary IP is an example of this. The seller can repeatedly touch the individual during the complete lifetime of the encounter ("visit"), not just at the time of the transaction. Imagine someone invisible joining you as you walk in the door of some brick & mortar store and directing other workers to put things in front of and to the side of you as you walk through the store, with the goal of maneuvering you to the checkout aisle with a shopping cart full of useless goodies.

Most digital property/website visitors have Transitory Identity. There's been lots of studies published since 2005 that indicate cookies are deleted, purged, expurgated, dunked in the coffee and milk you picked up at the corner store when you thought you were Anonymous and otherwise gotten rid of.[4,45,109, 166,188,191,204,229,379,413,414,418,459,473,573,585]

The next identity level is *Persistent Identity*. Persistent Identity occurs when the individual can be touched over several encounters, transactions or visits. A snail-mailbox, a direct access phone number, a permanent IP or personal email account are examples of being able to touch individuals over time, not just during the transaction (anonymity) or during a single encounter (transitory). If you thought being able to keep your mobile phone number from carrier to carrier was for your benefit, think again. Persistent Identity is a one-way affair, and doesn't offer the seller much more than transitory or anonymous identity save two things:

- Persistent Identity allows the seller to leave and/or place messages for the individual at the address. In other words, Persistent Identity is where mass-marketing ends and direct-marketing begins.
- Persistent Identity allows the seller to begin "branding" the individual according to that individual's worth to the seller by differentiating this individual from that individual (at another address).

These two items come together in a single word, relationship, and for all things there is a cost. Sellers asked for something, now they must give something, and here is where it gets really interesting because you haven't really asked for a mailbox, virtual or otherwise, a phone number or anything like that. When we seek to establish a relationship we are really asking for trust and how that trust is solicited influences the rest of the relationship. People who've read my iMediaCommunications *Usability Studies 101*[h] columns or attended my seminars know I preach about what goes on in the consumer's head a great deal, and trust is a key element in the equation of the visitor's mind. You have to let the individual know you trust them[i] before they'll trust you, so the cost of Persistent Identity is relationship and the price tag is the

---

[h] – http://nlb.pub/d
[i] – There are an amazing number of techniques available to demonstrate you trust your audience. Some were covered in *Reading Virtual Minds Volume I: Science and History*, others are explained and taught through NextStage's many trainings (see http://nlb.pub/G for trainings and schedulings). I also discuss this a bit when explaining the use of Anonymous-Expressive Identity on page 192. Alternately, you can become a NextStage member and have access to presentations and podcasts on these topics (see http://nlb.pub/4).

individual's trust that you will behave according to some mutually agreed to standard. Watch this because it will bite you. People don't read EULAs and Terms-of-Use disclosures before clicking on the "I Accept" box, but they definitely believe you're going to play fair(-exchange. I know, it's all over the place) and when you don't, you'll be saying "Ouch!", not them. Consumer trust is one of the most easily lost, hardest to gain and expensive commodities in the world today.

Next comes *Role-Specific Identity*. Role-Specific Identity begins a two-way exchange between the individual and the seller because the seller has created a role for the individual and to enjoy the benefits of that role the individual needs to play by some rules set by the seller. Credit cards brand individuals via role-specific identities.

For example, everybody knows what a Gold Card is, and that certain financial and other bona fides are required to get one, and most people know about what's involved in the getting and keeping of Platinum Cards.

But how many know what's involved in getting or keeping a Black AmEx? How about a Signature card?

For real credit cards, travel cards, club cards, etc., role-specific identity is the point. The seller controls the role the individual plays. Of course, the individual enjoys certain benefits by taking on the seller's predefined role. You get automatic upgrades on flights, you get preferred treatment at hotels, you get better tables at restaurants and guaranteed reservations. Also, the seller knows more about you than you know about yourself, but you have decided that you want it that way because that's part of the role you've been assigned. The only way to break out of the role is to be denied the benefits conferred by the role and most people don't want to do that. In the 1970s, you had to prove yourself to the credit card supplier before getting a silver, gold or platinum card and only a select few knew what a black card was. Now platinum cards are the gateway drugs that start capturing our macro-behaviors in our identity-hungry digital culture.

7.3 – Ego Identification by device, anyone? (circa 2010, anyways)

The last identity of common commerce is *Self-Expressive Identity*. In common commerce, Self-Expressive Identity is the goal because it's where the individual internalizes the seller's brand as part of their own identity. Examples of self-expressive identity can be found among owners of BMWs, Harley-Davidson motorcycles, BlackBerries (at one point in time), iPhones, Androids and drinkers of selected beverages. In these and many other cases individuals become billboards for the products they've identified with. This kind of personal identification with a brand or product is called *ego identification* and occurs when the seller's brand is integrated into the individual's Identity to the point that it influences that individual's Personality.

Self-Expressive identity isn't something relegated only to product and service branding. It is the first stage of *tribal identity* and can be seen in those wearing school jackets, gang colors, body piercings and tattoos (literally where the individual brands their body so that they'll be easily recognized by society as possessing a group affiliation).

Self-Expressive Identity is used in community building, as in the seller creating a community within which the individual gets to express their identity by being around people who think the way the individual thinks and do what the individual does and like what the individual likes. Being part of such a community is one of the most identity affirming things anyone can do. Example: I have a cap with my favorite cigar brand's name and logo on it. Other cigar smokers walk up to me and share their experiences with the brand, I share mine, we gossip, we exchange favorite stories and *we are known to each other via the mutually shared branded ego identity*. I mean, I smoke this brand of cigars and I'm handsome, viral, intelligent, kind to animals and children, etc., so everyone else who smokes this brand of cigars must be handsome, viral, intelligent, kind to animals and children, etc., correct?

Self-Expressive Identity is also where individuals become a brand that is shared with others. Consider the following press release (emphasis mine):

> Happy Birthday, *Ginuwine*! The award-winning R&B singer, whose real name is Elgin Baylor Lumpkin, turns 45 today! Born in Washington, D.C., *Ginuwine* began his music career as a member of the group Swing Bop, a record label

and music compound based in Rochester, NY. There, he met world-renowned rapper *Missy Elliott* and producer *Timbaland* with whom he collaborated throughout the 90's. *Ginuwine*'s debut album, "Genuwine ... The Bachelor", features the hit song "Pony" written by Static Major, which rose to number 6 on the Billboard Hot 100 chart. In the early 2000's after losing both parents within less than a year, *Ginuwine* recorded another hit "Two Reasons I Cry" as a tribute to them before starting his own record label, Bag Entertainment. Today, *Ginuwine* holds a number of multi-platinum and platinum albums and singles, and is referred to as one of the top R&B artists of the late 90's early 2000's. Cheers, *Ginuwine!*

Genuwine, Missy Elliott and Timbaland? Really?

But such self-expressive identities are much more closely tied to the cultures they are drawn from than *Marilyn Monroe* is from *Norma Jeane Mortenson*.

Self-Expressive Identity leads us into a new identity specific to information exchange and ecommerce systems, *Anonymous-Expressive Identity*. Anonymous-Expressive Identity occurs when the individual creates a role for themselves and the seller accepts it and uses it to communicate with the individual. This is true tribal identity in the information age because by understanding the anonymous-identity the individual presents, we know a great deal about them, their life, their hopes, dreams and aspirations, without invading their privacy at all. For example, you can tell a great deal about the owners of the following emailnyms (email pseudonyms) with a little thought and cultural understanding:

- tuboricuamary4u
- kzinlaw
- a company in which the privately used, internal email addresses used by top management include tex, reno, philly, kc, fresno
- a company in which in the privately used, internal email addresses include mightydan, brainchild and wondergirl
- paladin

- suemist
- grannygoodwitch
- newbillyland
- sueoboe
- meows7
- stonewall

What about the icons we choose as digital surrogates?

Reading Virtual Minds Volume I: Science and History[j] readers know we're getting into Core, Identity and Personality concepts here. People always project their Personalities when they're communicating and regardless of medium. Real-world exchanges allow us to also evaluate other people's Identity and Core while modifying our own based on the exchanges. In the digital world, the images we use to represent ourselves online are our Core, Identity and Personality[17,19,22,27,69,70,94,95,166,188,190,229,240,256,273, 316,347,379,413,414,436,462,467,473,482,489,492,553,585] reaching out into the virtual world.[76,98]

I've seen Twitter and Facebook ID images that I couldn't figure out at all. Take a look at the following and make a note as to what you think it is:

7.4 – Go ahead. Guess. What is it?

I understand that there's meaning, purpose and power in how we choose to self-identify in the digital world.[98] The above may be recognizable once you're told what it is[k] and there's little doubt (or at least I hope there's little doubt) regarding what the following image is:

---

[j] – http://nlb.pub/RVMV14th And get a copy now if you haven't already!
[k] – It's a chicken. No, really. Or so we were told. Once identified as a chicken, it's easy to see and hard not to see (which is an example of Adaptation Method described on page 91).

7.5 – No guesses required. You may not recognize *who*[l] it is and
there's no difficulty recognizing *what* it is.

Let me ask all red-blooded, American males (and any other heterosexual males in the audience), "Knowing nothing else except what the individual has chosen as an icon, do you want to Twitter, Skype or IM with the person behind Figure 7.4 or Figure 7.5?"

Adds a whole new dimension to Monty Hall's "Door #1 or Door #2?", doesn't it? And forget Stockton's *The Lady or the Tiger?*[m].

And these self-selected images of ourselves that we project into the online world? They can be just as indecipherable as the business cards, flyers, brochures, digital properties and related collateral material that lone-wolf entrepreneurs create for themselves when they're uncomfortable in their lone-wolf role, or have created for them by people who don't know a thing about the solopreneurs' audience or subject. A dark business card, difficult to read or with an image difficult to understand easily, or a self-selected online image (such as used on Twitter, LinkedIn, etc.), indicates a psychology not yet wanting to be known in their self-described or assigned social network role, or unsure of themselves in the new, chosen setting. We need to be careful what we project, especially in business.

Consider the following three images, the first used on both Twitter and LinkedIn and the last two of yours truly (and all are shown actual size):

---

[l] – This is the "Susna" character from the animated Star Trek(TM) series. One NextStageologist always misspells "Susan" as "Susna". Another NextStageologist told us that "Susna" exists in the Star Trek(TM) universe and Susan has used it for her online persona ever since.
[m] – http://www.eastoftheweb.com/short-stories/UBooks/LadyTige.shtml

7.6

7.7

7.8

All three pictures were used so we can accept their use was intentional. What is Figure 7.6's intention? A dark face on a dark background. Perhaps mystery? An homage to film noirs? Does not being able to clearly make out the individual or their setting inspire trust or trepidation? Figures 7.7 and 7.8 were also used with intention. Figure 7.7 presents a friendly face in a natural setting with lots of visual contrast. The communication is both approachability and trustworthiness. Figure 7.8 is me literally presenting another face. The darker colors highlight the books in the background, the lighting on the face and presentation suggest a knowledgeable, authoritative figure, one who understands and can be understood.

Finally, consider Maunik Patel's LinkedIn image below (7.9, again shown actual size).

7.9 – A smiling face, canted to show emotional curiosity (friendliness,
a desire to know about the person, not the position), staring directly
at the visitor. Excellent!

It is so near a perfect general purpose publicity headshot that I contacted him to learn how it came to be. Dr. Patel replied:

> I'm flattered you were impressed by the headshot, I actually did quite a bit of graphic design in college and I will admit it is a little bit 'touched up'. ... I am a self learned neuroscience lover! I've been a long fan of social/marketing psychology a la Robert Cialdini, Daniel Kahneman etc.

Compare Figures 7.7 and 7.8 with my Skype, Twitter and IM image:

7.10 – A visual ice-breaker guaranteed to start conversations...
or stop them from occurring in the first place.

The only people who'll chat with me or follow me on Twitter are those who know something about me (I routinely twit and post to Facebook the activities of NextStage's several mascots[n]). All others are non-consciously warned away. Each of these

---

[n] – http://nlb.pub/U

images demonstrates that there are two sides to the advertising coin: "Make sure what you're advertising is what you're selling" and "You can't sell what you don't advertise". All such images are our surrogates in the online world.,[760]

Now I will share with you something you may be beginning to appreciate by reading this book: chances are that any values and histories you assigned to the people using those emailnyms and icons above came more from you than from the emailnyms, icons or the people themselves. In each case, the question to be asked is "Who either accepts or refers to themselves as 'kzinlaw', 'paladin', 'meows7', etc., anonymously?" Ditto Figures 7.4, 7.6 and 7.10.

Because the individual has created the role, they present it and use it. Because the individual reuses the role often, the seller has much higher quality interactions with the individual. This is where Persistent Identity's direct-marketing becomes *direct-request-marketing*, meaning the individual now makes specific requests of the seller and gives the seller a direct means of contact with which to fulfill those requests. In more psychological terms, the individual tells the seller, "I have created this image of myself. Please give me things which fit this image I have of myself because by doing so, you reinforce an identity I've created for myself!"

A short paraphrase of the above is the individual crying out "Believe in me!" in the hope and belief that the seller will respond with "I believe in you!" and, when the seller does, they've created a customer for life. Nobody but a fool would walk away from that kind of recognition. The seller is no longer saying "I trust you" nor do they have a need to because the consumer now says to the seller, "I trust you" and they are requesting the relationship instead of the other way around.

---

[o] – NextStage Members can download the "That Smile, Those Eyes, That Face" research paper that explains facial image use in detail.

TakeAway #53 - Allow your visitors/users/audience Anonymous-Expressive Identity and they're yours forever.

Allow users, visitors and audience to use Anonymous-Expressive Identity and you've essentially let them know that with you, they're safe. People always go where they feel safe.

Do recognize that this type of relationship comes at a very high price. The buyer is trusting the seller with something more than the dollar they bring home from work; the buyer is trusting the seller to foster and nourish their identity. Destroy that trust and you've broken faith, destroyed confidence and most likely made an enemy for life. When this happens the seller has debranded the individual and has created an advocate for any and all competing products, regardless of the competing products' real worth in the market.

In other words, Anonymous-Expressive Identity is where individuals create their own, personal brand based on their beliefs about themselves. What they create in the marketplace is a "branding" identity and they ask the market to accept their own, personal brand just as much as the market asks the individual to accept its brand.

Digital property visitors, in particular, want to remain anonymous for the most part. At the same time, you want them to tell you who they are and what they want, which means you want them to express themselves. What we need to do is create a method for this equation – what they want and what you want – to achieve balance. So your job is to accept their brand if you want them to accept yours (it's fair-exchange all over again).

How does this benefit you, the marketer or seller or information designer?

1 - Because the individual has created the role, they present it and use it.

2 - When the seller/designer/marketer accepts the presented role, the individual becomes dependent on the seller/designer/marketer to reinforce that role.

3 - The individual is essentially saying to the seller/designer/marketer "Do this and you'll have me right where you want me."

4 - Because the individual reuses the role often, the seller/designer/marketer has much higher quality interactions with the individual.

Our task is to create a method for digital property visitors (regardless of device...or perhaps in spite of it? because of it?) to retain their sense of anonymity while telling you who they are and what they want. Creating a sense of anonymity while getting the individual to tell you about themselves is easy to do providing the buy-in to Anonymous-Expressive Identity obeys the following rules:

1 – The buy-in must be easy for the individual to take part in.

2 – The buy-in must be available to everyone. If not, then individuals automatically lose their anonymous status.

3 – There must be a compelling reason for the individual to take part in the buy-in.

4 – There must be no penalty for not taking part in the buy-in, but...

5 – ...there must be a high reward for taking part in the buy-in.

6 – Taking part must lead to higher trust relationships between the seller/designer/marketer and the individual so that...

7 – ...the seller/designer/marketer can touch the individual at will.

This is where we begin separating Tourists from Locals.[p] Two different home pages are shown in Figures 7.11-12[q] (pages 200-

---

[p] – Services that provide steaming, device-independent information (such as Netflix and Amazon Prime) are examples of this.
[q] – We'll be using simplified pages as examples, the better to draw your attention to what we're discussing.

201). The difference between the two pages is that the home page in Figure 7.12 has a login area and one less menu button. The "one less" menu button is actually two items removed and one added. Think of elements of the web page as screen targets, like targets in an arcade or a video game. We've removed two *low-worth, high-interest* screen targets – those targets which catch your eye and are easy to hit but don't give you lots of points for your effort – and replaced them with a single *high-worth, high-interest* screen target. The two removed menu items are "White Papers" and "Case Studies". The new menu item is "Access".

7.11 – Low-Worth, High-Interest Screen

Why do this? Low-worth, high-interest targets are screen points or decision points which benefit the visitor more than they benefit the site owner. The goal is to get them to express themselves in a way which allows them to believe they're controlling the exchange and which actually allows you to control the exchange. High-worth, high-interest targets start you down that control path.

Why "Access"?

Because "Access" is both a verb and a noun, and anything which can have more than one meaning is a source of confusion and curiosity. For example, you're on holiday. You want to go to a nice restaurant. You ask the concierge where to go. Google (that's the concierge's name) suggests two, no, three good places to go and a bunch of other places that might be nice, too, but those top two or three, by golly, they really are good.

7.12 – High-Worth, High-Interest Screen

As long as the majority of visitors to your site come to you through a search, you should spend your time attracting Tourists. If the majority of your visitors come to you through word of mouth or a known link, you should spend your time attracting Locals.

Locals are the people who know the city, know where the best restaurants are, know how to get where they want to go quickly, easily and would never ask Google about how to get there. Tourists are the people who don't know the city, need directions, may or may not have a good reason for their visit, may have performed a blind search – vacations – versus an intentional search – Walking Tours of Dublin, Ireland.

You want Locals. They are your regular customers because they're so familiar with your site that they won't go anywhere else. Familiarity breeds loyalty and the faster you can make people familiar with the layout of your site the more loyal they'll be to your offerings. More importantly for design purposes, Locals will forgive you a lack of flash (in fact, they might be turned off by anything that catches their attention but doesn't help them achieve their goal. Such attention grabbing, non-helpful things are *distractions* and frequent users/visitors won't forgive you if you keep putting them in their faces[120]).

Both Tourists and Locals can be vocal but the real separator between Tourists and Locals is that Locals will tell you what they want and how to make things easier for them. Tourists have nothing vested in your making things easier so if you hear from them it'll be when they close the door on their way out.

Here's an example: a pet supply company with a print catalog started an online store. One NextStageologist has been a catalogue customer for several years (she owns dogs, cats and horses) and was willing to make the switch to the company's website until she browsed it. She called them and finally got in touch with their senior web person, introduced herself, gave her background and credentials, and suggested two changes that would make the transition from print buyer to web buyer a snap. The company instituted the changes and sent her a wonderful thank you note...and bags of dog treats, kitty towers, catnip, chew toys, braiding combs, sweat scrapers and hoof picks.

This woman was a Local. She knew the company had good products at good prices. She also knew their website wasn't optimal. She was vocal. She told them how to fix it. They can't wait for her next call.

Most companies already have Tourist-Friendly sites. Tourist-Friendly sites are designed to quickly get information from the user. Tourist-Friendly sites focus on qualifying, nurturing and closing visitors. The design belies the fact that the visitor might be on the site only once and that the visitor has to be quickly placed in the sales cycle in order to justify the site's existence. Typically these sites require high traffic volume because the conversions numbers are low.

Local-friendly websites aren't concerned with closing, nurturing or qualifying in the traditional sense, they want to help. Specifically, they want to help or offer more to visitors who've already provided value by purchasing, providing contact information, etc. Sales people will recognize this as a chance to create a continuous revenue stream. Customer service representatives will recognize this as customer relationship management and providing a channel with which to touch the visitor. All businesses that want to touch their online customers repeatedly can benefit from providing a Local-Friendly site.

Local-Friendly site designs follow some simple rules in order to meet the goals of all parties concerned. First, they are generally smaller than their Tourist-Friendly cousins and are simpler to both navigate and create because they're designed to provide information quickly and cleanly. Where Tourists become Locals is up to you.

Small businesses probably already have a semi-Local-Friendly site due to development costs of a traditional Tourist-Friendly site, and this is fine. Small businesses build their businesses one client at a time. Until they reach that critical mass of clients where they can advertise broadly, there's no need for a Tourist-Friendly site.

So if you have a site which is excellent at capturing Tourists and rotten at retaining Locals, or if you're making the transition from a Local-Friendly site to a Tourist-Friendly site, go through your files and find a simpler, cleaner, more elegant version of your website. You're not done with them yet. They served you well when everybody knew your name, right? Now you're dealing with visitors who can't even pronounce your name and you still want them to do business with you. All businesses want to make Tourists into Locals as quickly as possible and a simple way to do it is by giving them "Access".

Make sure whatever visitors "Access" causes more curiosity than confusion and you are now leading people through your site rather than having them wander wondering where what they're looking for can be found. Keep in mind that a properly designed Local-Friendly site is a good offline conversion tool, too. Many companies' customer service staffs and offline sales people are told to direct potential customers to the corporate website before, during and after the sale. However, offline or telephoning customers are usually directed to a Tourist-Friendly site. Imagine giving a potential customer, especially one experiencing buyer remorse, access to a "backdoor" site that's A) easy to navigate and B) explains easy-to-implement, non-obvious and real benefits to using your products or services. Now you have a double-use marketing tool that goes well beyond its original purpose.

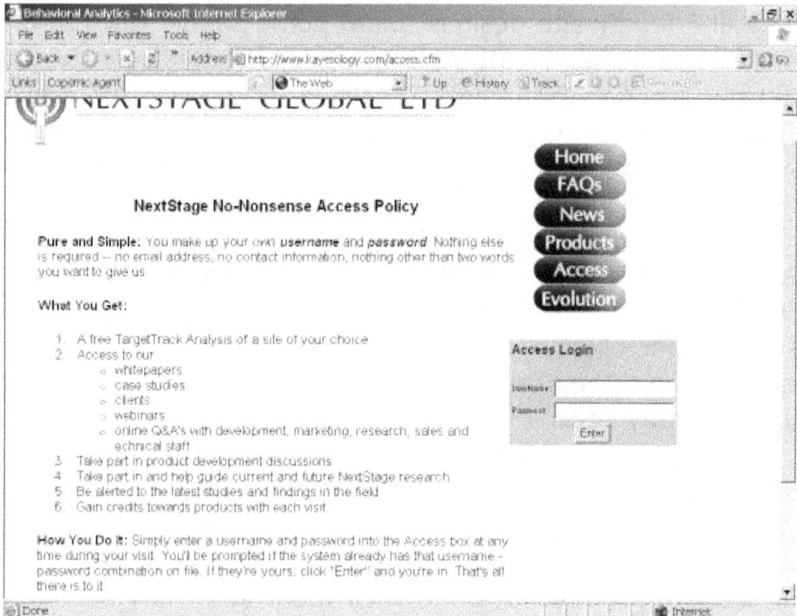

7.13 - Rewarding visitors who create an Anonymous-Expressive Identity

Okay, we've designed the gateway to the Local-Friendly site and explained its use, now it's time to reward visitors who are willing to create an Anonymous-Expressive Identity. The reward comes in two parts; part one is the immediate reward for going through the trouble of creating the identity in the first place. Part two is the promise of future rewards in order to keep them coming back (thus creating loyalty and increasing branding). Both rewards are demonstrated in Figure 7.13 (page 204).

Before listing the rewards, remember how this works – a visitor comes to a site, makes up a username and password on the spot and clicks enter.

For little effort on their part they get an instantaneous reward: access to Item 2 - white papers, case studies, reference accounts, Webinars, all sorts of stuff, and all without revealing their name, email address, phone number...

And I will be the first to admit that everything offered in Item 2 is interesting, it's nice, and it's really nothing special. The case studies and white papers menu items probably offered the same.

So we're going to up the ante by giving the visitor access to that most precious commodity, items 3 and 4 on the "Access" screen (Figure 7.13), your time, as in:

3 - Take part in product development discussions
4 - Take part in and help guide current and future research

The goal is to reward or incentivize visitors to become high-worth quickly and easily, with little risk or effort on their part. We've given them some reason so far and now we need to add some loyalty rewards. That's done with Item 5:

5 - Be alerted to the latest studies and findings in the field

Item 5 is where you define yourself as the resource point for industry knowledge. Industry knowledge is something visitors can get lots of other places but they can't get everything else you've offered and industry knowledge anywhere else but through you.

Now comes the time to offer them something which validates your uniqueness in the marketplace. This comes as Item 1:

1 - A free TargetTrack analysis of a site of your choice[r]

---

[r] – In NextStage's case, this takes the form of one of NextStage Membership, http://nlb.pub/4

Regardless of what you offer for Item 1, the goal of making visitor experience optimal (in this example and in the sense of an escalating reward) has these requirements on both the visitor and your side:

Visitor's Perspective	Your Perspective
• The reward must be something real	• The reward must place the visitor directly into the conversion process
• The reward must be something tangible	• Ideally the reward should require minimal effort on your part, such as a computer generated report
• The reward must have recognizable value and demonstrated worth in the market[s]	
• The reward must be a genuine product, something you've established through sales and for which you've published a price tag[t]	

Meeting these requirements allows you to short-circuit the conversion process. Meeting these requirements as part of a reward for providing an Anonymous-Expressive Identity gives

---

[s] – A user/visitor/audience testimonial will do this. The more the merrier.
[t] – Note, a *genuine* product, something that you'd normally actually sell, not something with "a $99 value". If you give it away for free and aren't selling it anywhere then it has no value. Until you've sold it at least once, it's valueless to everybody but you.

visitors reasons to return, which leads to Item 6: points towards rewards down the road for repeat visit:

6 - Gain credits towards products with each visit

First entry, complimentary something which has recognizable value to them. When they return, points towards something of equal or greater value.

And all for the time and energy involved in creating something which reveals (almost) nothing about them – an expression of themselves into the cyber reality of your site. At this point you don't need to know anything more about them. They're qualified, yes. They're warm, yes. Possibly hot.

And experience has shown that you now have a way to touch them beyond the first encounter and at will. Variations of this technique have increased visitor return ratios 3x, increased branding and led to ROI increases of 160-170% in 3-6 months' time.

7.B - Removing "Outs" from Conversion Pages (Improvements - TOS: 4m, SP: 60%, PCR: 96%, CR: 49%)

You'll notice some obvious differences between Figures 7.14 and 7.15 on page 208. Figure 7.15 has a large title, WhitePapers, and the column width on the white papers page is wider (which serves as a visual cue to the visitor to spend more time on the page, to go into a more cognitive, internal and receptive analysis mode).

The WhitePapers page is sometimes called a *conversion page*. It's a conversion page because we want the visitor to make a commitment here and the demonstration of that commitment is the download of information we're providing them for free...kind of sort of maybe.

7.14 - A traditional webpage

7.15 - A webpage with the "outs" removed.

The most important thing to notice about the conversion page is that it's lacking a menu. There's a very good reason for that.

Visitors who've clicked on this link have already made a commitment – for that matter, visitors who've clicked on any link beyond the home or landing page have made a capitalizable commitment to your site, they're waiting for their reward and it's up to you to deliver. The commitment they've made is that they're interested enough in what you offer that they're looking for information about it, so give it to them.

The catch is that most visitors will convert when:

1 - The risk is low
2 - It's something they probably want anyway
3 - And (here's the big one) there's no way to avoid the conversion

TakeAway #54 - Make sure visitors take what they've asked for by removing any "outs" from the conversion pages.

Remove the menu and most visitors will complete the form and submit the page. One Massachusetts company saw a 4:1 increase in conversions in a week with that suggestion alone. This concept is being used on an increasingly wide variety of properties. Figure 7.16 demonstrates this concept applied to a lead-swapping site.

OPP⊙TUNITY

① Hello ❭   ② I Offer ❭   ❸ I Need ❭   ④ My Pitch ❭ · ❺ Connect ❭

I Need

Industry*

Please select a minimum of 1

❮ Previous   Next ❯

7.16 - The only way out is through on this page. Visitors either closed the window or entered a "need". Visitors without a recognized "need" (exploring the site, for example), may make a need up in order to continue.

7.C - Removing Barriers to Entry and Qualification Upon Re-Entry
(Improvements - TOS: 1m10s, SP: 64%, PCR: 98%, CR: 48%)

So far we've given visitors a reason to internally brand your site via Anonymous-Expressive Identity (page 183), and removed any reasons for them not to convert by removing outs from conversion pages (page 207). Now we're going to make it easy for them to convert by removing one of the greatest pains, nuisances and aggravations to anyone involved with navigating or designing for the web. The industry calls this *permission marketing*.

7.17 - This type of page is a *buy-in* or conversion page, and is also a barrier to entry

What we're talking about is shown in Figure 7.17 on page 210, the Barrier to Entry screen, where a visitor is asked to give information before they get information.

The visitor won't cross such a barrier unless they really, *really, really!* want something and the site owner really, *really,*

really! doesn't want the aggravation of having to pay to have this coded, spend time separating valid entries from invalid entries, so on and so forth. And Figure 7.17 on page 210 is a very simple barrier to entry in the sense that we're not asking for lots of information. Some sites have barriers to entry that want to know your mother's maiden shoe size and your great aunt Floyd's sleep number.

Now, Gentle Readers, I will ask you a question (breaking down the fourth wall, as it were, but didn't I tell you there would be a test at some point?) How many of you get to a barrier to entry like this and think to yourself, "Oh, yeah! Hot Dang! I just can't wait to fill this out!"

And even though that is your thought, you as marketers and site owners want this information. More exactly, you want this information from people who want to give it to you because those people are not only Anonymous-Expressive, they're self-qualified.

But you yourself balk at filling something like this out. First law of social exchange (okay, probably not the first but who's going to know?): don't ask others to do something you yourself are loathe to do. You set them up for failure and yourself for disappointment. Not a good scenario when you're wanting people to have an experience so desirable they'll want to repeat it without prompting, tell others how wonderful it is and that they should take part as well, and when you want the social exchange to eventually involve something more.

Getting visitors to self-qualify is not a difficult thing to do and, as do so many things in this section of the book, it involves the concept of Fair-Exchange[u].

Figure 7.18 on page 213 shows the end of the white paper the visitor downloaded above once we removed the barrier to entry. It also shows a link (circled in red) embedded in the paper (something easy to do with today's web and related technologies).

The visitor can only get to this link if they've navigated the paper. They will only navigate the paper to the end if they've read

---

[u] – covered in *Reading Virtual Minds Volume III: Fair-Exchange and Social Networks.*

it or skimmed it. At this point they've either enjoyed it or not, found it useful or not.

The key to this discussion is the concept of "navigation". People don't read an electronic document in the same way they read or skim a physical document such as a magazine article, book or newspaper. To get to the end of an electronic document the reader has to navigate it while they're reading it. One of the primary reasons eBook devices didn't catch on in the USA as well as they could have had to do with migrating people from traditional reading to *navigational-reading*, something which is currently happening due to the ability of mobiles, tablets and similar devices to send and receive SMS, TXT, email messages and transfer content hither and yon. People have to be much more engaged in order to move through an electronic document than a physical document (assuming the paper is short enough to be read on-screen without taking up too much of the visitor's day, say 2-3 screens/pages at most).

Take a moment to recap what's happened so far in the mind of the visitor. They've qualified themselves in two ways: they downloaded the paper in the first place and they got to the end of it. Now there's this link (highlighted in red in Figure 7.18, page 213). If you've done your job and you provided value for their effort, they will follow that link to learn what else you can offer them and, of course, you now know you have them right where you want them because they came back to you for something only you can provide.

Good work and nicely done.

TakeAway #55 - Ask for value after you've given value and what you value shall be yours.

This method has been used on properties ranging from food sales to vacation packages and always delivered minimum double-digit ROI (as determined by development costs of collateral to final conversion dollar values).

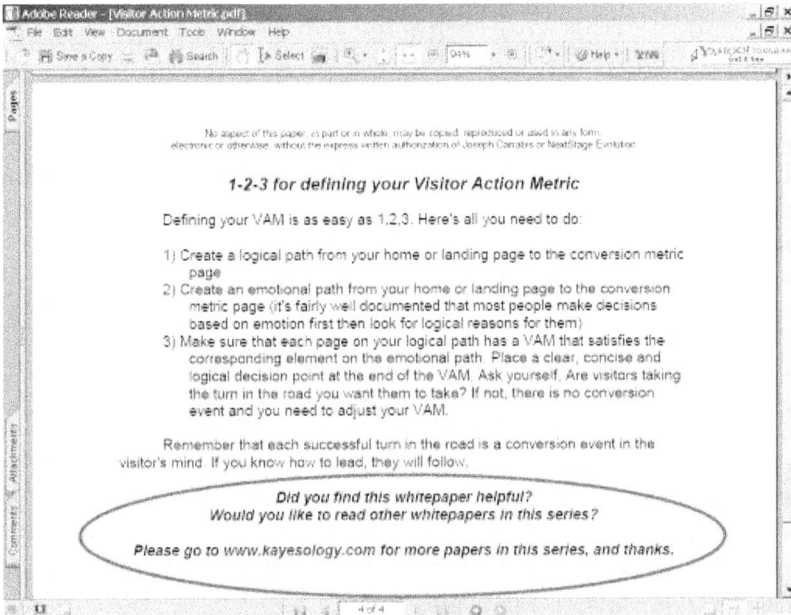

7.18 - Remove the Barrier to Entry and allow the visitor to self-qualify upon Re-Entry and you'll win most of the time.

7.D - Visitor-Designed Navigation (Improvements - TOS: 1m3s, SP: 100%, PCR: 73%, CR: 33%)

Figures 7.19-20 (pages 214-215 are identical save one simple change to the screen in Figure 7.20: we've added a new button at the top of the menu, "Next" (circled in red).

Now consider this: you come to a property with which you're unfamiliar. You see the logo, you see what's above the fold, you see the menu system.

At the top of the menu is a button which reads "Next". NextStage research has shown that Tourists click on "Next" 8:1 over Locals. When we interviewed Locals (repeat visitors) about their selection of "Next" it was usually because they wanted to know if anything had changed.

I'll admit this one requires some coding and time to implement, but the rewards are worth it. Start by having your web system keep track of most often requested pages[v]. For example, let's say your site is laid out with a home page, A, and 5 main pages – B, C, D, E and F – and that each main page has three sub pages – 1, 2 and 3 – as shown in the Figure 7.21 on page 215.

You go through your web logs and discover that the most popular pages on your site as a function of time on page and requests are, first to last, A, D1, E2, B2, F3 and C as demonstrated by the menutree charts shown in Figures 7.22-27 on pages 216-217. By definition, if these pages are the pages visitors always go to and spend the most time on, over time you've learned that these are the most popular pages on your site. Regardless of the order in which pages are actually called up, these are the pages which are the most interesting to people coming to your site to learn about you.

7.19 – Why Jonnie can't navigate

---

[v] – Note that the "most often requested" pages are not necessarily the "most popular" pages. A page can be repeatedly requested because it's confusing, amusing, eye-catching. An aspect of popularity is that people talk about whatever they deem popular, i.e., it has *viral capacity*. People may repeatedly access a page and never discuss their frustration with it. At least that's your hope.

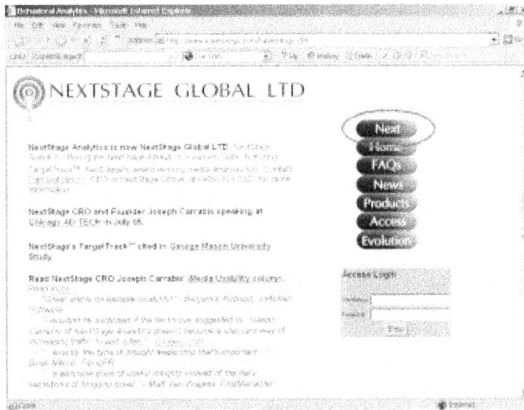

7.20 – Let all the Jonnies design the product path and individual Jonnies will navigate through the site every time

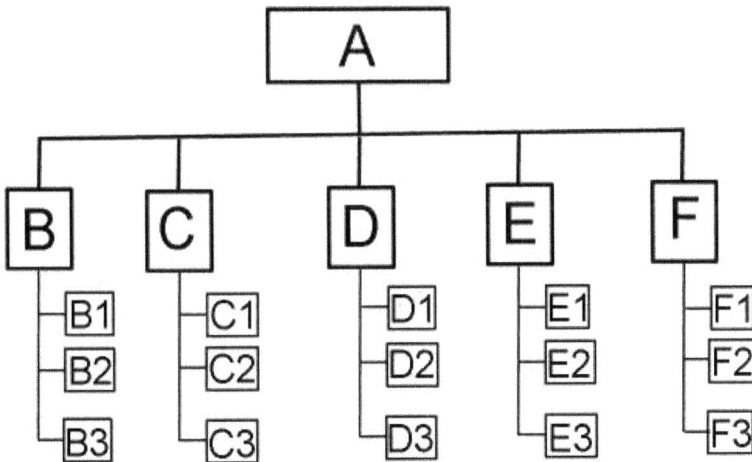

7.21 - MenuTree, MenuTree, Where oh Where is my MenuTree?

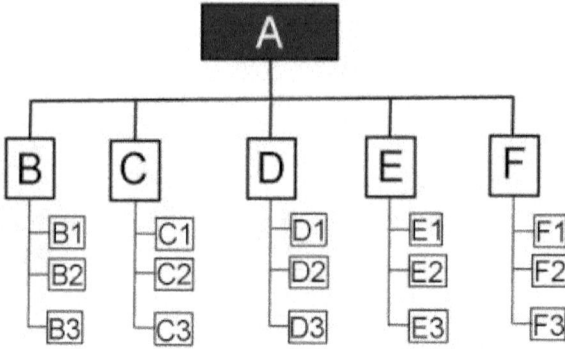

7.22 - A, your visitors' most favorite page

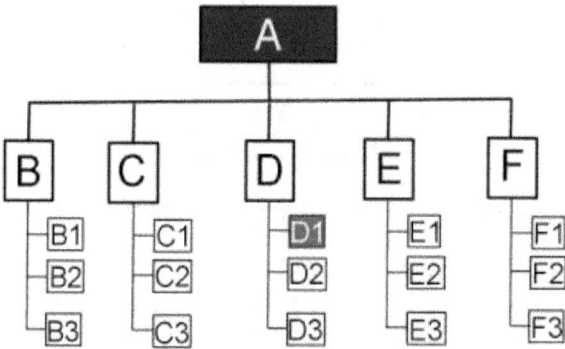

7.23 – D1, the second most favorite nightspot on
your website

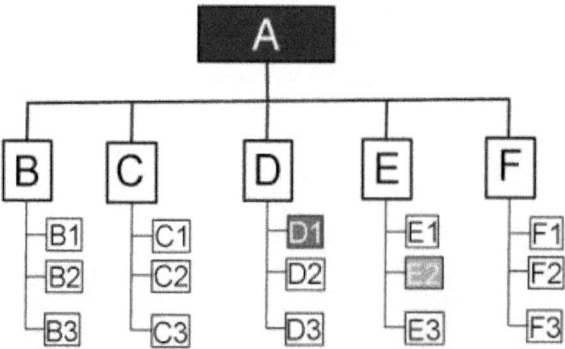

7.24 - E2, page #3 in your visitors' webpage hit
parade

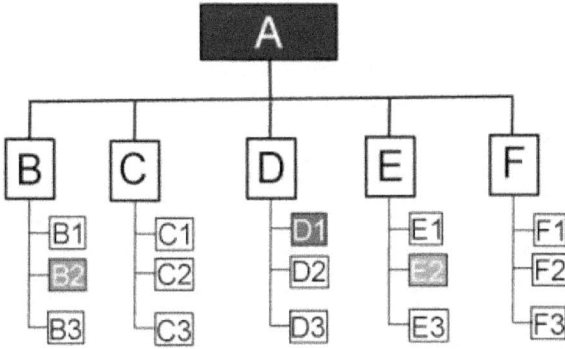

7.25 - B2, fourth most popular page on your site

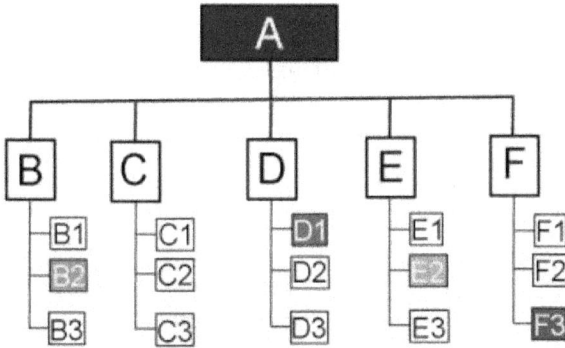

7.26 - F3, fifth most popular page on your site

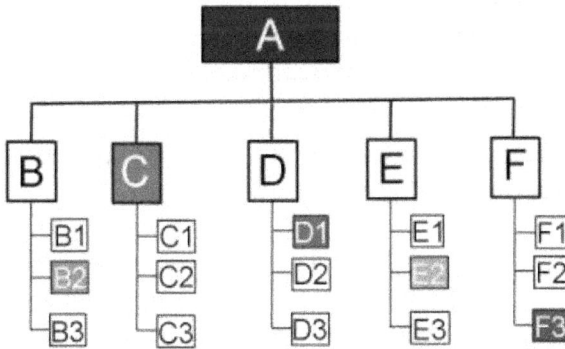

7.27 - C, the last of the most popular pages on your site

Then those are the most interesting pages to visitors on your site. All that is required at this point is to make it easy for them to get the information that history has demonstrated most people want or need, and the easiest way to do that is to show them what's "Next".

The difficulty can be that the way people are navigating your site isn't the way you intended or want them to navigate it, and sometimes the continuity between these pages is lacking because they weren't designed with this particular navigation scheme in mind.

Not a problem because people are easier to steer when they're already moving than when they're standing still. Once you know where people are going you can put your message in front of them and steer them to where you want them to be. However, until you're willing to let them go where they want to go you'll never be able to steer them at all.

NextStage has been advocating Visitor-Designed Navigation since the late 2000s on a variety of properties (mostly B2B and B2E). The recent move to a single, massive page that requires massive amounts of scrolling to navigate is a bow to "responsive" sites that are meant to be a one-size-fits-all property transcending everything from mobile to desktop platforms. It's not. There was a time when "best practices" were to put useless and low-value information below the fold because most people never navigated there, anyway. This is still true and things are further complicated by the increased load-times of massive single page properties; what people want to scroll to may not have loaded yet and frustration is the result. Save your money and put audience-desired information within easy reach.

TakeAway #56 - Always put what the audience values most within easy reach.

7.E - Reciprocal Evolution as Reciprocal Evaluation (Improvements - TOS: 2m21s, SP: 62%, PCR: 90%, CR: 26%)

Visitor-Designed Navigation is based on the concept of Reciprocal Evaluation which is based on the concept of Reciprocal Evolution.

"Of course it is, Joseph. We knew that," you say.

Well, it's true. Reciprocal Evaluation as Reciprocal Evolution is more often seen in ethology and behavioral studies. Borrowing from those fields and paraphrasing slightly, we get the following:

A tendency to create (or "evolve") a design that then causes the audience to create (or "evolve") a response.

If you've ever read or heard of a particular species of bird evolving to feed on specific seeds or in specific parts of trees and these same seeds or parts of trees evolving to be better available to these specific bird, you've heard or read of reciprocal evolution at work. The concept is perhaps more familiar to people as "finding their niche". Businesspeople will recognize this concept as finding the niche market and going for it, thus knowing the market change which caused the business to change which caused the...

It is amazing to me how many companies go through a complete rebranding and then wonder why they've lost regular customers. It is, to me, a demonstration that most companies don't appreciate the fact that their interface is more of their brand online than their brand is their brand.[75]

This leads us to the second aspect of reciprocal evolution as reciprocal evaluation; sites grow stale as a function of number of visitors/time period. Visitors will get bored with a site regardless of what is offered and move on to other sites unless there is a marked, compelling and specific reason to continue at a stale site.

The solution is to have an evolving website – not a completely redesigned website – which encourages the audience to also evolve, but in ways you wish them to evolve.

TakeAway #57 - It's easier to meet your audience's expectations if you tell your audience what to expect.

Doing so prevents a site from going stale because the site is constantly renewed with new information or presentations thereof.

Why do this?

Abrupt changes are shocks to the system and when someone is familiar with something they are comfortable with it. They may have contempt for whatever it is, and they'll also be comfortable with it (hence the expression "He was comfortable in his contempt").

You want to maximize the value of that comfort. Destroy the comfort and you need to build trust and acceptance all over again. The goal is to make many subtle changes over time. One way to think of this is to imagine someone you see every day losing weight. Most people don't notice their friend's weight loss until the friend gets some new clothes. You know it's your friend but now you take some time to admire the new view.

This "new view" also works with digital properties regardless of platform. Many subtle changes over time allow the comfort and trust to remain while new features, functionality and pages are added. An example of abrupt changes being shocks to the system is demonstrated in Figures 7.28-29 on page 221.

Figure 7.28 is our old friend, the NextStage Global website home page. Figure 7.29 is one of the contenders for the redesign.

And even though you're reading this in a book or perhaps as in eBook or on-screen in a PDF file or as a printout, I can tell without knowing anything else about you that each and every one of you spent time looking for features you were familiar with, couldn't find them in an obvious way, had a moment of confusion and frustration (nothing major, yet enough to register as fatigue and disappointment neurophysiologically), then gave up looking for your old friends and started out establishing relationships anew.

Sigh. Visitors who are subjected to radical rebrandings and interface redesign put in so much work for so little reward. Not a good thing when you want visitors to trust, accept and recognize you.

Yet if you look at the two home pages, you'll see that there's not a lot different form-wise. The menu is still on the right of the page, the logo is still at the top of the page and information text is still the first thing most people consciously see. What's new is the boxed "now just looky here" text, the image, and a site search capability.

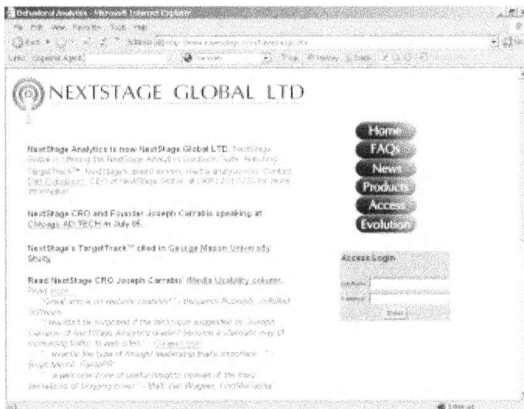

7.28 - Our old friend, the NextStage Global
homepage as of 03 Oct 2005

7.29 – A candidate for the next NextStage
Global Interface

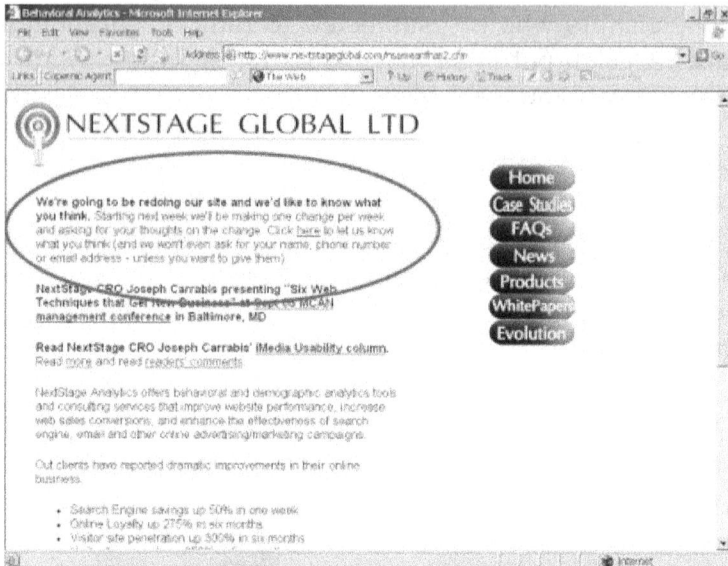

7.30 – Ask visitors to let you know what they think and chances
are they will. Remember to be careful what you wish for.

Let's say you come to the old site once a week. One week, you come to the site and see a message highlighted at the top left of the home page (Figure 7.30, page 222), "We're going to be redoing our site and we'd like to know what you think", followed by some explanatory material as to what's going to be changed and the reason for those changes.

Again, assuming your material is gravitating enough for visitors to show any level of interest, you've now given them a reason to become vested in your site because they'll have input into what it will become. Having input into a site's design is a digital visitor's dream. Much like the NextStageologist who was able to help create the pet company website she wanted by being vocal, here you're giving visitors a chance to help craft a site which will be one they want to navigate (and again, they'll be doing so Anonymous-Expressively). Without the visitor's knowledge you've established rapport and a line of communication you might not have had before.

Each week announce the one change which will appear in next week's site, and invite an anonymous response - Let us know what you think.

> "We're going to shrink our logo. Let us know what you think!"
> "We're going to redesign our menu system, same options, just prettier. Let us know what you think!"
> "We're going to add this big, honking graphic. Totally worthless, really, just makes us look more professional. Let us know what you think!"

The next thing you know casual visitors become regular visitors because there's a sense of community growing about your site. Here's a company whose visitors' thoughts are valued! Your regular visitors are now sending new visitors to your site because, heck, they had input into your site design. They're telling their friends, "Come see what I did," and you know word-of-mouth marketing is the best kind of marketing there is, correct?

TakeAway #58 - Brand visitors/users/audience and gain viral reach by inviting visitors/users/audience to become proactive in your site's redesign.

You'll be shocked to know there's an equation which determines how often material needs to be changed in order to keep an individual's attention and inquisitiveness to learn if that material has changed since it was last seen. The equation is called a *Time-Phase Learning Loop*. Time-Phase Learning Loops are based on Adaptation Method (page 91) and are used to determine the length of time it takes people to become desensitized to information (such as a digital property). The equation itself applies to many communication channels and resolves to a simple set of rules when it comes to digital design.

For most sites (you and the client have to be the judge), when the average Visitor-Time/page either equals or is less than 1/3 of the original values, it's time for a new design. Written down as steps, this becomes:

1) Put up a site
2) Pick a time interval (day, week, month)
3) Multiply the number of visitors during that time interval by the average time on a page
4) Label the answer V_0
5) Each equal time interval, do the same arithmetic. Label each new value V_1, V_2, ..., V_n
6) When $V_n = 1/3 * V_0$ it's time for a new design

TakeAway #59 - Keep visitor/user/audience interest maximized on your digital property by introducing proactivity before they tire of your property.

7.F - Improving Visual Search Results (Improvements - TOS: 10m41s, SP: 50%, PCR: 85%, CR: 44%)

By now you've seen the NextStage Global home page so much you're completely branded to it (sneaky me sneaky me! Pity it no longer exists!). Most people who view our sites tell us that the sites are simple and not professional (and if you've read *Reading Virtual Minds Volume I: Science and History*[w] of this book you know what the statement being made really is).

By the way, we agree. The NextStage Global, NextStage Evolution and other obvious NextStage sites tend to be simple in both design and function. There are reasons to make things simple (not necessarily as simple as NextStage does, and simp*ler*

---

[w] – GO BUY A COPY! http://nlb.pub/RVMV14th

never-the-less). Having read through this chapter, you probably appreciate that NextStage's sites (as of this writing) are designed for Locals, not Tourists, and are designed to attract and keep a very specific audience which isn't necessarily a business audience.

There is, however, another reason our properties are so simple and it's a reason you may want to apply to your own design work:

> Our society relies on accurate performance in visual screening tasks...if observers do not find what they are looking for fairly frequently, they often fail to notice it when it does appear.[301,603]

Functional designs make things obvious because when something isn't obvious, it is lost. If visitors can't find it quickly, they'll stop looking. When they stop looking you've lost their attention, their interest and the sale. Use simplistic designs because it encourages visitors' eyes to fall exactly where you want them to and visitors don't have to hunt for what they're looking for. Visitors/Users/Audiences who can easily find what they're looking for remain engaged and active in what you're presenting them instead of thinking about what they can't find but know should be there hence seeking for it on a competitor's site.

TakeAway #60 - Simpler designs make task execution simpler and simple task execution makes interested audience members more interested because simple task execution equals rapid, repeated success on interfaces, properties,

...

7.G - Always Tell a Story
(Improvements - TOS: 3m50s, SP: 44%, PCR: 92%, CR: 37%)

This last item is actually the most important in this chapter because, as readers of *Reading Virtual Minds Volume I: Science and History*[x] can tell you, humans seek out and create communities. One of the best ways to create a functional community is by telling stories. The stories you tell will be based on what your goals are for the material you're developing, and tell a story you must if you want the people interacting with your material to turn the page (electronic or otherwise).[y]

A good use of storytelling is keeping visitors engaged throughout a *product path*. A product path is the taxonomic or logical steps involved in getting someone from low-interest to conversion. Just as storytellers have known since we gathered around campfires to keep the booguns at bay, you need to set seeds in the individual's mind "here" that will be harvested by the individuals "there", you need to set and keep expectations, to prime them[77,123,126,127,181,227,315,350,355,406,554,610] and you need to give them a reason to return to hear the next story you want to tell. Good salespeople will tell you that this is the case. Psycho-, socio- and neural-linguists will tell you this is the art of conversation, establishing and building rapport at the individual's level – not your own – and engaging individuals where they want to be engaged, not where you want to engage them.

Generally you want to touch people with your brand at least three times[178] in order for them to remember it. This goes beyond getting them to navigate through three pages of your site or pick

---

[x] – And you bought a copy by now, correct? If for no other reason than to shut me up? http://nlb.pub/RVMV14th

[y] – Please don't confuse this with the "Storytelling" craze of the early to mid-2010s. I'm using "story" in the ethnographic, anthropologic, cultural mythology sense and using the concept's cultural power for marketing purposes. That and I've won awards, been nominated for awards, et cetera, for my fiction writing (you can find some at http://nlb.pub/jdcamazon), taught fiction writing, taught non-fiction writing, been a journalist, contributing editor, editor-in-chief, blah blah blah, so I know there's a difference and explain it in some of our trainings. See our schedule (http://nlb.pub/G) for more information.

up your brochure three times. You need to direct their attention to a branding event and keep them focused on that branding event long enough so that those three touches happen without the visitors' knowing it. Branding events occur when the prospect wants to get to know you. Inviting the prospect to take part in a branding event is where art meets science and determining branding events goes well beyond the realm of behavioral analytics. You're now in the world of behavioral mechanics and persuasive analytics.

One of the easiest ways to do simple behavioral mechanics and persuasive analytics on a digital property is to slow the visitor down to the point where they willingly stop navigating to see what's going on. It's like people driving along, paying attention to the road and traffic. When they stop at a light, a stop sign or a traffic jam, they start looking around to see what's going on beyond the immediate flow of traffic. When people stop navigating through a digital property it's because something else has their attention. You want that something else to be what's on the page.

Slowing a website visitor down long enough to brand them is often and best achieved via a simple animation/video which tells people a story. Here are the rules that apply:

1 - Initial visitors need to be slowed down just enough to pay attention to the story without realizing they're doing so.

2 - The story must be short enough so that it doesn't interfere with the visitors' continued navigation through the site.

3 - The purpose of the story is to get the visitor branded.

4 - The way to brand visitors is by getting them to associate something you (the site owner) do or offer with who and what you are.

5 - Visitors should continue to brand themselves without realizing they're doing so once the story is finished and they've continued to navigate the site.

6 - The story should leave the visitor with an implied question which the website can answer.

The animated/video story you tell can't stop navigation completely because you want them to continue navigating once the story's finished. Later on they'll demonstrate enough interest to warrant a longer, navigation-stopping story by downloading a white paper or some such, and they'll have expressed sufficient interest for you to exchange some of their time for one of your longer stories.

You can direct an individual's attention where you want it via a moving object. Only people with a great deal of training can focus their attention towards stillness when there's movement in their field of view because of the way the human brain is wired. Movement directs attention (as any stage magician can tell you) but in the case of telling a story on a website the movement must deliver on the promise paid for by the visitor's directed attention. A site can have an extremely beautiful animation loop which draws and keeps the visitor's attention, but if the entire purpose of the animated loop is to add some animation to the site, the visitor will lose interest, not pay attention to other animations being offered, and eventually become debranded because the promise wasn't kept.

Let the animation/video tell a story and make sure the story is being told in visual association with your brand. How is this done?

1 – The stories being told are visually attached to the logo and company name, so each new element in the animation keeps the visitor's attention focused on the brand.
2 – The stories convey what the company does without making the visitor work to understand the outcome.
3 – Neither story interferes with the visitors' continued navigation through the site.
4 – The last element of each story becomes part of the logo banner on all pages as the visitor navigates the

site. Making the last element of the story part of the logo on all other pages is done because visitors who go through the story once will check it again and again to make sure the story hasn't changed. The way they will do this is by briefly focusing their attention back on the brand, thus rebranding themselves on each page they navigate.

5 – The stories create an association in the visitors' mind between what the company does and the brand.

6 – The stories leave an implied question in the visitor's mind that further navigation can answer.

As stated previously, the best use of animated graphics or video on a site is to brand and attract visitors into exploring further. The best way to do all of these things is to tell the visitors a little story. This is behavioral mechanics and persuasive analytics done for a nickel or a dime rather than behavioral analytics done for dollars or a ten-spot.

Storytelling on a website should be like storytelling throughout history; make people comfortable – even if you make them comfortable with their discomfortableness (such as when people gleefully sit through a terrifying movie) – and they'll return because with you they can find something that is (usually) missing from every other aspect of their lives, psycho-logic and psycho-emotive peace and tranquility.

TakeAway #61 - Provide a branded story that satisfies and slightly exceeds the visitor's/user's/audience's expectation and you have them right where you want them: branded, returning and socially sharing your work with others.

7.G.i – Branded Stories and Storytelling

This section moves slightly from digital interface to personal interface, i.e., a spokesperson or demonstrator having to convince an audience that the brand being promoted should be the audience's chosen brand, chosen to the point where Anonymous-Expressive identity occurs and the audience self-brands.

This involves *storytelling* and I'm using the term in the sense mentioned in the previous footnote: ethnographic, anthropologic, cultural mythology, etc. Not as the term is used in marketing where (you're shocked, I know) classes are now offered on storytelling your brand.

Storytelling in the cultural anthropology sense goes back to our ancestors sitting around fires, talking about what was just beyond the edge of the fire's light. Such stories were and are mythic, educational and most of all entertaining. Without that last part any myths, fables, folklore, ancient wisdom, etc., wouldn't last.

So storytelling. The first objective any story is to get and keep the audience's attention until the story's end. It doesn't matter if the story is about Hercules, The Monkey King, Chi Lin, GrandMother Spider, SnowWalker, your brother baking his first pie or your sister beveling her first brick wall, whatever, if that story's not entertaining to your audience they won't pay attention and you're talking to air. Any time you're in a webinar and you start checking emails, browsing the web, typing a memo, editing a spreadsheet, reading a document, tra-la, your host has lost your attention. You're cruising, waiting for that one word or phrase or slide that'll catch your attention and cause you to focus on the presentation or training again.[z]

Once a storyteller has the audience's attention (and the more attention the better) the more you have them where you want them. It doesn't matter if you're rallying the troops, asking for votes, selling a car or talking to your children, nor does it matter cultural or language bias because all stories have a beginning, a

---

[z] – Amusingly, people never (yet) lose focus in a NextStage webinar or presentation. See **Comments from Live and Web Training Participants**, page 350.

middle and an end, all stories involve a protagonist, some goals, some obstacles, a plot, at least one theme, a setting and so on.

The point where most storytellers – especially brand storytellers – fail is not recognizing that the only way to change an audience's behavior (the goal of a branded story is to get the audience to stay loyal to a product, become disloyal to a competitive product, buy more product, evangelize the brand, ...) is to frame the story in the familiar. Most people on the planet were raised listening to stories, reading stories, watching stories, taking part in stories and that storyizing began at a very early age. Parents tell stories of hope and glory to their newborns in their arms and in their cribs. Nobody looks down upon their newborn child and gently whispers, "Whose going to grow up to be a nobody, a total incompetent, a burden to society, a derelict, a homeless vagabond who'll die in a gutter somewhere..."

My god I hope no one does! We whisper mythic stories of how wonderful they'll be, how beautiful or handsome they'll be, how successful they'll be. Such stories, both good and bad, stay with us forever.

Brand storytellers who wish to succeed must frame their brand stories in what the audience already knows and then add a bit more. That bit more is branding and brand-related action occurs. A story that has nothing new gets placed in the audience's "been there, done that" bucket and is quickly forgotten. A story that doesn't start in the audience's known environment and understandings is equally ignored and forgotten.

But a story that starts where they are and then moves them, provides emotional involvement along with entertainment and offers them change (based on brand-related actions, of course)? That's gold. Branded storytelling needs to take the audience from where they are and guide them through commitment to the brand. In the course of doing this the storyteller needs to convince them that they can change who they are, what they do, what they use, how they vote, what they believe, etc., is relevant and matters, first to the audience themselves, then to those around them.

TakeAway #62 - Branded stories must place the audience in the center of the storyteller's tale then move them to where the brand wants them to be.

TakeAway #63 - Branded stories must start with what the audience already knows – even if that prior knowledge is contrary to the brand's desires – then introduce new information that grows logically and emotionally out of that prior knowledge to create new, branded knowledge and behavior.

Afterword

This book has discussed the interplay of experience and expectation and how communication is shaped by it. Everything we've covered here – from Audience Knowledgeable Design to Always Tell a Story, from TakeAway 1 to TakeAway 63 (TakeAways 64-69 are covered in *Appendix A – Calculating Social Probabilities or "NeuroMathematics Proves Your Intuition Was Right All Along"*) – has been about it. Each item discussed serves two purposes.

First and foremost, it changes visitor's expectation of their interaction with your material. Imagine a site designed to make use of the visitor's knowledge base rather than to showcase development talent or overtly demonstrate product or service, yet which makes use of the visitor's knowledge base in order to demonstrate the product or service. That's real development talent. Imagine a site that gives information freely and asks for a return only if the visitor is satisfied by the encounter (shades of "I Trust You" leading to "You Can Trust Me"!).

Secondly, traditional web and media based expectation is channeled elsewhere and anon by the techniques we've covered here. From that rechanneling of expectation we've managed to alter visitors' experience of the material they're interacting with. Nothing of value is asked for yet something of value is given – the proverbial casting of bread upon the waters to have it return seven-fold. Or asking for someone's help (where Audience Knowledgeable Design and Reciprocal Evolution as Reciprocal Evaluation meet) and having them return to request your help – in the form of business – a little later on.

We've covered a lot and given examples of ways to change expectation in order to optimize experience. Hope you enjoyed and more so, hope your work benefits from what is covered here.

Now go forth and conquer!

Appendices

Appendix A – Calculating Social Probabilities or "NeuroMathematics Proves Your Intuition Was Right All Along"[a]

This appendix digs a little deeper into the discussion presented in *Chapter 1 – Of Coin Tosses and Card Tricks* (page 71). There's some math, not much, and it's more important you get the TakeAways than get the mathematics.

Developers, designers, information and education architects and anybody involved in communication knows that the easiest interface to design is for something intended users have no experience with. The hardest interface to design is for something intended users have lots of prior experience with.

> **TakeAway #64 - Design with your audience's experience and prior knowledge as guides and your designs will always be accepted by your audience.**

You really don't need to read any further if you're comfortable with that.

A.1 – Probability Solids

Traditional probability teaches that an ideal world coin toss should be 50/50. Therefore if I have two ideal world coins and ideal world toss each, one right after the other, then the probability of getting a Tails-Tails (TT) combination is ($\frac{1}{2}$ x $\frac{1}{2}$) or $\frac{1}{4}$. Extend this and we recognize that the ideal world probability of any combination ((TT), (TH), (HT), (HH)) is $\frac{1}{4}$.

Let's introduce a little notation for simplicity's sake.

I have two coins, C_1 and C_2.

The ideal world probability, I, of any two coin toss is

---

[a] – Social probabilities were demonstrated in a audience-participation exercise given during NextStage's 2008 SNCR TS Eliot, Ezekiel, Beehives and Mighty Mouse presentation.147

$$I(C_1) \times I(C_2) = \tfrac{1}{2} \times \tfrac{1}{2} = \tfrac{1}{4}$$

But we know I can "stack the deck" in my favor therefore the *real* world probability, R, of my getting TT is determined by a bunch of other factors, the least of which is whether or not the coins are tossed in an ideal world or not. So our *real* world notation for some single coin, C, looks like this

$$R(C) = \text{a whole bunch of other factors}(C)$$

Let's call all those deck-stacking factors "g" and go back to two coins. Now the probability of my getting TT on any toss looks something like

$$R = g(C_1) \times g(C_2)$$

But wait a second.

I'm able to adjust the "whole bunch of other factors" on the second toss based on my results from the first toss, so those *g*s are different. That first *g* in the equation above? That's based on all my practicing and training and experience tossing a coin but (*but!*) it's the first toss in this set of tosses and because it is the first toss in this set it sets the stage (so to write) for all the tosses that come after it. A mathematical notation for that very first *g* would be $g_0{}^b$. That second *g* is influenced by what happened with g_0 so it's different from g_0. Being mathematical again we call that second *g* g_1. That equation above should really look something like

$$R = g_0(C_1) \times g_1(C_2)$$

And if we really want to be sticklers, the whole bunch of factors that are g_1 may not even be the same whole bunch of

---

[b] – Mathematicians like to start at 0 when counting things like this. That's why it's g_0 instead of g_1.

factors that were g_0 because I modified g_1 based on the results of $g_0{}^c$. All the *gs* share factors but each factor's value changes based on the values in the previous *gs*, therefore the above equation probably (ha!) looks something like

$$R = g_0(C_1) \times [g_1 \times g_0](C_2)$$

That "×" between g_1 and g_0 in the above translates to "is influenced by" as in g_1 "is influenced by" g_0. It's a kind of multiplication on steroids[d]. And if there's a third toss?

$$R = g_0(C_1) \times [g_1 \times g_0](C_2) \times [g_2 \times [g_1 \times g_0]](C_3)$$

And as there's more and more tosses those *gs* build up right quickly into something that looks like.

$$g_0 [X_0{}^n g_i]$$

It doesn't matter if you toss different but identical (whatever "identical" means at this point) coins or the same coin, you get something like

$$R = g_0 [X_1{}^n g_i](C_i)$$

The only item close to being random (i.e., ideal world probability) is the g_0 factor because all other "g"s are influenced by it, and even then and as noted above, g_0 is itself influenced by

---

[c] – Readers with a background in systems analysis may recognize a state equation taking shape. Most state equations are a function of the current system state and the previous moment's inputs. Here the previous moment's inputs include the previous moment's system state and the system state is a function of the state equation itself. This is 2nd Order Cybernetics applied as referenced in *Reading Virtual Minds Volume I: Science and History*.87
[d] – Readers of *Reading Virtual Minds Volume 1: Science and History* may remember "ET figures things via *engines* and *channels*. An engine is a mathematical equation that adapts itself to what is being calculated, as if the equation first determines which types of variables its been given then decides which parts of itself need to be used in order to perform the calculation. A channel is like a variable in an equation, except that a channel knows when it needs other variables in order for the equation to calculate correctly." What I write here are rudimentary examples of engines and channels.

all my experience, muscle memory, training, mood, situational ethics, ...[e] So *g* itself looks like

$$G = \alpha f(\text{experience}) + \beta f(\text{muscle memory}) + \gamma f(\text{training}) + \eta f(\text{mood}) + \mu f(\text{situational ethics}) + \upsilon f(...)$$

Each of those "$f()$" above are highly subjective and many of them can be likened to sums of several equally subjective factors. "Situational ethics", for example, is itself a complex and rich set of equally rich and complex factors. Further, each "$f()$" is preceded by its own *relevancy* coefficient and none of those are necessarily fixed because some factors may be ignored from one calculation to the next, hence their individual relevancy tends to zero.[f]

Talk about a dialectic leading to an identity!

Okay, let's catch our breaths and go back to the beginning for a moment or two.

Let's say (for the sake of argument), that the probability of Tails-Tails really is ¼. That's at the very center, the very core, of what we're doing.

But we're not actually interested in what the probability of Tails-Tails really is, we're much more interested in whether or not I can repeatedly toss Tails, and we know that's influenced more by g than by ideal world probabilities, and we know that "g" is based on a whole bunch of other factors.

---

[e] – Readers familiar with these concepts may recognize that social probabilities are greatly influenced by the individual's situational awarenss.71,153,321,523 QBists love this.

[f] – Hopefully readers are beginning to understand that ET's experiential engine couldn't function semantically and has to function semiotically. Semantics would allow for a sender and a receiver to agree on the detonation of a symbol (both agree that the symbol occurred in some transmitting medium) but not necessarily on the connotation of that symbol (both agree on the meaning of the symbol). Experience is what allows both sender and receiver to agree on the connotation of a symbol, the "what I'm pointing at when I say it" and from there semantics grows. The exercise here demonstrates that communication is a multivariable process that requires both sender and receiver to first agree on the variables. This is the semioticist's "The first communication must be instructions on how to build a receiver".

Never the less, the core probability of Tails-Tails is ¼ and we're 100% sure that's the core probability. Let's chart just that (Figure AA.1, page 239).

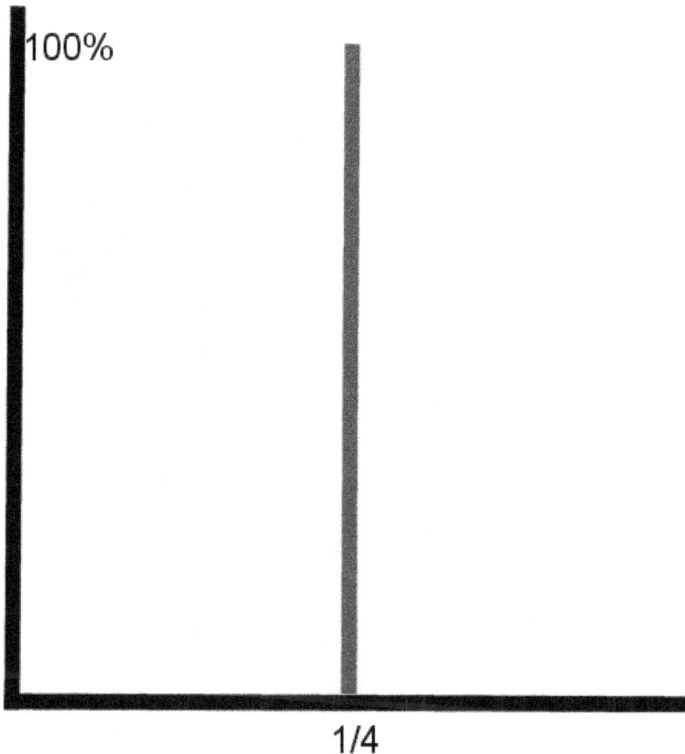

100%

1/4

A.1 - The surety that a Tails-Tails toss will be 1/4 is 100%

That's pretty clean and neat, don't you think? Can't argue much with that.

But what about those *g*s. Each g adds a layer of probabilities to the core, let's say each g's "whole bunch of factors" is countable, meaning we can count (for example) 100 factors that contribute to g. Those are the ones we know of.

So that clean and neat 100% surety that a Tails-Tails toss will be 1/4 neuromathematically looks like Figure AA.2 on page 240.

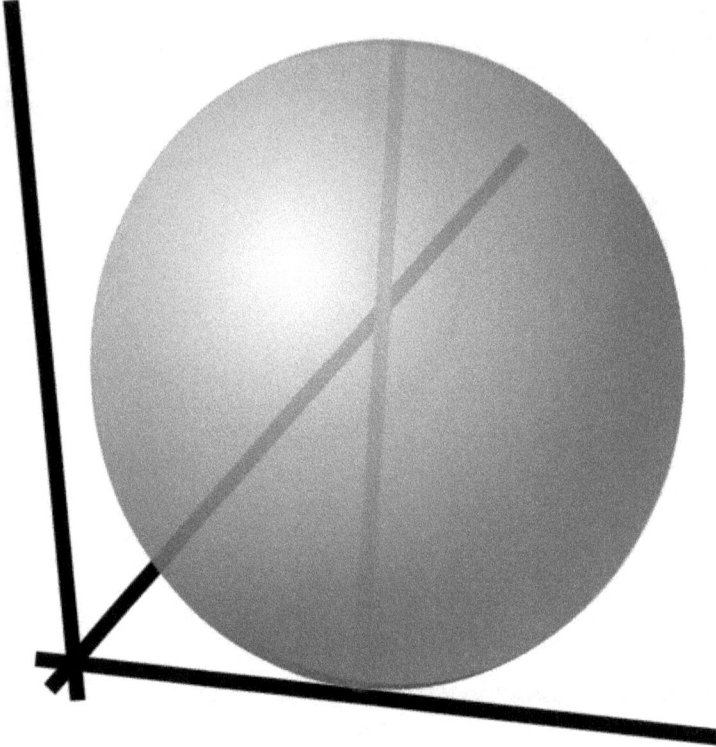

A.2 - The Tails-Tails toss engulfed in a cloud of g

And we can control in our favor each of those 100 factors to its own degree of probability, meaning we can either fix each factor or randomize at will and to what degree at will, meaning we can focus the cloud so that we have something like Figure A.3 on page 241.

So now that core probability we can be absolutely sure of is surrounded by a layer we can equally be absolutely sure of and that layer we can be equally sure can be described as:

"I've just watched Joseph flip a coin ten times and get tails ten times. I think he can flip it and get what he wants each and every time. I'm not so sure about that ¼ anymore."
"Well, then how sure are you?"
"Oh, 30%".[9]

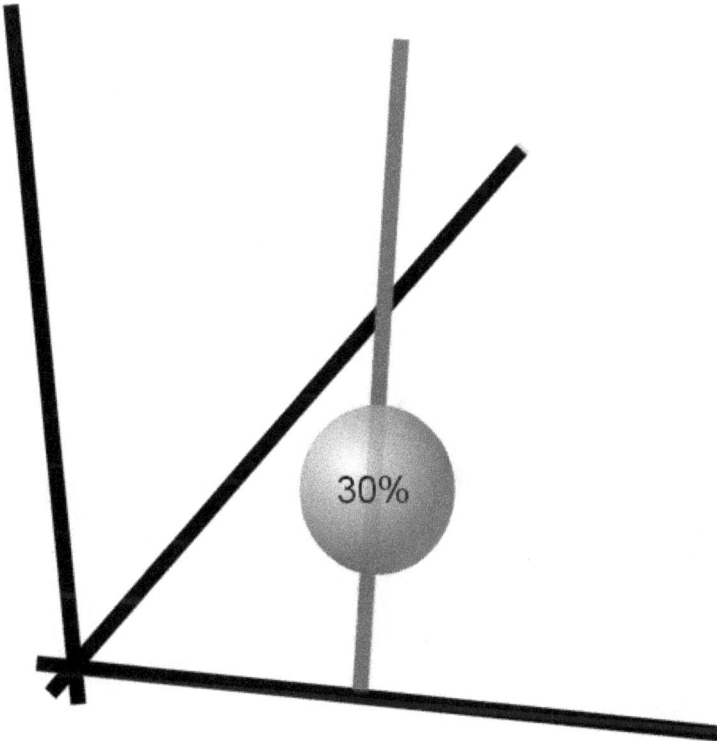

A.3 - The g cloud focuses on just a part of the Tails-Tails toss

And that cloud layer is surrounded by other cloud layers, like layers on an onion, as time moves on. The more we fix all the factors that go into each cloud layer, the more solid that cloud

---

[9] – Again, "How much of p is required for q to exist?" and Logical Calculus rules.

becomes. We can also fix some factors while letting others randomize as they wish.

Doing so allows us to see along some line of interest originating outside the clouds to the original core and based on where that line intersects the original core we can say with great certainty "We're very close to 100% surety" or "We're very near 0% surety" or "We're just about 50% surety" or...

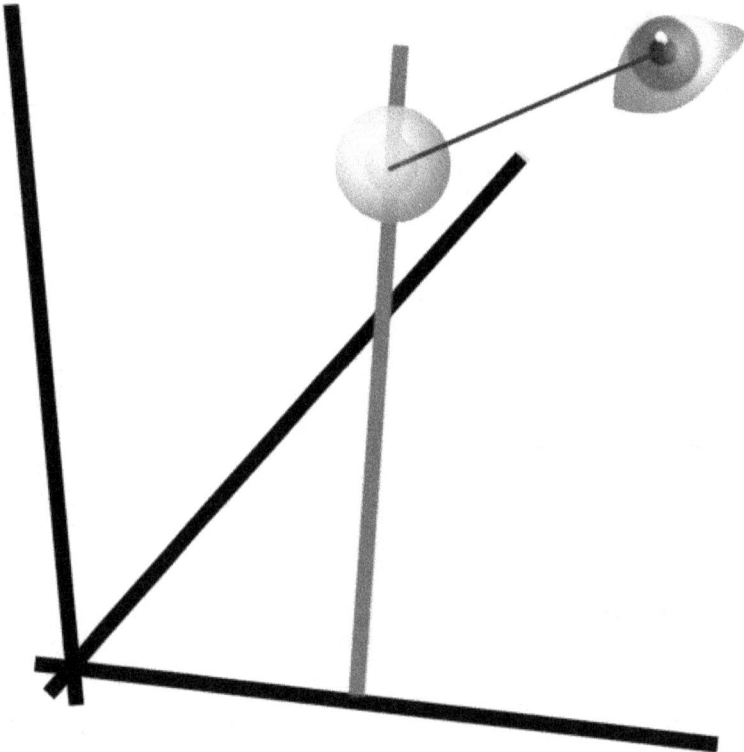

A.4 - We can control each g cloud layer to allow ourselves to "see" how much surety really exists

So if we know there's 100% probability of getting ¼ at the ideal world result of a Tails-Tails toss and we control what factors are in play in each g cloud layer, we know how sure we are of the probability really being 100%.

Or 60%.

Or 12%.

The end result of this exercise is actually quite simple and is a solid probability. Arrange the factors to be fixed or not, and determine which factors will be fixed and which won't, and you know with great surety whether you'll get 0, ¼, ½, ¾ or 1.

The probability cloud solidifies into a fixed, or solid, representation along certain factors or "axes", each axis corresponding to one of the g factors (and as I write this NextStage counts about 100 of them).

And if you can predict with 100% accuracy whether you'll get 0, ¼, ½, ¾ or 1, you can predict anything.

Social probabilities are constantly evolving. Determine the connection between some individual and some event and neuromathematics helps determine what people want or believe will happen (their expectation) and the influence (their experience) of that on their actions.

For example, get one hundred people sitting in a room hoping/wishing/praying that some other person survives cancer. I won't get into whether or not so many people wanting something to happen actually affects the outcome of that thing happening, and what is completely predictable is how such desire affects those with that desire. You can predict the future although you may not be able to change it. Better than that, however, is the ability to predict how a given future will affect the people who dwell there, and that's neuromathematics.

For those who wish to explore on their own,

TakeAway #65 - Consciousness tends to be discrete, hence enumerative.

TakeAway #66 - Non-consciousness tends to be continuous, hence measurable.

TakeAway #67 - You can count how many times someone does something but where they are on

the decision curve is measurable at any given point.

TakeAway #68 - Non-conscious activity is integrative, conscious activity is differentiative.

TakeAway #69 - At any point in time, someone's momentary identity is a solution to their behavior at that moment in time. Their behavior is a function of their identity at that time, t.

First law of PsychoLingualStatistics - Exact statements are not necessarily accurate. The first determination must be how accurate the information is that comprises the exact statement.

Second Law of PsychoLingualStatistics - The accuracy of any statement is determined by isolating the significant words (digits) and recognizing the how much variance in included in each one (how red is red?).

The significance of a word is determined grammatically. In a simple subject-verb-object statement ("I am male") the significant word is "male" because we need to determine what the speaker means by "male". In "I am" we need to determine what the speaker means by identity (I) and existence (am).

Appendix B – Coin Toss Outcomes

Toss	Series 1	Series 2	Series 3	Series 4	Series 5
1	H	H	H	H	H
2	H	H	T	H	H
3	H	H	H	H	H
4	T	H	H	H	H
5	T	H	T	H	T
6	H	H	T	H	T
7	H	H	T	H	H
8	H	H	T	H	H
9	H	H	T	H	H
10	H	H	T	H	T
11	H	H	T	H	T
12	H	H	T	H	T
13	H	H	T	H	T
14	H	H	T	H	H
15	H	H	T	H	T
16	H	H	T	T	H
17	H	H	T	T	T
18	H	H	T	T	H
19	H	H	T	T	H
20	H	H	T	T	H
21	H	H	T	T	T
22	H	H	T	T	T
23	H	H	T	T	T
24	H	H	T	T	T
25	T	T	T	T	T
26	H	H	T	T	T
27	T	T	T	T	T
28	H	T	T	T	T
29	T	T	T	T	T
30	T	T	T	T	T
31	H	T	T	T	T

32	H	T	T	T	T
33	H	T	T	T	T
34	H	T	T	T	T
35	H	T	T	T	T
36	H	T	T	T	T
37	H	T	T	T	T
38	H	T	T	T	T
39	H	T	T	T	T
40	T	T	T	T	T
41	T	T	T	T	T
42	T	T	T	T	T
43	T	T	T	T	T
44	T	T	T	T	T
45	T	T	T	T	T
46	T	T	T	T	T
47	T	T	T	T	T
48	T	T	T	T	H
49	T	T	T	T	H
50	T	T	T	T	H
51	T	T	T	T	H
52	T	T	T	T	H
53	T	T	T	T	H
54	T	T	T	T	H
55	T	T	T	T	H
56	T	T	T	T	T
57	T	T	T	T	T
58	T	T	T	T	T
59	T	T	T	T	T
60	T	T	T	T	T
61	T	T	T	T	T
62	T	T	T	T	T
63	T	T	T	T	T
64	T	T	T	T	T
65	T	T	T	T	T
66	T	T	T	T	T
67	T	T	T	T	T

68	T	T	T	T	T
69	T	T	T	T	T
70	T	T	T	T	T
71	T	T	T	T	T
72	T	T	T	T	T
73	T	T	T	T	T
74	T	T	T	T	T
75	T	T	T	T	T
76	T	T	T	T	T
77	T	T	T	T	T
78	T	T	T	T	T
79	T	T	T	T	T
80	T	T	T	T	T
81	T	T	T	T	T
82	T	T	T	T	T
83	T	T	T	T	T
84	T	T	T	T	T
85	T	T	T	T	T
86	T	T	T	T	T
87	T	T	T	T	T
88	T	T	T	T	T
89	T	T	T	T	T
90	T	T	T	T	T
91	T	T	T	T	T
92	T	T	T	T	T
93	T	T	T	T	T
94	T	T	T	T	T
95	T	T	T	T	T
96	T	T	T	T	T
97	T	T	T	T	T
98	T	T	T	H	T
99	T	T	T	H	T
100	T	T	T	H	T

Appendix C – eCommerce Wine Shop Example

What follows was originally from a demonstration we did in Feb 2000, before NextStage was officially NextStage. Nothing has changed from the original other than correcting a few typos, fixing some grammar, some formatting and using "Evolution Technology" or "ET" in place of what we originally thought to call it.

Some notes: the following uses some NextStage specific terms (at least I haven't heard or seen anybody else using them), most of which come from two papers, *Information Driven Web Systems* and *Information Mechanics* written in 1994 and 1997, respectively. Both were released only to other researchers and haven't been made publicly available (although if you have lots of money and an overriding desire for a massive headache, they're available). For example, when the following references something like "2,880 possible presentations" it's describing ET's ability to direct a content management system (CMS). Our original demonstrations of ET had it driving a CMS via *atomized* (a term from the above papers) site content. A CMS that can deliver any of three banners with any of three text blocks and any of three images for a single presentation (page delivery) can actually deliver any of 27 presentations (content permutations). If the same is true on the second instantiation (2nd page delivered) then there are 27^2 possible content permutations and so on.

Web usage studies have shown that eBusiness and eCommerce sites have at most three-to-five clicks (modern sites have three-to-five scrolls) to capture their audience before it wanders to another site. *Evolution Technology* links the latest in web technology to psycholinguistic, psychodynamic and neural linguistic research to create a rewarding, fulfilling, compelling and *uniquely individualized* user experience, one that so engages each member of your audience that it all but guarantees each visitor to your site stays on your site until they've completed a transaction or converted.

The following is an example of a user's experience between two wine sites, BeneVino using ET and Wines4U not using ET:

You're interested in purchasing a bottle of wine for a friend who lives across the country. They just landed a big deal and, although you can't be with them, you want to help them celebrate. You already have in mind how much you want to spend and will go somewhere around $100 plus another $20 for shipping.

Zeroth Click - You come to the site
(Five Clicks to Go)

BeneVino using ET - You use your favorite search engine and click on BeneVino.com.

BeneVino's splashpage looks like a fairly standard eCommerce homepage. It has branding, menus and web tools placed where they can be easily found. There is a Wine-of-the-Month item, some specialty wine offerings, clicks to a free wine drawing, a sommelier section and an auction of rare wines.

There is some text on the left of the page and beside each paragraph there is a picture of a bottle of wine. There are links to pages further down BeneVino's website in both the text and in the pictures. The text and pictures aren't for specific wines, only for Reds, Whites and Chablis.

Wines4U not using ET - You use your favorite search engine and click on Wines4U.com.

Wines4U has a very elaborate and attractive splashpage complete with animation and crisp, clean graphics; very state of the art. It has branding, menus and web tools placed where they can be easily found. There is a Wine-of-the-Month item, some specialty wine offerings, clicks to a free wine drawing, a sommelier section and an auction of rare wines.

General wine offerings are listed by country, with neuvo-art renditions of the major wine growing countries at the bottom of the page. Each "country" is a link to a page further down in Wines4U.Com's website.

Differences in User's Experience - BeneVino, using ET and without using Cookies, has already gathered enough information from you to know if you've been to the site before, regardless of which computer you're working on.

BeneVino using ET - BeneVino's splashpage looks like a fairly standard eCommerce homepage. It has branding, menus and web tools placed where they can be easily found. There is a Wine-of-the-Month item, some specialty wine offerings, clicks to a free wine drawing, a sommelier section and an auction of rare wines.

There is some text on the left of the page and beside each paragraph there is a picture of a bottle of wine. There are links to pages further down BeneVino's website in both the text and in the pictures. The text and pictures aren't for specific wines, only for Reds, Whites and Chablis.

Wines4U not using ET - Wines4U.Com has a very elaborate and attractive splashpage complete with animation and crisp, clean graphics; very state of the art. It has branding, menus and web tools placed where they can be easily found. There is a Wine-of-the-Month item, some specialty wine offerings, clicks to a free wine drawing, a sommelier section and an auction of rare wines.

General wine offerings are listed by country, with neuvo-art renditions of the major wine growing countries at the bottom of the page. Each "country" is a link to a page further down in Wines4U.Com's website.

Differences in User's Experience - Using principles of psychomotor response, BeneVino's ET enhanced site has started capturing how you think, how you internalize experience. It has started to make a well-informed guess about your psychological makeup and personality at this instant in time and is doing it passively, without intruding on your shopping experience. If the ET system determines you've been to the site before, it has already modeled it's zeroth page presentation according to your psychological makeup and personality.

Wines4U.Com is relying on information you entered five months ago when you were buying a bottle of wine for your niece's Christening. If not based on information entered weeks or months ago, it asks you a bunch of questions and hopes you're giving accurate, honest answers.

BeneVino using ET - You're not really sure what your friend would like, but you know she speaks French and likes red wines, so you click on "Red".

Wines4U not using ET - You're not really sure what your friend would like, but you know she speaks French and likes red wines, so you click on "France".

First Click - You start to navigate the site
(One Click Down, Four to Go)

BeneVino using ET - BeneVino's next page brings up a world map with red wine growing regions highlighted. As you mouse over the map, boxes pop up describing the types of wines and their prices. There's some text underneath the map describing the types of wines from the various regions. There are also links similar to those on the home page and a listing of other buyers' thoughts on the wines purchased, along with some suggestions for gift ideas.

You're not really sure what your friend would like, but you know she speaks French and likes red wines, so you click on "Red".

Wines4U not using ET - Wines4U.Com shows a map of the wine growing regions of France. You can click on the map for a region. As you mouse over the map, boxes pop up describing the types of wines and their prices. There are also links similar to those on the home page and a listing of other buyers' thoughts on the wines purchased, along with some suggestions for gift ideas.

You're not really sure what your friend would like, but you know she speaks French and likes red wines, so you click on "France".

Differences in User's Experience - BeneVino's ET has already determined which of 120 possible presentations is most likely to both keep you on the site and stimulate you into increasing your order. This unique presentation is displayed on your browser. Although similar to what someone else would receive at their browser, ET has already started customizing the presentation and content delivered to the way you think, the way you feel, the way you believe things should be. Specifically, it noticed that you spent time considering the Italian wines even though you selected the French wines.

The Wines4U.Com site is sending you the same information on French red wines it sends everyone. It is useful, but doesn't really encourage or help you.

First Click - You start to navigate the site
(One Click Down, Four to Go)

BeneVino using ET - BeneVino's next page brings up a world map with red wine growing regions highlighted. As you mouse over the map, boxes pop up describing the types of wines and their prices. There's some text underneath the map describing the types of wines from the various regions. There are also links similar to those on the home page and a listing of other buyers' thoughts on the wines purchased, along with some suggestions for gift ideas.

You click on "France".

Wines4U not using ET - Wines4U.Com shows a map of the wine growing regions of France. You can click on the map for a region. As you mouse over the map, boxes pop up describing the types of wines and their prices. There are also links similar to those on the home page and a listing of other buyers' thoughts on the wines purchased, along with some suggestions for gift ideas.

You don't know much about wines, so you click on "Ask our Wine Expert".

Differences in User's Experience - BeneVino's ET has already determined which of 120 possible presentations is most likely to both keep you on the site and stimulate you into increasing your order. This unique presentation is displayed on your browser. Although similar to what someone else would receive at their browser, ET has already started customizing the presentation and content delivered to the way you think, the way you feel, the way you believe things should be. Specifically, it noticed that you spent time considering the Italian wines even though you selected the French wines.

The Wines4U.Com site is sending you the same information on French red wines it sends everyone. It is useful, but doesn't really encourage or help you.

You want to get some wine for your friend so you go on.

Second Click - You're refining your search for a good wine
(Two Clicks Down, Three to Go)

BeneVino using ET - BeneVino displays a map of France's major wine growing regions. There are pop up boxes as you mouse over the regions. Beneath the map and as you mouse over the regions, different graphics appear. Some are just bottles of a wine, others show people enjoying themselves at a party, some show a more intimate, candlelit setting. The text describing the various wines is very enlivening and engaging. You can almost smell the bouquet and taste the wines as you mouse over the regions.

You notice some sounds coming from your computer's speakers and turn up the volume to hear it better, then laugh.

You notice that the background audio is for a wine that costs $45 a bottle, more than you wanted to spend, but it can be sent as part of a gift pack which includes some cheese and crackers in a basket for only $5 more. Other, less expensive wines can also be sent as gifts, but not in baskets like in the picture and your friend does speak French.

You click on "I'll take this one".

Wines4U not using ET - Wines4U.Com's Expert wants you to fill out a screen and a half long questionnaire so that it can help you pick out the best wine.

All you wanted to do was send your friend a bottle of wine, not conduct a census. You half-heartedly fill in the questionnaire.You've finished the questionnaire and gotten yourself a glass of wine out of the fridge. Because you're alone, you're using a Fred Flintstone jelly jar your mother picked up at a yard sale. The wine tastes a little yeasty and you're wondering if wine is a good gift to send. You have to be on the road early tomorrow for a meeting sixty miles away.

You click on "submit" and check your watch.

Differences in User's Experience - BeneVino's ET has now selected which of 2,880 possible presentations fits your current mood and delivered it to your browser. It has tested its theory about how you think and internalize experience, and made modifications to the presentation and content as necessary.

While doing this, it has also determined if your internet connection has sufficient bandwidth to send you some background audio as part of its presentation. You do have sufficient bandwidth for some audio and you laugh as you hear a bottle of wine being uncorked, a man speaking English and a woman speaking French.Wines4U.Com was suppose to be making this easy. Now they've asked you a bunch of questions and you really didn't like the "Is this a special friend?" one. You're yawning and want to know how long this is going to take. *Worse, Wines4U.Com has allowed an outside experience to dominate the user's web-based experience.*

Third Click - On BeneVino, You're feeling pretty good about getting your friend a gift basket.
On Wines4U.Com, you're deciding that sending a congratulatory email is a pretty good idea.
(Three Clicks Down, Two to Go)

BeneVino using ET - You've done what you wanted to do; selected a wine for your friend. You move your cursor over the "Proceed to checkout" icon and a box pops up beside the icon. Inside the box is "Before you go, we're having a special on two very high quality yet inexpensive wines from Italy. Click here for more info." The cursor is already in the center of the box. You had a good Italian wine when you went out for dinner last week.

You click on the box.

Wines4U not using ET - Wines4U.com's Wine Expert is telling you you forgot to answer all the questions and that you'll have to go back and fill them in again, and this time please make sure you answer questions 9, 17, 23 and 39. If there is no answer, please enter "N/A" in the space provided.

You remember that your friend owes you money and didn't introduce you to her friend, the good looking blonde with the big...eyes.

You remember that somewhere on the main page there was a "quick buy" button for some wine. You don't remember what kind of wine it was or what it cost, but you're sure that button was there.

Differences in User's Experience - BeneVino's ET has engaged you in extending your shopping session because it paid attention to everything you did on the site and the way you did it. The current presentation was selected from 17,280 possible combinations as the one most likely to encourage you into extending your BeneVino web session.

Meanwhile, Wines4U.Com's lack of an individually tuned presentation is costing them the immediate sale and possibly return business.

Fourth Click - You're staying on BeneVino for more than your intended purpose.
You're looking for a quick way out on Wines4U.Com.
(Four Clicks Down, One to Go)

BeneVino using ET - The wines BeneVino is offering seem pretty good. They're normally $15 a piece but the sale will send them both to you for $20 total plus $5 shipping.

You hear mellow sax music over your computer's speakers along with the "ting" of two wine glasses clinking in a toast. Underneath that, you can hear a woman and a man laugh. You're smiling. You're even thinking, "Damn, this site is good."

You add the wines to your cart and click on checkout.

Wines4U not using ET - You can't find that damn "quick buy" button on Wines4U.Com's homepage. You can't find anything that looks like a quick anything. You're tired and the wine probably won't taste good, anyway. You decide "The hell with it. I'll call her while I'm driving to my meeting in the morning and wish her well."

You log off the internet and shut down your computer. This has been a fiasco. You feel miserable because you didn't get your friend some wine, you're alone, the wine you're drinking from the Fred Flintstone jelly jar tastes like crap and is probably going to give you a hangover which will last through your meeting tomorrow. Who was the jerk who thought up the internet, anyway?

Differences in User's Experience - BeneVino's ET has now refined it's presentation and content, selecting the combination which is right for you from 34,560 possible combinations. Because ET deals with you at this instant, the next time you log on it will refine itself for you at that instant, doing so passively, never intruding itself into your experience or diverting you from your goal.

Fifth Click - BeneVino made the sale and created a memory of a pleasurable experience, an experience so pleasurable you'll mention the site for days to come.
Wines4U.Com is a painful memory. When you talk about it to others, you'll talk about the trouble you had and how frustrating it was. You'll remember the site name and vow never to go back.
(Five Clicks Down, None to Go)

BeneVino using ET - You've filled out the credit card information for the purchase and are ready to click on "I'll buy it" when you see a box pop up as you mouse over the purchase button. The text in the box says "Click here to complete your purchase AND to add BeneVino to your personal bookmarks." The mouse is already in the center of the box and this site's been fun. Sure, go for it. You already know you'll come back.

Wines4U not using ET -

Differences in User's Experience - BeneVino, using ET, has made a lasting customer and a site evangelist. ET has done its job.

Your bookshelf is your medicine cabinet.
— Stephen Guerra

Further Readings

My *Further Readings* sections are extensive, yes. My goal is to provide breadcrumbs for others' explorations. Enjoy!

1.   Abbott, A. (2011, 22 Jun). City living marks the brain. *Nature, 474*(429). (Http://www.nature.com/news/2011/110622/pdf/474429a .pdf)

2.   Ackerley, R., Wild, K., & Makin, A. (2008, 3 Sep). Cognitive Influences on the Generation of Eye Movements. *The Journal of Neuroscience, 28*(36), 8863–8864. (Http://www.jneurosci.org/content/28/36/8863.full.pdf+ht ml)

3.   Ackerman, J. M., Shapiro, J. R., Neuberg, S. L., Kenrick, D. T., Becker, D. V., Griskevicius, V., et al. (2006, 1 Oct). They All Look the Same to Me (Unless They're Angry). *Psychological Science, 17*(10), 836–840. (Http://www.nature.com/nature/journal/v439/n7072/pdf/ nature04340.pdf)

4.   Acquisti, A., Brandimarte, L., & Loewenstein, G. (2015, 30 Jan). Privacy and human behavior in the age of information. *Science, 347*(6221), 509–514. (Http://www.sciencemag.org/content/347/6221/509.full.p df)

5.   Adam J. Rubenstein. (2005, Oct). Variation in Perceived Attractiveness. *Psychological Science, 16*(10), 759–762. (Http://www3.interscience.wiley.com/cgi- bin/fulltext/118661656/PDFSTART)

6.   Adam, S., & Shaw, R. (2001). Experiential Dimensions in Internet Marketing: An Exploratory Investigation. Australian and New Zealand Marketing Academy Conference. Massey University, Auckland, NZ. (Http://www.stewartadam.com/publications/adam_shaw_ ANZMAC_2001.pdf)

7.   Adams, R. B., Jr., Gordon, H. L., Baird, A. A., Ambady, N.,
        & Kleck, R. E. (2003, 6 Jun). Effects of Gaze on Amygdala
        Sensitivity to Anger and Fear Faces. *Science, 300*(5625).

8.   Adolphs, R. (2010, 13 Aug). Emotion. *Current biology:
        CB, 20*(13), R549-R552.
        (Http://download.cell.com/current-
        biology/pdf/PIIS0960982210006494.pdf)

9.   Afraz, A., Pashkam, M. V., & Cavanagh, P. (2010, 7 Dec).
        Spatial Heterogeneity in the Perception of Face and Form
        Attributes. *Current biology: CB, 20*(23), 2112–2116.
        (Http://download.cell.com/current-
        biology/pdf/PIIS0960982210014429.pdf)

10.   Aharon, I., Etcoff, N., Ariely, D., Chabris, C. F., O'Connor,
        E., & Breiter, H. C. (2001, 8 Nov). Beautiful Faces Have
        Variable Reward Value: FMRI and Behavioral Evidence.
        Neuron, 32(3), 537–551.
        (Http://download.cell.com/neuron/pdf/PIIS089662730100
        4913.pdf)

11.   Albouy, G., Sterpenich, V., Balteau, E., Vandewalle, G.,
        Desseilles, M., Dang-Vu, T., et al. (2008, 24 Apr). Both the
        Hippocampus and Striatum Are Involved in Consolidation
        of Motor Sequence Memory. *Neuron, 58*(2), 261–272.
        (Http://www.sciencedirect.com/science/article/pii/S08966
        2730800130X)

12.   Almeida, J., Mahon, B. Z., & Caramazza, A. (2010, 1 Jun).
        The Role of the Dorsal Visual Processing Stream in Tool
        Identification. *Psychological Science, 21*(6), 772–778.
        (Http://pss.sagepub.com/content/21/6/772.full.pdf+html)

13.   Anderson, B. A., Laurent, P. A., & Yantis, S. (2013, 11
        Jun). Reward predictions bias attentional selection.
        Frontiers in Human Neuroscience, 7.
        (Http://www.frontiersin.org/Journal/DownloadFile.ashx?pd
        f=1&FileId=256363&articleId=50195&Version=1&Content
        TypeId=21&FileName=fnhum-07-00262.pdf)

14.   Armstrong, J. S., & Overton, T. (1971, Feb). Brief v
        Comprehensive Descriptions in Measuring Intentions to
        Purchase. *Journal of Marketing Research, 8,* 114–117.

(Http://marketing.wharton.upenn.edu/ideas/pdf/armstron g2/brief.pdf)

15. Arthur, R., & Diamond, J. (2011, 18 Nov). Understanding Tribal Fates. *Science, 334*(6058), 911–912. (Http://www.sciencemag.org/content/334/6058/911.full.p df)

16. Arthur, /. B. (2009). *The nature of technology: What it is and how it evolves.* New York: Free Press.

17. Ashton, D. (2011, 3 Jan). Awarding the self in Wikipedia: Identity work and the disclosure of knowledge. *First Monday, 16*(1). (Http://firstmonday.org/htbin/cgiwrap/bin/ojs/index.php/f m/article/view/3156/2747)

18. Assad, J. A. (2014, 27 Mar). Updating views of visual updating. *Nature, 507*(7493), 434–435. (Http://www.nature.com/nature/journal/v507/n7493/pdf/ 507434a.pdf)

19. Atkinson, Q. D., Meade, A., Venditti, C., Greenhill, S. J., & Pagel, M. (2008/2/1). Languages Evolve in Punctuational Bursts. *Science, 319*(5863). (Http://www.sciencemag.org/cgi/reprint/sci;319/5863/58 8.pdf)

20. Aunger, R. (2002). *The Electric Meme: A New Theory of How We Think.* Simon&Schuster.

21. Austen, K. (2015, 3 Sep). The Trouble With Wearables. *Nature, 252.* (Http://www.nature.com/news/what-could-derail-the-wearables-revolution-1.18263)

22. Awofeso, N., & Green, S. (2001, Oct). Numismatics: Australian two-dollar coin, and Aboriginal Identity. *Journal of Mundane Behavior, 2*(3), 345–353.

23. Bainbridge, W. S. (2007, 27 Jul). The Scientific Research Potential of Virtual Worlds. *Science, 317*(5837), 472–476. (Http://www.sciencemag.org/content/317/5837/472.full.p df)

24. Barinaga, M. (1995, 23 June). Remapping the motor cortex. *Science, 268*(5218), 1696–1698.

(Http://www.sciencemag.org/cgi/reprint/sci;268/5218/16
96.pdf)

25.   Barnes, N. G., & Lescault, A. M. (2014). *Millennials Drive
Social Commerce: Turning Their Likes, Follows or Pins Into
a Sale.* UMass Dartmouth: Center for Marketing Research.

26.   Baumann, O., Skilleter, A. J., & Mattingley, J. B. (2011, 24
May). Short-Term Memory Maintenance of Object
Locations during Active Navigation: Which Working
Memory Subsystem Is Essential? *PLoS ONE, 6*(5).

27.   Bekoff, M. (2002, 19 Sep). Animal reflections.
Nature, 419(6904), 255–255.
(Http://www.nature.com/nature/journal/v419/n6904/pdf/
419255a.pdf)

28.   Ben Harush, O. (2007). Reflections on women using
mobile phones. In M. (. Albion & P. (. Collins, *Education,
Employment, and Everything: The triple layers of a
woman's life.* University of Southern Queensland,
Toowoomba, Queensland, Australia: IWC (International
Women's Conference) 2007.

29.   Berger, D., & Schneck, D. (2003, Winter). The Use of
Music Therapy as a Clinical Intervention for Physiologic
Functional Adaptation. *Journal of Scientific
Exploration, 17*(4), 689.

30.   Berns, G. S., Capra, C. M., Moore, S., & Noussair, C.
(2010, 1 Feb). Neural mechanisms of the influence of
popularity on adolescent ratings of music.
NeuroImage, 49(3), 2687–2696.
(Http://www.sciencedirect.com/science/article/pii/S10538
11909011410)

31.   Berns, G. S., & Moore, S. E. (2012, Jan). A neural
predictor of cultural popularity. *Journal of Consumer
Psychology, 22*(1), 154–160.
(Http://www.sciencedirect.com/science/article/pii/S10577
40811000532)

32.   Bernstein, M. J., Sacco, D. F., Brown, C. M., Young, S. G.,
& Claypool, H. M. (2010). A preference for genuine smiles
following social exclusion. *Journal of Experimental Social*

Psychology, 46(1), 196–199.
(Http://www.sciencedirect.com/science?_ob=MImg&_imag
ekey=B6WJB-4X3N47F-1-
7&_cdi=6874&_user=10&_pii=S0022103109002133&_ori
gin=search&_coverDate=01%2F31%2F2010&_sk=999539
998&view=c&wchp=dGLbVzb-
zSkWA&md5=456c81b5fb9adb79272420ab3ffdf933&ie=/s
darticle.pdf)

33. Bhattacharjee, Y. (2006, 2 Mar). A Timely Debate About
     the Brain. *Science, 311*(5761), 596–598.
     (Http://www.sciencemag.org/content/311/5761/596.full.p
     df)

34. Bhattacharjee, Y. (2008, 10 Mar). Is Internal Timing the
     Key to Mental Health? *Science.*

35. Bi, G.-q., & Poo, M.-m. (1999, 21 Oct). Distributed
     synaptic modification in neural networks induced by
     patterned stimulation. *Nature, 401*(6755), 792–796.
     (Http://www.nature.com/nature/journal/v401/n6755/pdf/
     401792a0.pdf)

36. Bilkey, D. K. (2004, 27 Aug). In the Place Space.
     Science, 305(5688), 1245–1246.
     (Http://www.sciencemag.org/cgi/reprint/sci;305/5688/12
     45.pdf)

37. Blackmore, S. (2003). Consciousness in meme machines.
     Journal of Consciousness Studies, 10(4–5), 19–30.

38. Blood, A. J., & Zatorre, R. J. (2001, 25 Sep). Intensely
     pleasurable responses to music correlate with activity in
     brain regions implicated in reward and emotion.
     *Proceedings of the National Academy of Sciences of the
     United States of America, 98*(20), 11818–11823.
     (Http://www.pnas.org/content/98/20/11818.full.pdf+html
)

39. Bohorquez, J. C., Gourley, S., Dixon, A. R., Spagat, M., &
     Johnson, N. F. (2009, 17 Dec). Common ecology quantifies
     human insurgency. *Nature, 462*(7275), 911–914.
     (Http://www.nature.com/nature/journal/v462/n7275//pdf/
     nature08631.pdf)

40. Bonini, F., Burle, B., Liageois-Chauvel, C., Ragis, J., Chauvel, P., & Vidal, F. (2014, 21 Feb). Action Monitoring and Medial Frontal Cortex: Leading Role of Supplementary Motor Area. *Science, 343*(6173), 888–891. (Http://www.sciencemag.org/content/343/6173/888.full.pdf)

41. Borgatti, S. P., Mehra, A., Brass, D. J., & Labianca, G. (2009, 13 Feb). Network Analysis in the Social Sciences. *Science, 323*(5916), 892–895. (Http://www.sciencemag.org/cgi/reprint/sci;323/5916/892.pdf)

42. Bower, B. (1999, 7 Aug). Personality Conflicts. *Science News, 156,* 88.

43. Brewer, G., & Riley, C. (2009). Height, Relationship Satisfaction, Jealousy, and Mate Retention. *Evolutionary Psychology, 7*(3), 477–489. (Http://www.epjournal.net/filestore/ep07477489.pdf)

44. Brian P. Meier, M. D. R., Benjamin M. Wilkowski. (2006, Feb). Turning the Other Cheek - Agreeableness and the Regulation of Aggression-Related Primes. *Psychological Science, 17*(2), 136–142.

45. Brown, C. M., young, S. G., Sacco, D. F., Bernstein, M. J., & Claypool, H. M. (2009, 1 Jan). Social inclusion facilitates interest in mating. *Evolutionary Psychology, 7*(1), 1–11. (Http://www.epjournal.net/wp-content/uploads/EP075455592.pdf)

46. Bruce, V., & Young, A. (1998). *In the Eye of the Beholder: The Science of Face Perception.* Oxford: Oxford University Press.

47. Bruyn, S. T. (2002, Jun). Studies of the Mundane by Participant Observation. *Journal of Mundane Behavior, 3*(2).

48. Burgess, N., Maguire, E. A., & O'Keefe, J. (2002, 15 Aug). The Human Hippocampus and Spatial and Episodic Memory. *Neuron, 35*(4), 625–641. (Http://linkinghub.elsevier.com/retrieve/pii/S0896627302008309)

49.   Burke, D., & Sulikowski, D. (2010). A New Viewpoint on the Evolution of Sexually Dimorphic Human Faces. *Evolutionary Psychology, 8*(4), 573–585. (Http://www.epjournal.net/filestore/EP08573585.pdf?utm _source=MadMimi&utm_medium=email&utm_content=No vember+2010+Newsletter&utm_campaign=November+20 10+Newsletter&utm_term=A+new+viewpoint+on+the+ev olution+of+sexually+dimorphic+human+faces_)

50.   Buzsaki, G. (2005, 11 Aug). Neurons and navigation. *Nature, 436*(7052), 781–782. (Http://www.nature.com/nature/journal/v436/n7052/pdf/ 436781a.pdf)

51.   Buzsaki, G. (2013, 30 May). Time, space and memory. *Nature, 497*(7451), 568–569. (Http://www.nature.com/nature/journal/v497/n7451/pdf/ 497568a.pdf)

52.   Calero, C. I., Salles, A., Semelman, M., & Sigman, M. (2013, 17 Jun). Age and gender dependent development of theory of mind in 6 to 8-years old children. *Frontiers in Human Neuroscience, 7.* (Http://www.frontiersin.org/Journal/DownloadFile.ashx?pd f=1&FileId=261468&articleId=51848&Version=1&Content TypeId=21&FileName=fnhum-07-00281.pdf)

53.   Campbell-Meiklejohn, D. K., Bach, D. R., Roepstorff, A., Dolan, R. J., & Frith, C. D. (2010, 13 Aug). How the Opinion of Others Affects Our Valuation of Objects. *Current biology: CB, 20*(13), 1165–1170. (Http://download.cell.com/current-biology/pdf/PIIS0960982210005956.pdf)

54.   Carpenter, A. F., Georgopoulos, A. P., & Pellizzer, G. (1999, 12 Mar). Motor Cortical Encoding of Serial Order in a Context-Recall Task. *Science, 283*(5408), 1752–1757. (Http://www.sciencemag.org/cgi/reprint/sci;283/5408/17 52.pdf)

55.   Carrabis, J., Bratton, S., & Evans, D. (2008, 9 Jun). *Guest Blogger Joseph Carrabis Answers Dave Evans, CEO of Digital Voodoo's Question About Male Executives Weilding*

Social Media Influence on Par with Female Executives.
PersonalLifeMedia.
(Http://blogs.personallifemedia.com/dishymix/guest-
blogger-joseph-carrabis-answers-dave-evans-ceo-of-
digital-voodoos-question-about-male-executives-weilding-
social-media-influence-on-par-with-female-
executives/2008/06/09/)

56.   Carrabis, J., & Bratton, S. (2011). *Joseph Carrabis on
Neuro-Economics and Reading Virtual Minds Part 2 of 2.*
PerosnalLifeMedia.
(Http://personallifemedia.com/podcasts/232-
dishymix/episodes/125970-joseph-carrabis-neuro-
economics-reading)

57.   Carrabis, J., Carrabis, S., & Hamel, S. (2013, Dec). Want
to be loved? Go Mobile! *International Journal of Mobile
Marketing.*

58.   Carrabis, J., & Carrabis, S. (2009). *Designing Information
for Automatic Memorization (Branding).* Scotsburn, NS:
NextStage Evolution.

59.   Carrabis, J., & Carrabis, S. (2009). *Machine Detection of
Website Visitor Age and Gender via Analysis of
Psychomotor Behavioral Cues.* Scotsburn, NS: Northern
Lights Press.
(Http://www.nextstagevolution.com/membership.cfm)

60.   Carrabis, J., & Carrabis, S. (2014). *That smile, those eyes,
that face - Trust and Acceptance In a SnapShot.*
NextStage Evolution, LLC.

61.   Carrabis, J., Nesbitt, A., & Bratton, S. (2008, 14 Nov).
*Human Nature Meets Social Media – The Brain Science
Behind Participation by Joseph Carrabis, DishyMix Guest
Blogger.* PersonalLifeMedia.
(Http://blogs.personallifemedia.com/dishymix/human-
nature-meets-social-media-the-brain-science-behind-
participation-by-joseph-carrabis-dishymix-guest-
blogger/2008/11/14/)

62.   Carrabis, J., Nesbitt, A., & Bratton, S. (2008, 23 Jun).
Social Media: Exafference – Passive Participation (the

"They're Giving You Their Time" Part) – and Reafference, or Creating Active Participation. PersonalLifeMedia. (Http://blogs.personallifemedia.com/dishymix/social-media-exafference-%E2%80%93-passive-participation-the-%E2%80%9Cthey%E2%80%99re-giving-you-their-time%E2%80%9D-part-%E2%80%93-and-reafference-or-creating-active-participation/2008/06/23/)

63. Carrabis, J., & Peverill-Conti, G. (2011, Oct). The Selling Face - The Selling Face - A Study of Face and Body Biases in Marketing Communications(. *International Journal of Integrated Marketing Communications.*

64. Carrabis, J. (2000). *Thoughts into Movement: The Mechanics of Evolution Technology Part 1 - Modalities and Mathematics.* NextStage Evolution Research Paper.

65. Carrabis, J. (2000). *Thoughts into Movement: The Mechanics of Evolution Technology Part 2 - Browser and Sever Communications.* NextStage Evolution Research Paper.

66. Carrabis, J. (2001). Can Autonomous Entities Act on Non-Conscious Meaning in Human Applications? (Theory and Applications of Evolution Technology). IIAS.

67. Carrabis, J. (2001). *Internal Experience and the Web.* Scotsburn, NS: NextStage Evolution Research Paper. (Http://www.nextstagevolution.com/membership.cfm)

68. Carrabis, J. (2001, Jul). *Utilizing Visitor "Goal-Seeking" in eCommerce.* BizMediaScience. (Http://bizmediascience.hungrypeasant.com/2015/01/02/utilizing-visitor-goal-seeking-in-ecommerce/)

69. Carrabis, J. (2002). *Signatures and the Identity Matrix, Part 1: Neuromuscular Control of Fine Motor Reflexes.* NextStage Evolution Research Paper.

70. Carrabis, J. (2002). *Signatures and the Identity Matrix, Part 2: Psychomotor Behavioral Activity as an Indicator of Personal Identity.* NextStage Evolution Research Paper.

71. Carrabis, J. (2003). *Evaluation of Individuals as Cognitive Systems (Situational Awareness and Cognitive Readiness).* NextStage Evolution.

72.   Carrabis, J. (2004, 2006, 2009). *A Primer on Modality Engineering.* NextStage Evolution Research Whitepaper. Scotsburn, NS: Northern Lights Publishing. (Http://www.nextstagevolution.com/membership.cfm)

73.   Carrabis, J. (2004). *What We're Learning About Visitors From Websites.* NextStage Evolution. Scotsburn, NS: Northern Lights Publishing. (Http://www.nextstagevolution.com/membership.cfm)

74.   Carrabis, J. (2005, Oct). *Site ReDesign to Facilitate User Migration and Increase Branding.* Hungry Peasant. (Http://bizmediascience.hungrypeasant.com/2014/12/30/site-redesign-to-facilitate-user-migration-and-increase-branding/)

75.   Carrabis, J. (2005, 8 Apr). *Usability Studies 101: Brand Loyalty.* IMediaConnections. (Http://www.imediaconnection.com/content/5440.asp)

76.   Carrabis, J. (2005, 1 July). *Usability Studies 101: The X Funnel.* ImediaConnections. (Http://www.imediaconnection.com/content/6252.asp)

77.   Carrabis, J. (2006–2007). Priming BizMediaScience Blog Posts. In *BizMediaScience Blog Posts on Priming.* (Http://bizmediascience.hungrypeasant.com/category/sciences/neuroscience/priming/)

78.   Carrabis, J. (2006). *Author's Foreword, Reading Virtual Minds Volume I: Science and History.* Nashua, NH: Northern Lights Publishing. (Http://www.amazon.com/Reading-Virtual-Minds-Joseph-Carrabis/dp/0984140301)

79.   Carrabis, J. (2006). *Chapter 2, "History," Reading Virtual Minds Volume I: Science and History.* Scotsburn, NS: Northern Lights Publishing. (Http://nlb.pub/RVMV14th)

80.   Carrabis, J. (2006). *Chapter 3 "Behaviors, Offline to On," Reading Virtual Minds Volume I: Science and History.* Nashua, NH: Northern Lights Publishing. (Http://nlb.pub/RVMV14th)

81.   Carrabis, J. (2006). *Chapter 4 "Anecdotes of Learning," Reading Virtual Minds Volume I: Science and History.*

Nashua, NH: Northern Lights Publishing.
(Http://nlb.pub/RVMV14th)

82. Carrabis, J. (2006, 2 Dec). *DeBranding, Again...*
BizMediaScience.
(Http://bizmediascience.hungrypeasant.com/2014/12/30/
debranding-again/)

83. Carrabis, J. (2006). *Determining Prior Knowledge of
Information via PsychoMotor Behavioral Cuing.* Scotsburn,
NS: NextStage Evolution.

84. Carrabis, J. (2006, May). *Learning to Listen, Learning to
See.* Hungry Peasant.
(Http://bizmediascience.hungrypeasant.com/2014/12/30/l
earning-to-listen-learning-to-see/)

85. Carrabis, J. (2006, 9 Jun). *Listening to and Seeing
Searches.* IMediaConnection.
(Http://www.imediaconnection.com//content//9898.asp)

86. Carrabis, J. (2006, 10 Nov). *Mapping Personae to
Outcomes.*
(Http://www.imediaconnection.com/content/12358.asp)

87. Carrabis, J. (2006). *Reading Virtual Minds Volume I:
Science and History, 4th edition.* Nashua, NH: Northern
Lights Publishing. (Http://nlb.pub/RVMV14th)

88. Carrabis, J. (2006). *Use of Eye Images as Navigation and
Action Cues on Websites* [NSE WhitePaper]. NextStage
Evolution. Scotsburn, NS: Northern Lights Publishing.
(Http://www.nextstagevolution.com/membership.cfm)

89. Carrabis, J. (2007/2014, 30 May/28 Dec). *The Complete
Sweetness' Findings: Email Bankruptcy Arc.*
BizMedisScience.
(Http://bizmediascience.hungrypeasant.com/2014/12/28/t
he-complete-sweetness-findings-email-bankruptcy-arc/)

90. Carrabis, J. (2007/2015, 16 May/3 Jan). *The Complete
"KBar's Findings: Political Correctness in the Guise of a
Sandwich" Arc.* BizMediaScience.
(Http://bizmediascience.hungrypeasant.com/2015/01/03/t
he-complete-kbars-findings-political-correctness-in-the-
guise-of-a-sandwich-arc/)

91.   Carrabis, J. (2007/2015, 28 Sep/8 Jan). *The Complete
       "NextStage Evolution's Evolution Technology, Web
       Analytics, Behavioral Analytics and Marketing Analytics
       Reports for the BizMediaScience Blog, 7 day Cycle" Arc.*
       BizMediaScience.
       (Http://bizmediascience.hungrypeasant.com/2015/01/08/t
       he-complete-nextstage-evolutions-evolution-technology-
       web-analytics-behavioral-analytics-and-marketing-
       analytics-reports-for-the-bizmediascience-blog-7-day-
       cycle-arc/)

92.   Carrabis, J. (2007/2015, 9 Apr/22 Dec). *The Complete
       "Notes from UML's Strategic Management Class" Arc.*
       BizMediaScience.
       (Http://bizmediascience.hungrypeasant.com/2015/12/22/t
       he-complete-notes-from-umls-strategic-management-
       class-arc/)

93.   Carrabis, J. (2007/2015, 9 June/21 Dec). *The Complete
       "Nothing New Under the Sun: Designing for the Small
       Screen" Arc.* BizMediaScience.
       (Http://bizmediascience.hungrypeasant.com/2015/12/21/t
       he-complete-nothing-new-under-the-sun-designing-for-
       the-small-screen-arc/)

94.   Carrabis, J. (2007/2015, 20 June/22 Dec). *The Complete
       "WindKiller and the Drunken Pirate" Arc.* BizMediaScience.
       (Http://bizmediascience.hungrypeasant.com/2015/12/22/t
       he-complete-windkiller-and-the-drunken-pirate-arc/)

95.   Carrabis, J. (2007/2015, 10 May/3 Jan). *Drunken Pirates,
       Anyone? or "Interlife Realities 101.".* BizMediaScience.
       (Http://bizmediascience.hungrypeasant.com/2015/01/03/
       drunken-pirates-anyone-or-interlife-realities-101/)

96.   Carrabis, J. (2007/2015, 29 Jul/1 Jan). *The
       NextStageologists at the Edwards Rally.* BizMediaScience.
       (Http://bizmediascience.hungrypeasant.com/2015/01/01/t
       he-nextstageologists-at-the-edwards-rally/)

97.   Carrabis, J. (2007/2015, 14 Jan/22 Jan). *Quorum Sensing.*
       BizMediaScience.

(Http://bizmediascience.hungrypeasant.com/2015/01/22/
quorum-sensing/)

98.   Carrabis, J. (2007/2015, 25 Jun/1 Jan). *Second Life? I
      don't find you interesting in Real Life.* BizMediaScience.
      (Http://bizmediascience.hungrypeasant.com/2015/01/01/
      second-life-i-dont-find-you-interesting-in-real-life/)

99.   Carrabis, J. (2007/2015, 16 June/5 Apr). *So I declared
      Bankruptcy..or was it Voluntary Simplification applied to
      the 'Net?.* BizMediaScience.
      (Http://bizmediascience.hungrypeasant.com/2015/04/05/
      so-i-declared-a-bankruptcy-or-was-it-voluntary-
      simplification-applied-to-the-net/)

100. Carrabis, J. (2007/2015, 30 Mar/22 Dec). *Technology and
      Buying Patterns.* BizMediaScience.
      (Http://bizmediascience.hungrypeasant.com/2015/12/22/t
      echnology-and-buying-patterns/)

101. Carrabis, J. (2007/2015, 12 Jul1/ Jan). *What does
      NextStage do?.* BizMediaScience.
      (Http://bizmediascience.hungrypeasant.com/2015/01/01/
      what-does-nextstage-do/)

102. Carrabis, J. (2007, 29 Nov). *Adding sound to your brand
      website.* ImediaConnections.
      (Http://www.imediaconnection.com//content//17473.asp)

103. Carrabis, J. (2007, 13 Jul). *Attract and Stick, Part 1.*
      AllBusiness.com. (Http://www.allbusiness.com/marketing-
      advertising/internet-marketing/4353609–1.html)

104. Carrabis, J. (2007, 27 Jul). *Attract and Stick, Part 2.*
      AllBusiness.com. (Http://www.allbusiness.com/marketing-
      advertising/internet-marketing/4353761–1.html)

105. Carrabis, J. (2007, Dec). The Blogging Power Continuum:
      How Bloggers and Their Audience Share and Assign Power
      in a Knowledge-Based Medium [Holmes&Watsons]. Society
      for New Communications Research Symposium 2007.
      Boston, MA, USA.

106. Carrabis, J. (2007, 9 Mar). *Branding and Online Ad
      Placement.* IMediaConnections.
      (Http://www.imediaconnection.com//content//13969.asp)

107. Carrabis, J. (2007, 23 Feb). Branding in Online Video.
      ImediaConnections.
      (Http://www.imediaconnection.com/content/13782.asp)
108. Carrabis, J. (2007, 14 Jun). *Community Response Grids,
      Another Example.* BizMediaScience.
      (Http://bizmediascience.hungrypeasant.com/2015/01/08/
      community-response-grids-another-example/)
109. Carrabis, J. (2007, Feb). *The Complete Eventing Yourself
      Arc.* BizMediaScience.
      (Http://bizmediascience.hungrypeasant.com/2014/12/28/t
      he-complete-eventing-yourself-arc/)
110. Carrabis, J. (2007, Jul). *The Complete "Media Free? That
      Easy...And Scary. Know Why?" Arc.* BizMediaScience.
      (Http://bizmediascience.hungrypeasant.com/2014/12/28/t
      he-complete-media-free-that-easy-and-scary-know-why-
      arc/)
111. Carrabis, J. (2007, Jul). *The Curse of Social Networks.*
      BizMediaScience.
      (Http://bizmediascience.hungrypeasant.com/2014/12/28/t
      he-curse-of-social-networks/)
112. Carrabis, J. (2007, 25 Sept). *Expertise - Who Decides?.*
      BizMediaScience.
      (Http://bizmediascience.hungrypeasant.com/2014/12/28/
      expertise-who-decides/)
113. Carrabis, J. (2007, 14 Sept). Eye-Tracking Studies: Just
      Say "No!" *AllBusiness.com.*
      (Http://www.allbusiness.com/marketing-
      advertising/internet-marketing/4941677–1.html)
114. Carrabis, J. (2007, 7 Sep). *Fred Thompson: Is He
      Changing His Tune? And How Does He Compare with
      Governor Mitt Romney? Before and After NextStage
      Analysis of Campaign Messaging Styles.* BizMediaScience.
      (Http://bizmediascience.hungrypeasant.com/2015/09/25/f
      red-thompson-is-he-changing-his-tune-and-how-does-he-
      compare-with-governor-mitt-romney-before-and-after-
      nextstage-analysis-of-campaign-messaging-styles/)

115. Carrabis, J. (2007, 9 Nov). *God, Satan and your brand
      website.* ImediaConnections.
      (Http://www.imediaconnection.com//content//17287.asp)
116. Carrabis, J. (2007, 7 Sept). *Help visitors focus and reap
      the rewards.* ImediaConnections.
      (Http://www.imediaconnection.com//content//16533.asp)
117. Carrabis, J. (2007, 3 Jan). *Implications for Web 2.0 and
      Rich Media Developers.* Hungry Peasant.
      (Http://bizmediascience.hungrypeasant.com/2015/01/10/i
      mplications-for-web-2-0-and-rich-media-developers/)
118. Carrabis, J. (2007, Oct). *The Importance of Viral
      Marketing: Podcast and Text.* AllBusiness.com.
      (Http://www.allbusiness.com/4113507-1.html)
119. Carrabis, J. (2007, 6 Jul). *Intelligent Website Design:
      Expand Your Market.* ImediaConnections.
      (Http://www.imediaconnection.com//content//15697.asp)
120. Carrabis, J. (2007, 6 Jul). *Intrusive Little Windows or
      "DeBranding Made Easy.".* AllBusiness.com.
      (Http://www.allbusiness.com/marketing-
      advertising/internet-marketing/4353577-1.html)
121. Carrabis, J. (2007, 9 Oct). *Is Social Media a Woman
      Thing?.* AllBusiness.com.
      (Http://www.allbusiness.com/marketing-
      advertising/internet-marketing/4967764-1.html)
122. Carrabis, J. (2007, 11 May). *Make Sure Your Site Sells
      Lemonade….* IMediaConnections.
      (Http://www.imediaconnection.com//content//14904.asp)
123. Carrabis, J. (2007, 3 Aug). *Making Visitors Want It Now.*
      (Http://www.allbusiness.com/marketing-
      advertising/internet-marketing/4354179-1.html)
124. Carrabis, J. (2007, Aug). *The non-locality of Pizza Shops.*
      BizMediaScience.
      (Http://bizmediascience.hungrypeasant.com/2015/01/08/t
      he-non-locality-of-pizza-shops/)
125. Carrabis, J. (2007, 6 Jun). *Nothing New Under the Sun:
      Community Response Grids.* BizMediaScience.

(Http://bizmediascience.hungrypeasant.com/2015/01/08/
nothing-new-under-the-sun-community-response-grids/)

126. Carrabis, J. (2007, 10 Aug). *Priming the Conversion Pump with Color.* AllBusiness.com.
(Http://www.allbusiness.com/marketing-
advertising/internet-marketing/4354404–1.html)

127. Carrabis, J. (2007, 31 Aug). *Priming the Conversion Pump with Images.* AllBusiness.com.
(Http://www.allbusiness.com/marketing-
advertising/internet-marketing/4554354–1.html)

128. Carrabis, J. (2007, 29 Aug). *Romney, Mitt Romney, Governor Romney, Social, Social Networks, Social Media, Video, Multimedia, TV, Advertising.* BizMediaScience.
(Http://bizmediascience.hungrypeasant.com/2015/01/01/r
omney-mitt-romney-governor-mitt-romney-social-social-
networks-social-media-video-multimedia-tv-advertising/)

129. Carrabis, J. (2007, Jan). *Second Life is Experiencing Society's Woes! Surprise!.* BizMediaScience.
(Http://bizmediascience.hungrypeasant.com/2015/01/01/
second-life-is-experiencing-societys-woes-surprise/)

130. Carrabis, J. (2007, 27 Aug). *Stonewall's Findings: A New Kind of Community Response Grid.* BizMediaScience.
(Http://bizmediascience.hungrypeasant.com/2015/01/08/
stonewalls-findings-a-new-kind-of-community-response-
grid/)

131. Carrabis, J. (2007, 24 Aug). *Usability Studies 101: Get the attention you're already paying for.* ImediaConnections.
(Http://www.imediaconnection.com//content//16373.asp)

132. Carrabis, J. (2007, 23 Mar). *Websites: You've Only Got 3 Seconds.* ImediaConnections.
(Http://www.imediaconnection.com/content/7513.asp)

133. Carrabis, J. (2008/2015, 17 July/22 Dec). *Forget Influencers -- the New Metric of Interest will be "Saturation Point.".* BizMediaScience.
(Http://bizmediascience.hungrypeasant.com/2015/12/22/f
orget-influencers-the-new-metric-of-interest-will-be-
saturation-point/)

134. Carrabis, J. (2008/2015, 11 Jun/22 Dec). *Rocks, Hammers, Competition and How People Get Left Behind.* BizMediaScience. (Http://bizmediascience.hungrypeasant.com/2015/12/22/rocks-hammers-competition-and-how-people-get-left-behind/)

135. Carrabis, J. (2008/2015, 20 Jun/22 Dec). *The Stephane Hamel, Susan Bratton, Eric Peterson Convergence and more "Thoughts on Blogging.".* BizMediaScience. (Http://bizmediascience.hungrypeasant.com/2015/12/22/the-stephane-hamel-susan-bratton-eric-peterson-convergence-and-more-thoughts-on-blogging/)

136. Carrabis, J. (2008–9, 3 Jul/11 Jul). *From TheFutureOf (10 Jul 08): Back into the fray.* The Analytics Ecology. (Http://analyticsecology.hungrypeasant.com/index.php/2009/07/03/from-thefutureof-10-jul-08-back-into-the-fray/)

137. Carrabis, J. (2008–9, 15 Jul 09). *From TheFutureOf (11 Nov 08): Responding to Steve Jackson's 16 Sept 08 6:52am comment.* The Analytics Ecology. (Http://www.theanalyticsecology.com/?p=144)

138. Carrabis, J. (2008/9, 8–9 Feb/3 Jul). *From TheFutureOf (13 Feb 08): Response to Jim Novo, Part 2.* The Analytics Ecology. (Http://www.theanalyticsecology.com/?p=85)

139. Carrabis, J. (2008/9, 18 Jul/7 Jul). *From TheFutureOf (16 Jul 08): Responses to Geertz, Papadakis and others, 5 Feb 08.* The Analytics Ecology. (Http://www.theanalyticsecology.com/?p=106)

140. Carrabis, J. (2008/9, 18 Jul/7 Jul). *From TheFutureOf (16 Jul 08): Responses to Papadakis 7 Feb 08.* The Analytics Ecology. (Http://www.theanalyticsecology.com/?p=104)

141. Carrabis, J. (2008–9, 19 Aug/9 Jul). *From TheFutureOf (19 Aug 08): Response to Visitor Engagement Time for a reality check.* The Analytics Ecology. (Http://www.theanalyticsecology.com/?p=123)

142. Carrabis, J. (2008/9, 28 Jan/1 Jul). *From TheFutureOf (22 Jan 08): Starting the discussion: Attention, Engagement,*

Authority, Influence, …. The Analytics Ecology.
(Http://www.theanalyticsecology.com/?p=13)

143.   Carrabis, J. (2008/9, 29 Aug/9 Jul). *From TheFutureOf (28 Aug 08): Response to Jim Novo's 12 Jul 08 9:40am comment.* The Analytics Ecology.
(Http://www.theanalyticsecology.com/?p=127)

144.   Carrabis, J. (2008/9, 10 Nov/15 Jul). *From TheFutureOf (7 Nov 08): Debbie Pascoe asked me to pontificate on "What are we measuring when we measure 'engagement'?".* The Analytics Ecology.
(Http://www.theanalyticsecology.com/?p=137)

145.   Carrabis, J. (2008, 26 Jun). *The Complete "Canadian Based Business Differences -- Responding to June Li, Christopher Berry and Jaques Warren" Arc (also known as "Responding to Christopher Berry's 'A Vexing Problem.." and incorporating "The Language of Web Analytics - The Hard(er) Sell in Canada").* BizMediaScience.
(Http://bizmediascience.hungrypeasant.com/2015/01/28/the-complete-canadian-based-business-differences-responding-to-june-li-christopher-berry-and-jaques-warren-arc-also-known-as-responding-to-christopher-berrys-a-vexing-problem-and-incorpo/)

146.   Carrabis, J. (2008, Oct). *The Complete "Slew of emails about my political postings" Arc.* HungryPeasant.
(Http://bizmediascience.hungrypeasant.com/2015/04/06/the-complete-slew-of-emails-about-my-political-postings-arc/)

147.   Carrabis, J. (2008, 27 May). *The Complete "TS Eliot, Ezekiel, Beehives and Mighty Mouse – Why 'Whispering to Be Heard'?" Arc.* BizMediaScience.
(Http://bizmediascience.hungrypeasant.com/2015/03/14/the-complete-ts-eliot-ezekiel-beehives-and-mighty-mouse-why-whispering-to-be-heard-arc/)

148.   Carrabis, J. (2008, 30 Oct). *The Complete "What is an A6 or A11 or V6 or V21, etc. decision style?" Arc (Originally "Do McCain, Biden, Palin and Obama Think the Way We Do? (Part…)".* BizMediaScience.

(Http://bizmediascience.hungrypeasant.com/2015/01/28/t
he-complete-what-is-an-a6-or-a11-or-v6-or-v21-etc-
decision-style-arc-originally-do-mccain-biden-palin-and-
obama-think-the-way-we-do-part/)
149.   Carrabis, J. (2008). *Designing an Email Newsletter for
Maximum ROI.* Scotsburn, NS: NextStage Evolution.
(Http://www.nextstagevolution.com/membership.cfm)
150.   Carrabis, J. (2008, 31 Oct). *Governor Palin's (and
everybody else's) Popularity.* BizMediaScience.
(Http://bizmediascience.hungrypeasant.com/2015/03/14/
governor-palins-and-everybody-elses-popularity/)
151.   Carrabis, J. (2008, 21 May). *Meet Online Engagement's
Little Friend, Satisfaction.* AllBusiness.com.
(Http://www.allbusiness.com/marketing-
advertising/marketing-advertising/10174308–1.html)
152.   Carrabis, J. (2008, 31 July). *Programable method and
apparatus for real-time adaptation of presentations to
individuals (Patent #1).* US Patent Office (USPTO.GOV).
(Http://appft.uspto.gov/netacgi/nph-
Parser?Sect1=PTO2&Sect2=HITOFF&p=1&u=%2Fnetahtml
%2FPTO%2Fsearch-
bool.html&r=2&f=G&l=50&co1=AND&d=PG01&s1=Carrabi
s&OS=Carrabis&RS=Carrabis)
153.   Carrabis, J. (2008, 17 Mar). *Situational Awareness, Too
Much Information Too Fast, and Voting v Voting with your
Feet.* BizMediaScience.
(Http://bizmediascience.hungrypeasant.com/2015/01/29/
situational-awareness-too-much-information-too-fast-and-
voting-v-voting-with-your-feet/)
154.   Carrabis, J. (2008, 21 Jan). *VerizonWireless' 20 year plan.*
AllBusiness.com. (Http://www.allbusiness.com/media-
telecommunications/telecommunications/6347110–1.html)
155.   Carrabis, J. (2009/2015, 8 Sep/9 Jan). *Addendum to "I'm
the Intersection of Four Statements.".* BizMediaScience.
(Http://bizmediascience.hungrypeasant.com/2015/01/09/
addendum-to-im-the-intersection-of-four-statements/)

156.   Carrabis, J. (2009/2015, 10 Nov/22 Dec). *Counting Wristwatches at the SNCR Conference.* BizMediaScience. (Http://bizmediascience.hungrypeasant.com/2015/12/22/counting-wristwatches-at-the-sncr-conference/)

157.   Carrabis, J. (2009/2015, 5 Jun/8 Jan). *Sentiment Analysis, Anyone? (Part 1).* BizMediaScience. (Http://bizmediascience.hungrypeasant.com/2015/01/08/sentiment-analysis-anyone-part-1/)

158.   Carrabis, J. (2009, 12 Jun). *Canoeing with Stephane (Sentiment Analysis, Anyone? (Part 2)).* BizMediaScience. (Http://bizmediascience.hungrypeasant.com/2015/01/29/canoeing-with-stephane-sentiment-analysis-anyone-part-2/)

159.   Carrabis, J. (2009). *A Demonstration of Professional Test-Taker Bias in Web-Based Panels and Applications.* San Francisco, CA: Society for New Communications Research.

160.   Carrabis, J. (2009). *A Demonstration of Professional Test-Taker Bias in Web-Based Panels and Applications.* Nashua, NH: NextStage Evolution. (Http://www.nextstagevolution.com/membership.cfm)

161.   Carrabis, J. (2009). *Frequency of Blog Posts is Best Determined by Audience Size and Psychological Distance from the Author.* Scotsburn, NS: NextStage Evolution. (Http://www.nextstagevolution.com/membership.cfm)

162.   Carrabis, J. (2009, 18 Aug). *I'm the Intersection of Four Statements.* BizMediaScience. (Http://bizmediascience.hungrypeasant.com/2015/01/09/im-the-intersection-of-four-statements/)

163.   Carrabis, J. (2009, 1 Oct). *Learning to Use New Tools.* The Analytics Ecology. (Http://www.theanalyticsecology.com/?p=152)

164.   Carrabis, J. (2009). Machine Detection of and Response to User Non-Conscious Thought Processes to Increase Usability, Experience and Satisfaction - Case Studies and Examples. In *The 2nd International Multi-Conference on Engineering and Technological Innovation* (Vol. 3, pp. 69–

74). Orlando, FL: International Institute of Informatics and Systemics.

165.   Carrabis, J. (2009, 17 Aug). *They're Following Me! (More on Twitter)*. AllBusiness.com. (Http://www.allbusiness.com/population-demographics/population-size/12619840–1.html)

166.   Carrabis, J. (2010, 2 Feb). *Five Rules Re: Online Visibility Versus Privacy.* AllBusiness.com. (Http://www.allbusiness.com/population-demographics/population-size/13412393–1.html)

167.   Carrabis, J. (2010, 26 Oct). *Programmable method and apparatus for real-time adaptation of presentations to individuals (Patent #2).* US Patent Office (USPTO.GOV). (Http://patft.uspto.gov/netacgi/nph-Parser?Sect1=PTO2&Sect2=HITOFF&p=1&u=%2Fnetahtml%2FPTO%2Fsearch-bool.html&r=1&f=G&l=50&co1=AND&d=PTXT&s1=carrabis&OS=carrabis&RS=carrabis)

168.   Carrabis, J. (2011, 26 Apr). *I Can Crack My Knuckles Therefore I Must Be a Chiropractor! (Musings on Expertise).* TechnologyMarketers.com. (Http://technologymarketers.com/StatingTheObvious/i-can-crack-my-knuckles-therefore-i-must-be-a-chiropractor-musings-on-expertise/)

169.   Carrabis, J. (2012, 18 Dec). *System and Method for Obtaining Subtextual Information Regarding an Interaction Between an Individual and a Programmable Device (Patent #3).* US Patent Office (USPTO.GOV). (Http://appft.uspto.gov/netacgi/nph-Parser?Sect1=PTO2&Sect2=HITOFF&p=1&u=%2Fnetahtml%2FPTO%2Fsearch-bool.html&r=1&f=G&l=50&co1=AND&d=PG01&s1=Carrabis&OS=Carrabis&RS=Carrabis)

170.   Carrabis, J. (2013, 9 Oct). *Digital Divisivity.* An Economy of Meanings. (Http://aneconomyofmeaning.wordpress.com/2013/10/09/digital-divisivity/)

171. Carrabis, J. (2013, 23 Oct). *Joseph Carrabis' Under the Influence: Customer Service, Acquisition and Retention in the Age of Digital Divisivity.* IMediaConnection. (Http://blogs.imediaconnection.com/blog/2013/10/23/joseph-carrabis-under-the-influence-customer-service-acquisition-and-retention-in-the-age-of-digital-divisivity/)

172. Carrabis, J. (2013, 24 Apr). *Truth Be Told.* PersonalLifeMedia. (Http://think.personallifemedia.com/?p=526)

173. Carrabis, J. (2014, 5 Feb). *12 Mobile Marketing Secrets You Need to Know.* IMediaConnection. (Http://www.imediaconnection.com/content/35876.asp#multiview)

174. Carrabis, J. (2014, 10 Jul). *7 proven ways that facial cognition can drive business.* IMediaConnection. (Http://www.imediaconnection.com/content/36898.asp)

175. Carrabis, J. (2014, Dec). *Brilliantly Social – The Dancing Traffic Light.* BizMediaScience. (Http://bizmediascience.hungrypeasant.com/2014/12/29/brilliantly-social-the-dancing-traffic-light/)

176. Carrabis, J. (2014, 18 Feb). *System and method for determining a characteristic of an individual (Patent #4).* US Patent Office (USPTO.GOV). (Http://patft.uspto.gov/netacgi/nph-Parser?Sect1=PTO2&Sect2=HITOFF&p=1&u=%2Fnetahtml%2FPTO%2Fsearch-bool.html&r=1&f=G&l=50&co1=AND&d=PTXT&s1=8,655,804&OS=8,655,804&RS=8,655,804)

177. Carrabis, J. (2014, 4 Jun). *This puts a whole new meaning on impatience, doesn't it?.* LinkedIn. (Https://www.linkedin.com/today/post/article/20140604195942–112718-this-puts-a-whole-new-meaning-on-impatience-doesn-t-it?trk=mp-author-card)

178. Carrabis, J. (2015, 2 Mar). *Lock Your Brand into Consumers' Memory with The 3X Rule.* LinkedIn. (Https://www.linkedin.com/pulse/lock-your-brand-consumers-memory-3x-rule-joseph-carrabis)

179.   Carrabis, S. (2007). *DeBranding.* Hungry Peasant. (Http://bizmediascience.hungrypeasant.com/2015/01/05/debranding/)

180.   Carrier, D. R. (2011, 18 May). The Advantage of Standing Up to Fight and the Evolution of Habitual Bipedalism in Hominins. *PLoS ONE, 6*(5).

181.   Chambon, M. (2008, Jan). Embodied perception with others' bodies in mind: Stereotype priming influence on the perception of spatial environment. *Journal of Experimental Social Psychology, 45*(1), 283–287. (Http://www.sciencedirect.com/science?_ob=MImg&_imagekey=B6WJB-4TDK70V-3–5&_cdi=6874&_user=10&_orig=search&_coverDate=01%2F31%2F2009&_sk=999549998&view=c&wchp=dGLbVzW-zSkWA&md5=b1a78bae30578615af294c5e1ca517d5&ie=/sdarticle.pdf)

182.   Charron, S., & Koechlin, E. (2010, 16 Apr). Divided Representation of Concurrent Goals in the Human Frontal Lobes. *Science, 328*(5976), 360–363. (Http://www.sciencemag.org/content/328/5976/360.full.pdf)

183.   Chen, M. K. (2013). The Effect Of Language On Economic Behavior - Evidence From Savings Rates, Health Behaviors, And Retirement Assets. *American Economic Review.*

184.   Chicurel, M. (2002, 15 Mar). Neurons Weigh Options, Come to a Decision. *Science, 295*(5562), 1995b-1997. (Http://www.sciencemag.org/cgi/reprint/sci;295/5562/1995b.pdf)

185.   Chisholm, R., & Karrer, R. (1983). Movement-related brain potentials during hand squeezing in children and adults. *International Journal of Neuroscience, 19,* 243–58.

186.   Chisholm, R., & Karrer, R. (1988). Movement-related potentials and control of associated movements. *International Journal of Neuroscience, 42,* 131–48.

187. Chittka, L., & Dyer, A. (2012, 12 Jan). Your face looks familiar. *Nature, 481*(7380), 154–155. (Http://www.nature.com/nature/journal/v481/n7380/pdf/481154a.pdf)

188. Chris Fullwood, Mike Thelwall, & Sam O'Neill. (2011, 2 May). Clandestine chatters: Self-disclosure in U.K. chat room profiles. *First Monday, 16*(5). (Http://firstmonday.org/htbin/cgiwrap/bin/ojs/index.php/fm/article/view/3231/2954)

189. Clark, L., Ting, I.-H., Kimble, C., Wright, P., & Kudenko, D. (2006, Jan). Combining ethnographic and clickstream data to identify user Web browsing strategies. *informationresearch, 11*(2).

190. Cohen, G. L., Garcia, J., Purdie-Vaughns, V., Apfel, N., & Brzustoski, P. (2009, 17 Apr). Recursive Processes in Self-Affirmation: Intervening to Close the Minority Achievement Gap. *Science, 324*(5925), 400–403. (Http://www.sciencemag.org/cgi/reprint/sci;324/5925/400.pdf)

191. Cohn, A., Fehr, E., & Marechal, M. A. (2014, 4 Dec). Business culture and dishonesty in the banking industry. *Nature, 516*(7529), 86–89. (Http://www.nature.com/nature/journal/v516/n7529/pdf/nature13977.pdf)

192. Connor, C. E. (2010, 5 Nov). A New Viewpoint on Faces. *Science, 330*(6005), 764–765. (Http://www.sciencemag.org/content/330/6005/764.full.pdf)

193. Conway, C., Jones, B., DeBruine, L., & Little, A. (2008, 7 Jul). Evidence for adaptive design in human gaze preference. *Proceedings of the Royal Society B: Biological Sciences, 275*(1630), 63–69. (Http://rspb.royalsocietypublishing.org/content/275/1630/63.full.pdf+html)

194. Copas, G. M. (2003, Feb). Can Internet Shoppers Be Described by Personality Traits? *Usability News (Software Usability Research Laboratory (SURL) at Wichita State*

University), 5(1).
(Http://www.surl.org/usabilitynews/51/personality.asp)

195. Cox, D., Meyers, E., & Sinha, P. (2004, 2 Apr). Contextually Evoked Object-Specific Responses in Human Visual Cortex. *Science, 304*(5667), 115–117. (Http://www.sciencemag.org/cgi/reprint/sci;304/5667/115.pdf)

196. Cramer, P. (1999, Oct). Ego Functions and Ego Development: Defense Mechanisms and Intelligence as Predictors of Ego Level. *Journal of Personality, 67*(5), 735–760.

197. da Fontoura Costa, L., Oliveira, O. N., Jr., Travieso, G., Rodrigues, F. A., Boas, P. T. V., Antiqueira, L., et al. (2007). *Analyzing and Modeling Real-World Phenomena with Complex Networks: A Survey of Applications.* ArXiv:0711.3199v1.

198. Daniel Epstein. (2013). *The Sports Gene: : Inside the Science of Extraordinary Athletic Performance.* Current Hardcover. (Http://www.amazon.com/Sports-Gene-Extraordinary-Athletic-Performance/dp/1591845114/ref=tmm_hrd_title_0?_encoding=UTF8&sr=8–1&qid=1405017861)

199. Danziger, S., Levav, J., & Avnaim-Pesso, L. (2011, 26 Apr). Extraneous factors in judicial decisions. *Proceedings of the National Academy of Sciences, 108*(17), 6889–6892. (Http://www.pnas.org/content/108/17/6889.full.pdf+html)

200. Davidson, T. J., Kloosterman, F., & Wilson, M. A. (2009, 27 Aug). Hippocampal Replay of Extended Experience. *Neuron, 4,* 497–507. (Http://download.cell.com/neuron/pdf/PIIS0896627309005820.pdf)

201. Davies, J. (2014). *Riveted: The Science of Why Jokes Make Us Laugh, Movies Make Us Cry, and Religion Mkaes Us Feel One with the Universe.* Palgrave Macmillan.

202. Davis, N. (1984). *The Return of Martin Guerre*. Cambridge, MA: Harvard University Press.

203. Daw, N. D., & Dayan, P. (2004, 18 Jun). Matchmaking. *Science, 304*(5678), 1753–1754. (Http://www.sciencemag.org/cgi/reprint/304/5678/1753.pdf)

204. de Montjoye, Y.-A., Radaelli, L., Singh, V. K., & Pentland, A. .". (2015, 30 Jan). Unique in the shopping mall: On the reidentifiability of credit card metadata. *Science, 347*(6221), 536–539. (Http://www.sciencemag.org/content/347/6221/536.full.pdf)

205. De Smedt, J., & De Cruz, H. (2010, Dec). Toward an integrative approach of cognitive neuroscientific and evolutionary psychological studies of art. *Evolutionary Psychology, 8*(4), 695–719. (Http://www.epjournal.net/filestore/EP08695719.pdf?utm_source=MadMimi&utm_medium=email&utm_content=December+2010+Newsletter&utm_campaign=December+2010+Newsletter&utm_term=Toward+an+integrative+approach+of+cognitive+neuroscientific+and+evolutionary+psychological+studies+of+art_)

206. DeBruine, L. M., Jones, B. C., Crawford, J. R., Welling, L. L. M., & Little, A. C. (2010, 7 Aug). The health of a nation predicts their mate preferences: Cross-cultural variation in women's preferences for masculinized male faces. *Proceedings of the Royal Society B: Biological Sciences, 277*(1692), 2405–2410. (Http://rspb.royalsocietypublishing.org/content/277/1692/2405.full.pdf+html)

207. DeBruine, L. M., Jones, B. C., Little, A. C., Boothroyd, L. G., Perrett, D. I., Penton-Voak, I. S., et al. (2006, 7 Jun). Correlated preferences for facial masculinity and ideal or actual partner's masculinity. *Proceedings of the Royal Society B: Biological Sciences, 273*(1592), 1355–1360. (Http://rspb.royalsocietypublishing.org/content/273/1592/1355.full.pdf+html)

208. DeBruine, L. M., Jones, B. C., Little, A. C., Crawford, J. R., & Welling, L. L. M. (2011, 22 Mar). Further evidence for regional variation in women's masculinity preferences. *Proceedings of the Royal Society B: Biological Sciences, 278*(1707), 813–814. (Http://rspb.royalsocietypublishing.org/content/278/1707/813.full.pdf+html)

209. DeBruine, L. M. (2002, 7 Jul). Facial resemblance enhances trust. *Proceedings of the Royal Society of London. Series B: Biological Sciences, 269*(1498), 1307–1312. (Http://rspb.royalsocietypublishing.org/content/269/1498/1307.full.pdf+html)

210. DeBruine, L. M. (2004, 7 Oct). Facial resemblance increases the attractiveness of same-sex faces more than other-sex faces. *Proceedings of the Royal Society of London. Series B: Biological Sciences, 271*(1552), 2085–2090. (Http://rspb.royalsocietypublishing.org/content/271/1552/2085.full.pdf+html)

211. Decety, J., Grezes, J., Costes, N., Perani, D., Jeannerod, M., Procyk, E., et al. (1997). Brain activity during observation of actions (Influence of action content and subject's strategy). *Brain, 120,* 1763–1777.

212. Deecke, L. (1980). Influence of age on human cerebral potentials associated with voluntary movement. In D. G. Stein (Ed.), *The Psychobiology of Aging: Problems and Perspectives.* Elsevier.

213. Denning, S. (2014). An economy of access is opening for business: Five strategies for success. *Strategy and Leadership, 42*(4), 14–21. (Http://www.ingentaconnect.com/search/article?option1=tka&value1=%22sharing+economy%22&pageSize=10&index=4)

214. Dennis, C. (2004, 25 Mar). The sweet smell of success. *Nature, 428*(6981), 362–364.

(Http://www.nature.com/nature/journal/v428/n6981/pdf/
428362a.pdf)

215.   Desmurget, M., Reilly, K. T., Richard, N., Szathmari, A.,
       Mottolese, C., & Sirigu, A. (2009, 8 May). Movement
       Intention After Parietal Cortex Stimulation in Humans.
       Science, 324(5928), 811–813.
       (Http://www.sciencemag.org/cgi/reprint/sci;324/5928/81
       1.pdf)

216.   DeWeerdt, S. (2013, 23 May). The dark night.
       Nature, 497(7450), S14-S15.
       (Http://www.nature.com/nature/journal/v497/n7450_sup
       p/pdf/497S14a.pdf)

217.   Diedrichsen, J., Hashambhoy, Y., Rane, T., & Shadmehr,
       R. (2005, 26 Oct). Neural Correlates of Reach Errors. *The
       Journal of Neuroscience, 25*(43), 9919–9931.
       (Http://www.jneurosci.org/content/25/43/9919.full.pdf+ht
       ml)

218.   Diego A. Pizzagalli, R. J. S., Jeffrey B. Henriques. (2005,
       Oct). Frontal Brain Asymmetry and Reward
       Responsiveness. *Psychological Science, 16*(10), 805–813.
       (Http://www3.interscience.wiley.com/cgi-
       bin/fulltext/118661664/PDFSTART)

219.   Dixson, B., Grimshaw, G., Linklater, W., & Dixson, A.
       (2011, 1 Feb). Eye Tracking of Men's Preferences for
       Female Breast Size and Areola Pigmentation. *Archives of
       Sexual Behavior, 40*(1), 51–58. Springer Netherlands.

220.   Dixson, B., Grimshaw, G., Linklater, W., & Dixson, A.
       (2011, 1 Feb). Eye-Tracking of Men's Preferences for
       Waist-to-Hip Ratio and Breast Size of Women. *Archives of
       Sexual Behavior, 40*(1), 43–50. Springer Netherlands.

221.   Dobbins, I. G., Schnyer, D. M., Verfaellie, M., & Schacter,
       D. L. (2004, 18 Mar). Cortical activity reductions during
       repetition priming can result from rapid response learning.
       Nature, 428(6980), 316–319.
       (Http://www.nature.com/nature/journal/v428/n6980/pdf/
       nature02400.pdf)

222.   Dodds, P. S., Muhamad, R., & Watts, D. J. (2003, 8 Aug).
        An Experimental Study of Search in Global Social
        Networks. *Science, 301*(5634), 827–829.
        (Http://www.sciencemag.org/cgi/reprint/sci;301/5634/82
        7.pdf)

223.   Donoso, M., Collins, A. G. E., & Koechlin, E. (2014, 27
        Jun). Foundations of human reasoning in the prefrontal
        cortex. *Science, 344*(6191), 1481–1486.
        (Http://www.sciencemag.org/content/344/6191/1481.full.
        pdf)

224.   Dovidio, J. F. (2009, 18 Dec). Racial Bias, Unspoken But
        Heard. *Science, 326*(5960), 1641–1642.
        (Http://www.sciencemag.org/cgi/reprint/sci;326/5960/16
        41.pdf)

225.   Draaisma, D. (2001, 8 Nov). The tracks of thought.
        Nature, 414(6860), 153–153.
        (Http://www.nature.com/nature/journal/v414/n6860/pdf/
        414153a0.pdf)

226.   Dutton, W. H., & Shepherd, A. (2003). *Trust in the
        Internet: The Social Dynamics of an Experience
        Technology.* Oxford Internet Institute. University of
        Oxford: Oxford Internet Institute.
        (Http://www.oii.ox.ac.uk/resources/publications/RR3.pdf)

227.   Edward M. Bowden, & Mark Jung Beeman. (1998). Getting
        the Right Idea: Semantic Activation in the Right
        HemisphereMay Help Solve Insight Problems. *Psychological
        Science, 9*(6), 435–440.
        (Http://www3.interscience.wiley.com/cgi-
        bin/fulltext/119129846/PDFSTART)

228.   Eisenstein, M. (2013, 23 May). Stepping out of time.
        Nature, 497(7450), S10-S12.
        (Http://www.nature.com/nature/journal/v497/n7450_sup
        p/pdf/497S10a.pdf)

229.   Ellison, N., Heino, R., & Gibbs, J. (2006). Managing
        Impressions Online: Self-Presentation Processes in the
        Online Dating Environment. *Journal of Computer-Mediated
        Communication, 11*, 415–441.

230. Emlen, S. T. (1995, 29 Aug). An evolutionary theory of the family. *Proceedings of the National Academy of Sciences of the United States of America, 92*(18), 8092–8099. (Http://www.pnas.org/content/92/18/8092.full.pdf+html)

231. Engeström, Y., Engeström, R., & Kärkkäinen, M. (1995, Dec). Polycontextuality and boundary crossing in expert cognition: Learning and problem solving in complex work activities. *Learning and Instruction, 5*(4), 319–336. (Http://www.sciencedirect.com/science/article/pii/095947 5295000216)

232. Epstein, R., & Robertson, R. E. (2015, 18 Aug). The search engine manipulation effect (SEME) and its possible impact on the outcomes of elections. *Proceedings of the National Academy of Sciences, 112*(33), E4512-E4521. (Http://www.pnas.org/content/112/33/E4512.full.pdf)

233. Epstein, R., & Kanwisher, N. (1998, 9 April). A cortical representation of the local visual environment. *Nature, 392,* 598–601.

234. Ericsson, K. A., & Ward, P. (2007/12/01). Capturing the Naturally Occurring Superior Performance of Experts in the Laboratory: Toward a Science of Expert and Exceptional Performance. *Current Directions in Psychological Science, 16*(6), 346–350. (Http://cdp.sagepub.com/content/16/6/346.full.pdf+html)

235. Etcoff, N. (1999). *Survival of the Prettiest: The Science of Beauty.* NYC: Doubleday.

236. Ethofer, T., Van De Ville, D., Scherer, K., & Vuilleumier, P. (2009, 23 Jun). Decoding of Emotional Information in Voice-Sensitive Cortices. *Current Biology, 19*(12), 1028–1033. (Http://www.sciencedirect.com/science?_ob=ArticleURL&_ udi=B6VRT-4W929HC-4&_user=10&_coverDate=06%2F23%2F2009&_rdoc=1&_f mt=high&_orig=browse&_sort=d&view=c&_acct=C000050 221&_version=1&_urlVersion=0&_userid=10&md5=a57e0 7a3255950cfe2327d7f453d588e)

237.   Eysel, U. T. (2003, 31 Oct). Illusions and Perceived
        Images in the Primate Brain. *Science, 302*(5646), 789–
        791.
        (Http://www.sciencemag.org/cgi/reprint/sci;302/5646/78
        9.pdf)
238.   Fara, P. (2003, 7 Feb). Face Values: How Portraits Win
        Friends and Influence People. *Science, 299*(5608), 831–
        832.
        (Http://www.sciencemag.org/cgi/reprint/sci;299/5608/83
        1.pdf)
239.   Faris, R., & Felmlee, D. (2011, Feb). Network Centrality
        and Gender Segregation in Same- and Cross-Gender
        Aggression. *American Sociological Review.*
        (Http://www.asanet.org/images/journals/docs/pdf/Faris_F
        elmleeASRFeb11.pdf)
240.   Fast, N. J., & Tiedens, L. Z. (2010, Jan). Blame contagion:
        The automatic transmission of self-serving attributions.
        Journal of Experimental Social Psychology, 46(1), 97–106.
        (Http://www.sciencedirect.com/science?_ob=MImg&_imag
        ekey=B6WJB-4XGBG5S-1–
        7&_cdi=6874&_user=10&_pii=S0022103109002601&_ori
        gin=search&_zone=rslt_list_item&_coverDate=01%2F31
        %2F2010&_sk=999539998&wchp=dGLbVzW-
        zSkWA&md5=b1c159f3a704d634f53f77cebca90880&ie=/s
        darticle.pdf)
241.   Fenske, M. J., Raymond, J. E., Kessler, K., Westoby, N., &
        Tipper, S. E. (2005, Oct). Attentional Inhibition Has Social-
        Emotional Consequences for Unfamiliar Faces.
        Psychological Science, 16(10), 753–758.
        (Http://www3.interscience.wiley.com/cgi-
        bin/fulltext/118661655/PDFSTART)
242.   Fenske, M. J., & Raymond, J. E. (2006). Affective
        Influences of Selective Attention. *Current Directions in
        Psychological Science, 15*(6), 312–316.
        (Http://www3.interscience.wiley.com/cgi-
        bin/fulltext/118584121/PDFSTART)

243.   Ferster, D. (2004, 12 Mar). Blocking Plasticity in the Visual
        Cortex. *Science, 303*(5664), 1619–1621.
        (Http://www.sciencemag.org/cgi/reprint/303/5664/1619.p
        df)
244.   Fiedler, K. (2008, 1 Jan). Language: A Toolbox for Sharing
        and Influencing Social Reality. *Perspectives on
        Psychological Science, 3*(1), 38–47.
        (Http://pps.sagepub.com/content/3/1/38.full.pdf+html)
245.   Fitch, W. T. (2007, 11 Oct). An invisible hand.
        Nature, 449(7163), 665–667.
        (Http://www.nature.com/nature/journal/v449/n7163/pdf/
        449665a.pdf)
246.   Fraccaro, P. J., Feinberg, D. R., DeBruine, L. M., Little, A.
        C., Watkins, C. D., & Jones, B. C. (2010, Sep). Correlated
        Male Preferences for Femininity in Female Faces and
        Voices. *Evolutionary Psychology, 8*(3), 447–461.
        (Http://www.epjournal.net/filestore/EP08447461.pdf?utm
        _source=MadMimi&utm_medium=email&utm_content=Se
        ptember+2010+Newsletter&utm_campaign=September+2
        010+Newsletter&utm_term=Correlated%2Bmale%2Bprefe
        rences%2Bfor%2Bfemininity%2Bin%2Bfemale%2Bfaces%
        2Band%2Bvoices_)
247.   Francois-Lechanche, X. (1993). *L'ecornifleur d'Artigat:
        Histoire apocryphe de Martin Guerre.* Parage.
248.   Freedman, M. S., Lucas, R. J., Soni, B., von Schantz, M.,
        Mu&ntilde, oz, M., et al. (1999, 16 Apr). Regulation of
        Mammalian Circadian Behavior by Non-rod, Non-cone,
        Ocular Photoreceptors. *Science, 284*(5413), 502–504.
        (Http://www.sciencemag.org/cgi/reprint/sci;284/5413/50
        2.pdf)
249.   Froehler, M. T., & Duffy, C. J. (2002, 29 Mar). Cortical
        Neurons Encoding Path and Place: Where You Go Is Where
        You Are. *Science, 295*(5564), 2462–2465.
        (Http://www.sciencemag.org/cgi/reprint/sci;295/5564/24
        62.pdf)
250.   Fu, Y.-X., Djupsund, K., Gao, H., Hayden, B., Shen, K., &
        Dan, Y. (2002, 14 Jun). Temporal Specificity in the Cortical

Plasticity of Visual Space Representation.
Science, 296(5575), 1999–2003.
(Http://www.sciencemag.org/cgi/reprint/296/5575/1999.p
df)

251. Fukunaga, K. (1990). *Introduction to Statistical Pattern Recognition.* San Diego, CA: Academic Press.

252. Fukushima, K., Yamanobe, T., Shinmei, Y., Fukushima, J., Kurkin, S., & Peterson, B. W. (2002, 12 Sep). Coding of smooth eye movements in three-dimensional space by frontal cortex. *Nature, 419*(6903), 157–162.
(Http://www.nature.com/nature/journal/v419/n6903/pdf/
nature00953.pdf)

253. Furlong, E. E., & Opfer, J. E. (2009). Cognitive Constraints on How Economic Rewards Affect Cooperation.
Psychological Science, p. 8.

254. Fyhn, M., Molden, S., Witter, M. P., Moser, E. I., & Moser, M.-B. (2004, 27 Aug). Spatial Representation in the Entorhinal Cortex. *Science, 305*(5688), 1258–1264.
(Http://www.sciencemag.org/cgi/reprint/305/5688/1258.p
df)

255. Gaffan, D. (2005, 30 Sep). Widespread Cortical Networks Underlie Memory and Attention.
Science, 309(5744), 2172–2173.
(Http://www.sciencemag.org/cgi/reprint/309/5744/2172.p
df)

256. Gallagher, S. (2001). The Practice of Mind (Theory, Simulation or Primary Interaction). *Journal of Consciousness Studies, 8*(5–7), 83–108.

257. Ganel, T., & Goodale, M. A. (2003, 11 Dec). Visual control of action but not perception requires analytical processing of object shape. *Nature, 426*(6967), 664–667.
(Http://www.nature.com/nature/journal/v426/n6967/pdf/
nature02156.pdf)

258. Gardner, H. E. (2000). *Intelligence Reframed: Multiple Intelligences for the 21st Century.* Basic Books.
(Http://www.amazon.com/Intelligence-Reframed-Multiple-
Intelligences-

Century/dp/0465026117/ref=sr_1_1?s=books&ie=UTF8&q
id=1449594409&sr=1–
1&keywords=intelligence+reframed)
259. Gilbert, D. T., Killingsworth, M. A., Eyre, R. N., & Wilson,
      T. D. (2009, 20 Mar). The Surprising Power of Neighborly
      Advice. *Science, 323*(5921), 1617–1619.
      (Http://www.sciencemag.org/cgi/reprint/sci;323/5921/16
      17.pdf)
260. Gold, J. I., & Shadlen, M. N. (2000, 23 Mar).
      Representation of a perceptual decision in developing
      oculomotor commands. *Nature, 404*(6776), 390–394.
261. Golder, S. A., & Macy, M. W. (2011, 30 Sep). Diurnal and
      Seasonal Mood Vary with Work, Sleep, and Daylength
      Across Diverse Cultures. *Science, 333*(6051), 1878–1881.
      (Http://www.sciencemag.org/content/333/6051/1878.full.
      pdf)
262. Goldin-Meadow, S. (2003). *Hearing Gesture: How our
      Hands Help us Think.* Cambridge, MA: Harvard University
      Press.
263. Gore, J., & McAndrew, C. (2009, Mar). Accessing Expert
      Cognition. *The Psychologist, 22,* 218–219.
      (Http://www.thepsychologist.org.uk/archive/archive_home
      .cfm?volumeID=22&editionID=173&ArticleID=1483)
264. Le Grand, R., Mondloch, C. J., Maurer, D., & Brent, H. P.
      (2001, 19 Apr). Early visual experience and face
      processing. *Nature, 410*(6831), 890–890.
      (Http://www.nature.com/nature/journal/v410/n6831/pdf/
      410890a0.pdf)
265. Granovetter, M. (2003, 8 Aug). Ignorance, Knowledge, and
      Outcomes in a Small World. *Science, 301*(5634), 773–774.
      (Http://www.sciencemag.org/cgi/reprint/sci;301/5634/77
      3.pdf)
266. Green, C. B., & Menaker, M. (2003, 18 Jul). Clocks on the
      Brain. *Science, 301*(5631), 319–320.
      (Http://www.sciencemag.org/cgi/reprint/sci;301/5631/31
      9.pdf)

267.   Greenfield, P. M. (2009, 2 Jan). Technology and Informal
        Education: What Is Taught, What Is Learned.
        Science, 323(5910), 69–71.
        (Http://www.sciencemag.org/cgi/reprint/323/5910/69.pdf
)
268.   Greenspan, S. I., M.D., & Shanker, S. G., D. Phil. (2004).
        *The First Idea: How Symbols, Language, and Intelligence
        Evolved from Our Primate Ancestors to Modern Humans.*
        Da Capo Press.
        (Http://www.amazon.com/gp/product/0306814498?keywo
        rds=the%20first%20idea&qid=1444753591&ref_=sr_1_1
        &sr=8–1)
269.   Griffiths, T. L. (2015, Mar). Revealing ontological
        commitments by magic. *Cognition, 136*(0), 43–48.
        (Https://www.google.com/url?sa=t&rct=j&q=&esrc=s&sou
        rce=web&cd=1&cad=rja&uact=8&ved=0CB8QFjAA&url=ht
        tps%3A%2F%2Fcocosci.berkeley.edu%2Ftom%2Fpapers
        %2Fmagic.pdf&ei=P6FLVeHGKojZoASHxoCYDg&usg=AFQj
        CNHnZ2Zk7I95ZkN8FusbJoP337YwXA&bvm=bv.92765956
        ,d.cGU)
270.   Gwen Shaffer. (2011, 2 May). Banding together for
        bandwidth: An analysis of survey results from wireless
        community network participants. *First Monday, 16*(5).
        (Http://firstmonday.org/htbin/cgiwrap/bin/ojs/index.php/f
        m/article/view/3331/2956)
271.   Haarmeier, T., Bunjes, F., Lindner, A., Berret, E., & Thier,
        P. (2001, 8 Nov). Optimizing Visual Motion Perception
        during Eye Movements. *Neuron, 32*(3), 527–535.
        (Http://download.cell.com/neuron/pdf/PIIS089662730100
        486X.pdf)
272.   Hafting, T., Fyhn, M., Molden, S., Moser, M.-B., & Moser,
        E. I. (2005, 11 Aug). Microstructure of a spatial map in the
        entorhinal cortex. *Nature, 436*(7052), 801–806.
        (Http://www.nature.com/nature/journal/v436/n7052/pdf/
        nature03721.pdf)
273.   Haggard, P. (2009, 8 May). The Sources of Human
        Volition. *Science, 324*(5928), 731–733.

(Http://www.sciencemag.org/cgi/reprint/324/5928/731.pd
f)

274. Hagoort, P., & Levelt, W. J. M. (2009, 16 Oct). The
      Speaking Brain. *Science, 326*(5951), 372–373.
      (Http://www.sciencemag.org/cgi/reprint/sci;326/5951/37
      2.pdf)

275. Hallerberg, S., & Kantz H. (2008, 29 Jan). When are
      Extreme Events the better predictable, the larger they are?
      arXiv:0801.4525, 1, 14.

276. Hampson, R. E., Simeral, J. D., & Deadwyler, S. A. (1999,
      9 Dec). Distribution of spatial and nonspatial information
      in dorsal hippocampus. *Nature, 402*(6762), 610–614.
      (Http://www.nature.com/nature/journal/v402/n6762/pdf/
      402610a0.pdf)

277. Hang-Hyun Jo and MÃirton Karsai and JÃinos KertÃ©sz
      and Kimmo Kaski. (2012, Jan). Circadian pattern and
      burstiness in mobile phone communication. *New Journal of
      Physics, 14*(1), 013055. (Http://iopscience.iop.org/1367–
      2630/14/1/013055/pdf/1367–2630_14_1_013055.pdf)

278. Hare, T. (2014, 27 Jun). Exploiting and exploring the
      options. *Science, 344*(6191), 1446–1447.
      (Http://www.sciencemag.org/content/344/6191/1446.full.
      pdf)

279. Hartley, T., Maguire, E. A., Spiers, H. J., & Burgess, N.
      (2003, 6 Mar). The Well-Worn Route and the Path Less
      Traveled: Distinct Neural Bases of Route Following and
      Wayfinding in Humans. *Neuron, 37*(5), 877–888.
      (Http://linkinghub.elsevier.com/retrieve/pii/S0896627303
      000953)

280. Harvey, C. D., Collman, F., Dombeck, D. A., & Tank, D. W.
      (2009, 15 Oct). Intracellular dynamics of hippocampal
      place cells during virtual navigation.
      Nature, 461(7266), 941–946.
      (Http://www.nature.com/nature/journal/v461/n7266/pdf/
      nature08499.pdf)

281. Hasselmo, M. E. (2008, 7 Aug). The Scale of Experience.
      Science, 321(5885), 46–47.

(Http://www.sciencemag.org/content/321/5885/46.full.pd
f)
282.   Hasson, U., Nir, Y., Levy, I., Fuhrmann, G., & Malach, R.
(2004, 12 Mar). Intersubject Synchronization of Cortical
Activity During Natural Vision. *Science, 303*(5664), 1634–
1640.
(Http://www.sciencemag.org/cgi/reprint/sci;303/5664/16
34.pdf)
283.   Hauert, C., & Doebeli, M. (2004, 8 Apr). Spatial structure
often inhibits the evolution of cooperation in the snowdrift
game. *Nature, 428*(6983), 643–646.
(Http://www.nature.com/nature/journal/v428/n6983/pdf/
nature02360.pdf)
284.   Havlin, S. (2009, 22 May). Phone Infections.
Science, 324(5930), 1023–1024.
(Http://www.sciencemag.org/cgi/reprint/324/5930/1023.p
df)
285.   Haxby, J. V., Gobbini, M. I., Furey, M. L., Ishai, A.,
Schouten, J. L., & Pietrini, P. (2001, 28 Sep). Distributed
and Overlapping Representations of Faces and Objects in
Ventral Temporal Cortex. *Science, 293*(5539), 2425–2430.
(Http://www.sciencemag.org/cgi/reprint/sci;293/5539/24
25.pdf)
286.   Hayden, B. Y., Pearson, J. M., & Platt, M. L. (2009, 15
May). Fictive Reward Signals in the Anterior Cingulate
Cortex. *Science, 324*(5929), 948–950.
(Http://www.sciencemag.org/cgi/reprint/sci;324/5929/94
8.pdf)
287.   He, S., Dong, W., Deng, Q., Weng, S., & Sun, W. (2003,
17 Oct). Seeing More Clearly: Recent Advances in
Understanding Retinal Circuitry. *Science, 302*(5644), 408–
411.
(Http://www.sciencemag.org/cgi/reprint/sci;302/5644/40
8.pdf)
288.   Henkel, L. A. (2014, 1 Feb). Point-and-Shoot Memories:
The Influence of Taking Photos on Memory for a Museum

Tour. *Psychological Science, 25*(2), 396–402.
(Http://pss.sagepub.com/content/25/2/396.full.pdf+html)

289. Henrich, J. (2014, 9 May). Rice, Psychology, and
      Innovation. *Science, 344*(6184), 593–594.
      (Http://www.sciencemag.org/content/344/6184/603.full.p
      df)

290. Henson, R., Shallice, T., & Dolan, R. (2000, 18 Feb).
      Neuroimaging Evidence for Dissociable Forms of Repetition
      Priming. *Science, 287*(5456), 1269–1272.
      (Http://www.sciencemag.org/content/287/5456/1269.full.
      pdf)

291. Herbert, W. (2007, Aug). How Beliefs About the Self Shape
      Personality and Behavior. *APS Observer.*
      (Http://www.psychologicalscience.org/observer/getArticle.
      cfm?id=2187)

292. Hernández, A., Zainos, A., & Romo, R. (2002, 14 Mar).
      Temporal Evolution of a Decision-Making Process in Medial
      Premotor Cortex. *Neuron, 33*(6), 959–972.
      (Http://www.sciencedirect.com/science?_ob=MImg&_imag
      ekey=B6WSS-47MC579-D-
      3&_cdi=7054&_user=10&_orig=search&_coverDate=03%
      2F14%2F2002&_sk=999669993&view=c&wchp=dGLzVtb-
      zSkzk&md5=213a3365b29e25dcb74f5a9307df5ef5&ie=/s
      darticle.pdf)

293. Heyman, K. (2006, 4 Aug). Making Connections.
      Science, 313(5787), 604–606.
      (Http://www.sciencemag.org/content/313/5787/604.full.p
      df)

294. Heyman, K. (2006, 5 May). The Map in the Brain: Grid
      Cells May Help Us Navigate. *Science, 312*(5774), 680–681.
      (Http://www.sciencemag.org/cgi/reprint/312/5774/680.pd
      f)

295. Hickok, G. (2014). *The Myth of Mirror Neurons.* W.W.
      Norton & Co. (Http://www.amazon.com/Myth-Mirror-
      Neurons-Neuroscience-
      Communication/dp/0393089614/ref=sr_1_1?ie=UTF8&qid

=1441125903&sr=8–
1&keywords=the+myth+of+mirror+neurons)

296. Hindi Attar, C., MÃ¼ller, M. M., Andersen, S. K., BÃ¼chel,
      C., & Rose, M. (2010, 14 Apr). Emotional Processing in a
      Salient Motion Context: Integration of Motion and Emotion
      in Both V5/hMT+ and the Amygdala. *The Journal of
      Neuroscience, 30*(15), 5204–5210.
      (Http://www.jneurosci.org/content/30/15/5204.full.pdf+ht
      ml)

297. Hinkle, V. (2009, Oct). Using Tag Clouds to Visualize Text
      Data Patterns. *Usability News (Software Usability Research
      Laboratory (SURL) at Wichita State University), 11*(1).
      (Http://www.surl.org/usabilitynews/111/pdf/Usability%20
      News%20111%20-%20Hinkle.pdf)

298. Hodgson D. (2002). Three Tricks of Consciousness Qualia,
      Chunking and Selection. *Journal of Consciousness
      Studies, 9*(12), 65–88.

299. Hodkinson, C., & Kiel, G. (2006). WWW Consumer
      External Information Search: Do Traditional Predictors of
      Search Apply in this New Information Environment?
      University of Queensland.

300. Holden, C. (2001, 2 Nov). 'Behavioral' Addictions: Do They
      Exist? *Science, 294*(5544), 980–982.
      (Http://www.sciencemag.org/cgi/reprint/294/5544/980.pd
      f)

301. Horowitz, T. S., & Wolfe, J. M. (1998). Visual Search has
      no memory. *Nature, 394,* 575–577.

302. Hulleman, C. S., & Harackiewicz, J. M. (2009, 4 Dec).
      Promoting Interest and Performance in High School
      Science Classes. *Science, 326*(5958), 1410–1412.
      (Http://www.sciencemag.org/cgi/reprint/sci;326/5958/14
      10.pdf)

303. Huxter, J., Burgess, N., & O'Keefe, J. (2003, 23 Oct).
      Independent rate and temporal coding in hippocampal
      pyramidal cells. *Nature, 425*(6960), 828–832.
      (Http://www.nature.com/nature/journal/v425/n6960/pdf/
      nature02058.pdf)

304.   Iacoboni, M., Woods, R. P., Brass, M., Bekkering, H.,
        Mazziotta, J. C., & Rizzolatti, G. (1999, 24 Dec). Cortical
        Mechanisms of Human Imitation. *Science, 286,* 2526–
        2528.
        (Http://www.sciencemag.org/cgi/reprint/286/5449/2526.p
        df)
305.   Izquierdo, I., & Cammarota, M. (2004, 7 May). Zif and the
        Survival of Memory. *Science, 304*(5672), 829–830.
        (Http://www.sciencemag.org/cgi/reprint/304/5672/829.pd
        f)
306.   Jack P. Manno. (2010). Commoditization and oppression.
        *Annals of the New York Academy of
        Sciences, 1185*(Ecological Economics Reviews), 164–178.
307.   Jaffe, E. (2010, Dec). The Psychological Study of Smiling.
        APS observer, 23(10).
        (Http://www.psychologicalscience.org/index.php/publicati
        ons/observer/2010/december-10/the-psychological-study-
        of-smiling.html#.ULTquWdB5eU)
308.   Jaffe, E. (2011, Oct). The Complicated Psychology of
        Revenge. *APS Observer, 24.*
        (Http://www.psychologicalscience.org/index.php/publicati
        ons/observer/2011/october-11/the-complicated-
        psychology-of-revenge.html)
309.   Jaffe, E. (2011, Mar). Monkey Business. *APS
        Observer, 24*(3).
        (Http://www.psychologicalscience.org/index.php/publicati
        ons/observer/2011/march-11/monkey-
        business.html#.ULN8qWdB4xM)
310.   Jaffe, E. (2011, Mar). Remember When? *APS
        Observer, 24*(3).
        (Http://www.psychologicalscience.org/index.php/publicati
        ons/observer/2011/march-11/remember-
        when.html#.ULN4mmdB4xM)
311.   Johansson, P., Hall, L., Sikstrom, S., & Olsson, A. (2005, 7
        Oct). Failure to Detect Mismatches Between Intention and
        Outcome in a Simple Decision Task.
        Science, 310(5745), 116–119.

(Http://www.sciencemag.org/cgi/reprint/310/5745/116.pd
f)

312.   Johnstone, R. A., & Manica, A. (2011, 17 May). Evolution
        of personality differences in leadership. *Proceedings of the
        National Academy of Sciences, 108*(20), 8373–8378.
        (Http://www.pnas.org/content/108/20/8373.full.pdf+html
)

313.   Jones, B. C., DeBruine, L. M., Little, A. C., Burriss, R. P., &
        Feinberg, D. R. (2007, 22 Mar). Social transmission of face
        preferences among humans. *Proceedings of the Royal
        Society B: Biological Sciences, 274*(1611), 899–903.
        (Http://rspb.royalsocietypublishing.org/content/274/1611/
        899.full.pdf+html)

314.   Jones, B. C., Main, J. C., DeBruine, L. M., Little, A. C., &
        Welling, L. L. (2010, 1 Jun). Reading the Look of Love:
        Sexually Dimorphic Cues in Opposite-Sex Faces Influence
        Gaze Categorization. *Psychological Science, 21*(6), 796–
        798.
        (Http://pss.sagepub.com/content/21/6/796.full.pdf+html)

315.   Justin Storbeck, G. L. C. (2005, Oct). With Sadness Comes
        Accuracy; With Happiness, False Memory. *Psychological
        Science, 16*(10), 785–791.
        (Http://www3.interscience.wiley.com/cgi-
        bin/fulltext/118661661/PDFSTART)

316.   Kahan, D. (2010, 21 Jan). Fixing the communications
        failure. *Nature, 463*(7279), 296–297.
        (Http://www.nature.com/nature/journal/v463/n7279/pdf/
        463296a.pdf)

317.   Kahn, H. S., Ravindranath, R., Valdez, R., & Narayan, K.
        (2001). Fingerprint Ridge-Count Difference between
        Adjacent Fingertips (dR45) Predicts Upper-Body Tissue
        Distribution: Evidence for Early Gestational Programming.
        American Journal of Epidemiology, 153(4), 338–344.
        (Http://aje.oxfordjournals.org/content/153/4/338.full.pdf
        +html)

318.   Kaminski, G., Dridi, S., Graff, C., & Gentaz, E. (2009, 7
        Jul). Human ability to detect kinship in strangers' faces:

Effects of the degree of relatedness. *Proceedings of the Royal Society B: Biological Sciences, 276*(1670), 3193–3200.
(Http://rspb.royalsocietypublishing.org/content/276/1670/3193.full.pdf+html)

319.   Kanai, R., Feilden, T., Firth, C., & Rees, G. (2011, 26 Apr). Political Orientations Are Correlated with Brain Structure in Young Adults. *Current biology: CB, 21*(8), 677–680.
(Http://download.cell.com/current-biology/pdf/PIIS0960982211002892.pdf)

320.   Kara, P., & Boyd, J. D. (2009, 2 Apr). A micro-architecture for binocular disparity and ocular dominance in visual cortex. *Nature, 458*(7238), 627–631.
(Http://www.nature.com/nature/journal/v458/n7238/pdf/nature07721.pdf)

321.   Kaufman, M. T., & Churchland, A. K. (2013, 11 Apr). Sensory noise drives bad decisions.
Nature, 496(7444), 172–173.
(Http://www.nature.com/nature/journal/v496/n7444/pdf/496172a.pdf)

322.   Kaufmann, A. (1985). *Introduction to fuzzy arithmetic: Theory and applications (Van Nostrand Reinhold electrical/computer science and engineering series).* Van Nostrand Reinhold Co.
(Http://www.amazon.com/Introduction-fuzzy-arithmetic-applications-engineering/dp/0442230079)

323.   Kawakami, K., Dunn, E., Karmali, F., & Dovidio, J. F. (2009, 9 Jan). Mispredicting Affective and Behavioral Responses to Racism. *Science, 323*(5911), 276–278.
(Http://www.sciencemag.org/cgi/reprint/323/5911/276.pdf)

324.   Kätsyri, J., Hari, R., Ravaja, N., & Nummenmaa, L. (2013, 13 Jun). Just watching the game ain't enough: Striatal fMRI reward responses to successes and failures in a video game during active and vicarious playing. *Frontiers in Human Neuroscience, 7.*
(Http://www.frontiersin.org/Journal/DownloadFile.ashx?pd

f=1&FileId=258811&articleId=51641&Version=1&Content
TypeId=21&FileName=fnhum-07-00278.pdf)

325.   Kelley, T. C., & Hare, J. F. (2010). Pair-bonded humans
       conform to sexual stereotypes in web-based
       advertisements for extra-marital partners. *Evolutionary
       Psychology, 8*(4), 561–572.
       (Http://www.epjournal.net/filestore/EP085615722.pdf?ut
       m_source=MadMimi&utm_medium=email&utm_content=
       November+2010+Newsletter&utm_campaign=November+
       2010+Newsletter&utm_term=Pair-
       bonded+humans+conform+to+sexual+stereotypes+in+w
       eb-based+advertisements+for+extra-marital+partners_)

326.   Kemp, M. (2009, 15 Oct). Art history's window onto the
       mind. *Nature, 461*(7266), 882–883.
       (Http://www.nature.com/nature/journal/v461/n7266/pdf/
       461882a.pdf)

327.   Kikutani, M., Roberson, D., & Hanley, J. (2010, 1 Jun).
       Categorical Perception for Unfamiliar Faces: The Effect of
       Covert and Overt Face Learning. *Psychological
       Science, 21*(6), 865–872.
       (Http://pss.sagepub.com/content/21/6/865.full.pdf+html)

328.   Killian, N. J., Jutras, M. J., & Buffalo, E. A. (2012, 29 Nov).
       A map of visual space in the primate entorhinal cortex.
       Nature, 491(7426), 761–764.
       (Http://www.nature.com/nature/journal/v491/n7426/pdf/
       nature11587.pdf)

329.   Kim, A. S., Vallesi, A., Picton, T. W., & Tulving, E. (2009,
       Dec). Cognitive association formation in episodic memory:
       Evidence from event-related potentials.
       Neuropsychologia, 47(14), 3162–3173.
       (Http://www.sciencedirect.com/science/article/pii/S00283
       93209003108)

330.   Kimura, M., & Takeda, Y. (2013, 12 Jun). Task difficulty
       affects the predictive process indexed by visual mismatch
       negativity. *Frontiers in Human Neuroscience, 7.*
       (Http://www.frontiersin.org/Journal/DownloadFile.ashx?pd

f=1&FileId=257783&articleId=51841&Version=1&Content TypeId=21&FileName=fnhum-07-00267.pdf)

331.   Kirrane, E., & Carrabis, J. (2011, 28 Jan). *Joseph Carrabis - Fear Álainn.* Crepuscular Light.
       (Http://www.emerkirrane.com/2011/01/28/joseph-carrabis-fear-alainn/)

332.   Kitagawa, N., & Ichihara, S. (2002, 14 Mar). Hearing visual motion in depth. *Nature, 416*(6877), 172–174.
       (Http://www.nature.com/nature/journal/v416/n6877/pdf/416172a.pdf)

333.   Kjelstrup, K. B., Solstad, T., Brun, V. H., Hafting, T., Leutgeb, S., Witter, M. P., et al. (2008, 7 Apr). Finite Scale of Spatial Representation in the Hippocampus.
       Science, 321(5885), 140–143.
       (Http://www.sciencemag.org/content/321/5885/140.full.pdf)

334.   Knierim, J. J. (2009, 27 Aug). Imagining the Possibilities: Ripples, Routes, and Reactivation. *Neuron, 63*(4), 421–423.
       (Http://download.cell.com/neuron/pdf/PIIS089662730900587X.pdf)

335.   Knight, J. (2003, 23 Jan). Meeting aims to find brain's benchmarks for beauty. *Nature, 421*(6921), 305–305.
       (Http://www.nature.com/nature/journal/v421/n6921/pdf/421305b.pdf)

336.   Koechlin, E., & Hyafil, A. (2007, 26 Oct). Anterior Prefrontal Function and the Limits of Human Decision-Making. *Science, 318*(5850), 594–598.

337.   Koivisto, M., & Revonsuo, A. (2007, 1 Oct). How Meaning Shapes Seeing. *Psychological Science, 18*(10), 845–849.
       (Http://pss.sagepub.com/content/18/10/845.full.pdf+html)

338.   Kolling, N., Behrens, T. E. J., Mars, R. B., & Rushworth, M. F. S. (2012, 6 Apr). Neural Mechanisms of Foraging.
       Science, 336(6077), 95–98.
       (Http://www.sciencemag.org/content/336/6077/95.full.pdf)

339. Kording, K. P., & Wolpert, D. M. (2004, 15 Jan). Bayesian integration in sensorimotor learning.
      Nature, 427(6971), 244–247.
      (Http://www.nature.com/nature/journal/v427/n6971/pdf/
      nature02169.pdf)

340. Koren, Y., North, S. C., & Volinsky, C. (2007). *Measuring and Extracting Proximity in Networks.* Florham Park, NJ: AT&T Labs - Research.

341. Kounios, J., Frymiare, J. L., Bowden, E. M., Fleck, J. I., Subramaniam, K., Parrish, T. B., et al. (2006, 1 Oct). The Prepared Mind: Neural Activity Prior to Problem Presentation Predicts Subsequent Solution by Sudden Insight. *Psychological Science, 17*(10), 882–890.
      (Http://pss.sagepub.com/content/17/10/882.full.pdf+html
)

342. Koyama, T., McHaffie, J. G., Laurienti, P. J., & Coghill, R. C. (2005, 6 Sep). The subjective experience of pain: Where expectations become reality. *Proceedings of the National Academy of Sciences of the United States of America, 102*(36), 12950–12955.
      (Http://www.pnas.org/content/102/36/12950.full.pdf)

343. Kozlovic, A. K. (2004). Lights! Camera! Sermon!: Additional Research Notes on Sacred Servant Categories Within the Popular Cinema. *Journal of Mundane Behavior, 5*(1).

344. Kozlowski, S. W., & Ilgen, D. R. (2006, Dec). Enhancing the Effectiveness of Work Groups and Teams. *Psychological Science in the Public Interest, 7*(3), 77–124.
      (Http://www3.interscience.wiley.com/cgi-
      bin/fulltext/118600272/PDFSTART)

345. Krishna, A. (2013). *Customer Sense: How the 5 senses influence buying behavior.* Palgrave Macmillan.

346. Kruger, D. J. (2010, Jun). Socio-demographic factors intensifying male mating competition exacerbate male mortality rates. *Evolutionary Psychology, 8*(2), 194–204.
      (Http://www.epjournal.net/filestore/ep08194204.pdf?utm
      _source=MadMimi&utm_medium=email&utm_content=Ju

ne+2010+Newsletter&utm_campaign=June+2010+Newsle
tter&utm_term=Socio-
demographic%2Bfactors%2Bintensifying%2Bmale%2Bmat
ing%2Bcompetition%2Bexacerbate%2Bmale%2Bmortality
%2Brates_)

347.   Kurzban, R. (2010, 29 Sep). *Sex and Politics.* Evolutionary
       Psychology. (Http://www.epjournal.net/blog/2010/09/sex-
       and-politics/)

348.   Kuzmanovic, B., Jefferson, A., Bente, G., & Vogeley, K.
       (2013, 11 Jun). Affective and motivational influences in
       person perception. *Frontiers in Human Neuroscience, 7.*
       (Http://www.frontiersin.org/Journal/DownloadFile.ashx?pd
       f=1&FileId=256145&articleId=48408&Version=1&Content
       TypeId=21&FileName=fnhum-07–00266.pdf)

349.   Lakshmikantham, V., & Mohaptra, R. (2003). *Theory of
       Fuzzy Differential Equations and Inclusions (Mathematical
       Analysis and Applications).* CRC Press.
       (Http://www.amazon.com/Differential-Equations-
       Inclusions-Mathematical-
       Applications/dp/0415300738/ref=sr_1_9?ie=UTF8&qid=13
       02091977&sr=8–9)

350.   Lang, J. W., & Lang, J. (2010, 1 Jun). Priming Competence
       Diminishes the Link Between Cognitive Test Anxiety and
       Test Performance: Implications for the Interpretation of
       Test Scores. *Psychological Science, 21*(6), 811–819.
       (Http://pss.sagepub.com/content/21/6/811.full.pdf+html)

351.   Lappe, C., Steinsträter, O., & Pantev, C. (2013, 7 Jun).
       Rhythmic and melodic deviations in musical sequences
       recruit different cortical areas for mismatch detection.
       Frontiers in Human Neuroscience, 7.
       (Http://www.frontiersin.org/Journal/DownloadFile.ashx?pd
       f=1&FileId=254437&articleId=50190&Version=1&Content
       TypeId=21&FileName=fnhum-07–00260.pdf)

352.   Lau, H. C., Rogers, R. D., Haggard, P., & Passingham, R.
       E. (2004, 20 Feb). Attention to Intention.
       Science, 303(5661), 1208–1210.

(Http://www.sciencemag.org/cgi/reprint/sci;303/5661/12
08.pdf)

353.   Lederbogen, F., Kirsch, P., Haddad, L., Streit, F., Tost, H.,
        Schuch, P., et al. (2011, 23 Jun). City living and urban
        upbringing affect neural social stress processing in
        humans. *Nature, 474*(7352), 498–501.
        (Http://www.nature.com/nature/journal/v474/n7352/pdf/
        nature10190.pdf)

354.   Lee, J. L. C., Everitt, B. J., & Thomas, K. L. (2004, 7 May).
        Independent Cellular Processes for Hippocampal Memory
        Consolidation and Reconsolidation.
        Science, 304(5672), 839–843.
        (Http://www.sciencemag.org/cgi/reprint/sci;304/5672/83
        9.pdf)

355.   Leighton, J., Bird, G., Orsini, C., & Heyes, C. (2010, Nov).
        Social attitudes modulate automatic imitation. *Journal of
        Experimental Social Psychology, 46*(6), 905–910.
        (Http://www.sciencedirect.com/science?_ob=MImg&_imag
        ekey=B6WJB-50J9H8D-1-
        5&_cdi=6874&_user=10&_pii=S0022103110001526&_ori
        gin=search&_coverDate=11%2F30%2F2010&_sk=999539
        993&view=c&wchp=dGLbVlb-
        zSkzS&md5=2cb962e997fb4bcd7c7842c5c92c095f&ie=/sd
        article.pdf)

356.   Lerman, K. (2007). *Social Browsing & Information Filtering
        in Social Media.* University of Southern California,
        Information Sciences Institute, Marinadel Rey, CA: Cornell
        University Library. (Http://arxiv.org/abs/0710.5697)

357.   Lettvin, J. Y., Maturana, H. R., McCulloch, W. S., & Pitts,
        W. H. (1968). What the Frog's Eye Tells the Frog's Brain.
        Proc. Inst. Radio Engr., 47, 1940–1951.
        (Http://jerome.lettvin.info/lettvin/Jerome/WhatTheFrogsE
        yeTellsTheFrogsBrain.pdf)

358.   Leutgeb, S., Leutgeb, J. K., Barnes, C. A., Moser, E. I.,
        McNaughton, B. L., & Moser, M.-B. (2005, 22 Jul).
        Independent Codes for Spatial and Episodic Memory in
        Hippocampal Neuronal Ensembles.

Science, 309(5734), 619–623.
(Http://www.sciencemag.org/cgi/reprint/309/5734/619.pdf)

359.   Li, N., Chen, T.-W., Guo, Z. V., Gerfen, C. R., & Svoboda, K. (2015, 5 Mar). A motor cortex circuit for motor planning and movement. *Nature, 519*(7541), 51–56.
(Http://www.nature.com/nature/journal/v519/n7541/pdf/nature14178.pdf)

360.   Li, Y., Van Hooser, S. D., Mazurek, M., White, L. E., & Fitzpatrick, D. (2008, 18 Dec). Experience with moving visual stimuli drives the early development of cortical direction selectivity. *Nature, 456*(7224), 952–956.
(Http://www.nature.com/nature/journal/v456/n7224/suppinfo/nature07417_S1.html)

361.   Lida, B. (2002, Jul). Can Personality Be Used to Predict How We Use the Internet? *Usability News (Software Usability Research Laboratory (SURL) at Wichita State University), 4*(2).
(Http://www.surl.org/usabilitynews/42/e-shopping_personality.asp)

362.   Lieberman, M. D., & Eisenberger, N. I. (2009, 13 Feb). Pains and Pleasures of Social Life.
Science, 323(5916), 890–891.
(Http://www.sciencemag.org/cgi/reprint/323/5916/890.pdf)

363.   Lindsey, B. A., & Nagel, M. L. (2015, 17 Jul). Do students know what they know? Exploring the accuracy of students' self-assessments. *Physical Review Special Topics - Physics Education Research, 11*(2).
(Http://journals.aps.org/prstper/pdf/10.1103/PhysRevSTPER.11.020103)

364.   Lippa, R. A. Are 2D:4D finger-length ratios related to sexual orientation? Yes for men, no for women. *Journal of Personality and Social Psychology, 85*(1), 179–188.

365.   Little, A. C., DeBruine, L. M., & Jones, B. C. (2011, 7 Jul). Exposure to visual cues of pathogen contagion changes preferences for masculinity and symmetry in opposite-sex

faces. *Proceedings of the Royal Society B: Biological Sciences, 278*(1714), 2032–2039. (Http://rspb.royalsocietypublishing.org/content/278/1714/2032.full.pdf+html)

366.   Lleras, A., & Moore, C. M. (2006, 1 Oct). What You See Is What You Get: Functional Equivalence of a Perceptually Filled-In Surface and a Physically Presented Stimulus. *Psychological Science, 17*(10), 876–881. (Http://pss.sagepub.com/content/17/10/876.full.pdf+html)

367.   Loehlin, J. C., McFadden, D., Medland, S. E., & Martin, N. G. (2006, Dec). Population Differences in Finger-Length Ratios: Ethnicity or Latitude? *Archives of Sexual Behavior, 35*(6), 739–742. (Http://www.psy.utexas.edu/psy/faculty/Loehlin/pdf/EthLat.pdf)

368.   Lopez-Aranda, M. F., Lopez-Tellez, J. F., Navarro-Lobato, I., Masmudi-Martin, M., Gutierrez, A., & Khan, Z. U. (2009, 3 Jul). Role of Layer 6 of V2 Visual Cortex in Object-Recognition Memory. *Science, 325*(5936), 87–89. (Http://www.sciencemag.org/cgi/reprint/325/5936/87.pdf)

369.   Low, D. J. (2000, 28 Sep). Following the crowd. *Nature, 407*(6803), 465–466. (Http://www.nature.com/nature/journal/v407/n6803/pdf/407465a0.pdf)

370.   Lynch, A. (1996). *Thought Contagion: How Belief Spreads Through Society (The New Science of Memes).* Basic Books.

371.   Mack, A., & Rock, I. (1998). *Inattentional Blindness.* Cambridge, MA: MIT Press.

372.   Maguire, E. A., Frackowiak, R. S. J., & Frith, C. D. (1997, 15 Sep). Recalling Routes around London: Activation of the Right Hippocampus in Taxi Drivers. *The Journal of Neuroscience, 17*(18), 7103–7110. (Http://www.jneurosci.org/content/17/18/7103.full.pdf+html)

373.   Mahowald, M. W., & Schenck, C. H. (2005, 27 Oct).
       Insights from studying human sleep disorders.
       Nature, 437(7063), 1279–1285.
       (Http://www.nature.com/nature/journal/v437/n7063/pdf/
       nature04287.pdf)

374.   Maier, S. U., Makwana, A. B., & Hare, T. A. (2015, 28
       Sep). Acute Stress Impairs Self-Control in Goal-Directed
       Choice by Altering Multiple Functional Connections within
       the Brain's Decision Circuits. *Neuron, 87*(3), 621–631.

375.   Makeig, S., Westerfield, M., Jung, T.-P., Enghoff, S.,
       Townsend, J., Courchesne, E., et al. (2002, 25 Jan).
       Dynamic Brain Sources of Visual Evoked Responses.
       Science, 295(5555), 690–694.
       (Http://www.sciencemag.org/cgi/reprint/295/5555/690.pd
       f)

376.   Malmgren, R. D., Stouffer, D. B., Campanharo, A. S. L. O.,
       & Amaral, L. A. N. (2009, 25 Sep). On Universality in
       Human Correspondence Activity.
       Science, 325(5948), 1696–1700.
       (Http://www.sciencemag.org/cgi/reprint/325/5948/1696.p
       df)

377.   Mamassian, P. (2008). Overconfidence in an Objective
       Anticipatory Motor Task. *Psychological
       Science, 19*(6), 601–606.

378.   Mannucci, M. A., Sparks, L., & Struppa, D. C. (2007).
       Simplicial Models of Social Aggregation 1. HoloMathics,
       LLC.

379.   Marks-Tarlow, T., Robertson, R., & Comb, A. (2002).
       Varela and the Uroborus: The Psychological Significance of
       Reentry. *Cybernetics & Human Knowing, 9*(2), 31–47.
       (Http://www.ingentaconnect.com/search/download?pub=i
       nfobike%3a%2f%2fimp%2fchk%2f2002%2f00000009%2f
       00000002%2f114&mimetype=application%2fpdf&exitTarg
       etId=1297005474474)

380.   Marsh, R. L., Ellerby, D. J., Carr, J. A., Henry, H. T., &
       Buchanan, C. I. (2004, 2 Jan). Partitioning the Energetics
       of Walking and Running: Swinging the Limbs Is Expensive.

Science, 303(5654), 80–83.
(Http://www.sciencemag.org/cgi/reprint/sci;303/5654/80.
pdf)
381.   Martinez, G. M., & Abma, J. C. (2015). *Sexual Activity,
Contraceptive Use, and Childbearing of Teenagers Aged
15–19 in the United States.* CDC: CDC.
(Http://www.cdc.gov/nchs/data/databriefs/db209.pdf)
382.   Masum, H., & Zhang, Y.-C. (2008). Manifesto for the
Reputation Society. *First Monday.*
383.   Matsumoto, K., Suzuki, W., & Tanaka, K. (2003, 11 Jul).
Neuronal Correlates of Goal-Based Motor Selection in the
Prefrontal Cortex. *Science, 301*(5630), 229–232.
(Http://www.sciencemag.org/cgi/reprint/sci;301/5630/22
9.pdf)
384.   Maviel, T., Durkin, T. P., Menzaghi, F., & Bontempi, B.
(2004, 2 Jul). Sites of Neocortical Reorganization Critical
for Remote Spatial Memory. *Science, 305*(5680), 96–99.
(Http://www.sciencemag.org/cgi/reprint/305/5680/96.pdf
)
385.   May, A. (2012, Jun). What Exactly Do You Mean, "Scalar
Waves"? *EdgeScience, 11.*
(Http://www.scientificexploration.org/edgescience/edgesci
ence_11.pdf)
386.   Mazzucato, M. (2013). *The Entrepreneurial State:
Debunking Public vs. Private Sector Myths.* Anthem Press.
387.   McFadden, D., Loehlin, J. C., Breedlove, S. M., Lippa, R.
A., Manning, J. T., & Rahman, Q. (2005, Jun). A
Reanalysis of Five Studies on Sexual Orientation and
Relative Length of the 2nd and 4th Fingers (the 2D:4D
Ratio). *Archives of Sexual Behavior, 34*(3), 341–346.
(Http://www.ecfs.org/projects/pchurch/AT%20BIOLOGY/P
apers0809/sexualOrientationFingerLength.pdf)
388.   McMahon, J. A. (2000). Perceptual Principles as the Basis
for Genuine Judgments of Beauty. *Journal of
Consciousness Studies, 7*(8–9), 29–35.
(Http://www.ingentaconnect.com/content/imp/jcs/2000/0
0000007/F0020008/1039)

389. McNamara, J. M., Barta, Z., Fromhage, L., & Houston, A. I.
      (2008, 10 Jan). The coevolution of choosiness and
      cooperation. *Nature, 451*(7175), 189–192.
      (Http://www.nature.com/nature/journal/v451/n7175/pdf/
      nature06455.pdf)
390. McNeil, D. (1992). *Hand and Mind: What Gestures Reveal
      about Thought.* Chicago, IL: University of Chicago Press.
391. McNeil, D. (Ed.). (2000). *Language and Gesture.*
      Cambridge: Cambridge University Press.
392. Medin, D., & Waxman, S. R. (1999). Conceptual
      Organization. In *A Companion to Cognitive Science.*
      Blackwell Publishing.
      (Http://www.blackwellreference.com/public/tocnode?id=g
      9780631218517_chunk_g978063121851711)
393. Mevorach, C., Hodsoll, J., Allen, H., Shalev, L., &
      Humphreys, G. (2010, 28 Apr). Ignoring the Elephant in
      the Room: A Neural Circuit to Downregulate Salience. *The
      Journal of Neuroscience, 30*(17), 6072–6079.
      (Http://www.jneurosci.org/content/30/17/6072.full.pdf+ht
      ml)
394. Michael R. Waldmann, Y. H., Aaron P. Blaisdell. (2006).
      Beyond the Information Given: Causal Models in Learning
      and Reasoning. *Current Directions in Psychological
      Science, 15*(6), 307–311.
      (Http://www3.interscience.wiley.com/cgi-
      bin/fulltext/118584120/PDFSTART)
395. Miller, G. (2010, 1 Oct). Social Savvy Boosts the Collective
      Intelligence of Groups. *Science, 330*(6000), 22–22.
      (Http://www.sciencemag.org/content/330/6000/22.full.pd
      f)
396. Miller, J. (1991). The flanker compatibility effect as a
      function of visual angle, attentional focus,visual transients,
      and perceptual load: A search for boundary conditions.
      Perception and Psychophysics, 49, 270–288.
      (Http://www.psychonomic.org/search/view.cgi?id=5499)
397. Millikan, R. G. (1998). A common structure for concepts of
      individuals, stuffs, and real kinds: More Mama, more milk,

and more mouse. *Behavioral and Brain Sciences, 21*(01), 55–65.

398. Mitchell, J. F., Stoner, G. R., & Reynolds, J. H. (2004, 27 May). Object-based attention determines dominance in binocular rivalry. *Nature, 429*(6990), 410–413. (Http://www.nature.com/nature/journal/v429/n6990/pdf/nature02584.pdf)

399. Mitchell, M. (2010). Understanding Meaning.

400. Mobbs, D., Yu, R., Meyer, M., Passamonti, L., Seymour, B., Calder, A. J., et al. (2009, 15 May). A Key Role for Similarity in Vicarious Reward. *Science, 324*(5929). (Http://www.sciencemag.org/cgi/reprint/324/5929/900.pdf)

401. Le Moigne, J.-L. (2006). Modeling For Reasoning Socio-Economic Behaviors. *Cybernetics And Human Knowing., 13*(3–4), 9–26. (Http://www.ingentaconnect.com/search/article?journal=Human+Knowing&journal_type=words&year_from=2006&year_to=2006&database=1&pageSize=20&index=2)

402. Monteggia, L. M., & Kavalali, E. T. (2012, 22 Nov). Depression brought to light. *Nature, 491*(7425), 537–538. (Http://www.nature.com/nature/journal/v491/n7425/pdf/nature11752.pdf)

403. Montgomery, D. B., & Armstrong, J. S. (1970). Brand Trial After a Credibility Change. *Journal of Advertising Research, 10*(5), 26–32. (Http://marketing.wharton.upenn.edu/ideas/pdf/Armstrong/Brand%20Trial%20After%20a%20Credibility%20Change.pdf)

404. Moore, T., Rodman, H. R., Repp, A. B., & Gross, C. G. (1995, 29 Aug). Localization of visual stimuli after striate cortex damage in monkeys: Parallels with human blindsight. *Proceedings of the National Academy of Sciences of the United States of America, 92*(18), 8215–8218. (Http://www.pnas.org/content/92/18/8215.full.pdf+html)

405.   Morell, V. (2008, 16Feb). Setting a Biological Stopwatch.
        Science, 271.
406.   Morewedge, C. K., & Kahneman, D. (2010, Jan).
        Associative processes in intuitive judgment. *Trends in
        Cognitive Sciences, 14*(10), 435–440.
        (Http://linkinghub.elsevier.com/retrieve/pii/S1364661310
        001713)
407.   Mort, G. S., & Drennan, J. (2001, 45 Dec). M-Marketing:
        New Directions in B2C E-Business. ANZMAC2001.
        (Http://smib.vuw.ac.nz:8081/WWW/ANZMAC2001/anzma
        c/AUTHORS/pdfs/Mort.pdf)
408.   Moser, E. I., & Moser, M.-B. (2011, 20 Jan). Seeing into
        the future. *Nature, 469*(7330), 303–304.
        (Http://www.nature.com/nature/journal/v469/n7330/pdf/
        469303a.pdf)
409.   Mulder, M. B., Bowles, S., Hertz, T., Bell, A., Beise, J.,
        Clark, G., et al. (2009, 30 Oct). Intergenerational Wealth
        Transmission and the Dynamics of Inequality in Small-
        Scale Societies. *Science, 326*(5953), 682–688.
        (Http://www.sciencemag.org/cgi/reprint/326/5953/682.pd
        f)
410.   Müller, D., Widmann, A., & Schröger, E. (2013, 10 Jun).
        Object-related regularities are processed automatically:
        Evidence from the visual mismatch negativity. *Frontiers in
        Human Neuroscience, 7.*
        (Http://www.frontiersin.org/Journal/DownloadFile.ashx?pd
        f=1&FileId=255080&articleId=50374&Version=1&Content
        TypeId=21&FileName=fnhum-07-00259.pdf)
411.   Myrick, J. G. (2015, Nov). Emotion regulation,
        procrastination, and watching cat videos online: Who
        watches Internet cats, why, and to what effect? *Computers
        in Human Behavior, 52.*
        (Http://www.sciencedirect.com/science/article/pii/S07475
        63215004343)
412.   Nabel, G. J. (2009, 2 Oct). The Coordinates of Truth.
        Science, 326(5949), 53–54.

(Http://www.sciencemag.org/cgi/reprint/sci;326/5949/53. pdf)

413.   Nabeth, T. (. (2006). *Future of Identity in the Information Society - Set of use cases and scenarios.* INSEAD.

414.   Nabeth, T. (2005). *Understanding the Identity Concept in the Context of Digital Social Environments.* INSEAD CALT: INSEAD.

415.   Nardi, D. (2009). Neuroscience of Personality - Principles of the Psyche as a Living System. Los Angeles, CA: University of California. (Http://www.pdx.edu/sysc/sites/www.pdx.edu.sysc/files/n euro-systems.pdf)

416.   Negoita, C. V., & Ralescu, D. (1987). *Simulation, Knowledge-based Computing, and Fuzzy Statistics.* NYC: Van Nostrand Reinhold Company.

417.   Nelson, R. R., Peterhansl, A., & Sampat, B. (2004, 1 Oct). Why and how innovations get adopted: A tale of four models. *Ind Corp Change, 13*(5), 679–699. (Http://icc.oxfordjournals.org/cgi/reprint/13/5/679)

418.   Newman, A. L. (2015, 30 Jan). What the 'right to be forgotten' means for privacy in a digital age. *Science, 347*(6221), 507–508.

419.   Nick Yeung, J. D. C. (2006, Feb). The Impact of Cognitive Deficits on Conflict Monitoring. *Psychological Science, 17*(2), 164–171.

420.   Noe A. (2000). Experience and experiment in art. *Journal of Consciousness Studies, 7*(s 8–9), 123–136. (Http://docserver.ingentaconnect.com/deliver/connect/im p/13558250/v7n8/s12.pdf?expires=1375113890&id=7501 9194&titleid=3956&accname=Joseph+Carrabis&checksum =A936F17870D5C4A564E2B5264F88FC67)

421.   Nummenmaa, L., Hyana, J., & Hietanen, J. K. (2009, 1 Dec). I'll Walk This Way: Eyes Reveal the Direction of Locomotion and Make Passersby Look and Go the Other Way. *Psychological Science, 20*(12), 1454–1458. (Http://pss.sagepub.com/content/20/12/1454.full.pdf+ht ml)

422. O'Doherty, J., Dayan, P., Schultz, J., Deichmann, R., Friston, K., & Dolan, R. J. (2004, 16 Apr). Dissociable Roles of Ventral and Dorsal Striatum in Instrumental Conditioning. *Science, 304*(5669), 452–454. (Http://www.sciencemag.org/cgi/reprint/sci;304/5669/452.pdf)

423. O'Regan, J. K., & Noe, A. (2000, June 29-July 2). *Explaining sensory phenomenology.* (Http://nivea.psycho.univ-paris5.fr)

424. Offer, S., & Schneider, B. (2011, Dec). Revisiting the Gender Gap in Time-Use Patterns: Multitasking and Well-Being among Mothers and Fathers in Dual-Earner Families. *American Sociological Review.* (Http://www.asanet.org/images/journals/docs/pdf/asr/Dec11ASRFeature.pdf)

425. Oh! You pretty things. (2014, 12 Jul). *The Economist, 412.* (Http://www.economist.com/news/briefing/21606795-todays-young-people-are-held-be-alienated-unhappy-violent-failures-they-are-proving)

426. Ohbayashi, M., Ohki, K., & Miyashita, Y. (2003, 11 Aug). Conversion of Working Memory to Motor Sequence in the Monkey Premotor Cortex. *Science, 301*(5630), 233–236. (Http://www.sciencemag.org/cgi/reprint/301/5630/233.pdf)

427. Ohman, A. (2005, 29 Jul). Conditioned Fear of a Face: A Prelude to Ethnic Enmity? *Science, 309*(5735), 711–713. (Http://www.sciencemag.org/cgi/reprint/sci;309/5735/711.pdf)

428. Olsson, A., Ebert, J. P., Banaji, M. R., & Phelps, E. A. (2005, 29 Jul). The Role of Social Groups in the Persistence of Learned Fear. *Science, 309*(5735), 785–787. (Http://www.sciencemag.org/cgi/reprint/309/5735/785.pdf)

429. One Never Forgets a Face. (2010, Nov). *APS Observer, 23.* (Http://www.psychologicalscience.org/index.php/publicati

ons/observer/2010/november-10/one-never-forgets-a-face.html)

430. Onnela, J.-P., & Reed-Tsochas, F. (2010, 26 Oct). Spontaneous emergence of social influence in online systems. *Proceedings of the National Academy of Sciences, 107*(43), 18375–18380. (Http://www.pnas.org/content/107/43/18375.full.pdf+html)

431. Osland, J. Expert Cognition and Sense-Making in the Global Organization Leadership Context: A Case Study. San Jose, CA: San Jose State. (Http://www.cob.sjsu.edu/osland_j/Bus165A/EXPERT%25 20COGNITION%2520CASE%2520STUDY.pdf)

432. Otamendi, R. D., Carrabis, J., & Carrabis, S. (2009). *Predicting Age & Gender Online.* Brussels, Belgium: NextStage Analytics.

433. Otamendi, R. D. (2009, 22 Oct). *NextStage Announcements at eMetrics Marketing Optimization Summit Washington DC.* NextStage Analytics. (Http://makingmarketingactionable.com/2009/10/22/next stage-announcements-at-emetrics-marketing-optimization-summit-washington-dc/?CFID=148013&CFTOKEN=70102829)

434. Otamendi, R. D. (2009, 24 Nov). *NextStage Rich PersonaeTM classification.* NextStage Analytics. (Http://makingmarketingactionable.com/2009/11/24/next stage-rich-personaetm-classification/comment-page-1/)

435. Owens, B. (2013, 23 May). Heavy sleepers. *Nature, 497*(7450), S8-S9. (Http://www.nature.com/nature/journal/v497/n7450_sup p/pdf/497S8a.pdf)

436. Oyserman, D., Brickman, D., Bybee, D., & Celious, A. (2006). Fitting in Matters: Markers of In-Group Belonging and Academic Outcomes. *Psychological Science, 17*(10), 854–862.

437. Pagel, M. (2012, 16 Feb). Adapted to culture. *Nature, 482*(7385), 297–299.

(Http://www.nature.com/nature/journal/v482/n7385/pdf/
482297a.pdf)

438.   Palmer, L., & Lynch, G. (2010, 18 Jun). A Kantian View of
       Space. *Science, 328*(5985), 1487–1488.
       (Http://www.sciencemag.org/content/328/5985/1487.full.
       pdf)

439.   Pasquale, F. (2015). *The Black Box Society: The Secret
       Algorithms that Control Money and Information.* Harvard
       University Press.

440.   Paterson, S. J., Brown, J. H., Gs&ouml, dl, M. K., Johnson,
       M. H., & Karmiloff-Smith, A. (1999, 17 Dec). Cognitive
       Modularity and Genetic Disorders.
       Science, 286(5448), 2355–2358.
       (Http://www.sciencemag.org/cgi/reprint/286/5448/2355.p
       df)

441.   Paul E. Dux, V. C. (2005, Oct). The Meaning of the Mask
       Matters. *Psychological Science, 16*(10), 775–779.
       (Http://www3.interscience.wiley.com/cgi-
       bin/fulltext/118661659/PDFSTART)

442.   Pawar, S., Dell, A. I., & Van M. Savage. (2012, 28 Jun).
       Dimensionality of consumer search space drives trophic
       interaction strengths. *Nature, 486*(7404), 485–489.
       (Http://www.nature.com/nature/journal/v486/n7404/pdf/
       nature11131.pdf)

443.   Payne, B. K. (2006). Weapon Bias: Split-Second Decisions
       and Unintended Stereotyping. *Current Directions in
       Psychological Science, 15*(6), 287–291.
       (Http://www3.interscience.wiley.com/cgi-
       bin/fulltext/118584116/PDFSTART)

444.   Pearce, T. M., & Moran, D. W. (2012, 24 Aug). Strategy-
       Dependent Encoding of Planned Arm Movements in the
       Dorsal Premotor Cortex. *Science, 337*(6097), 984–988.
       (Http://www.sciencemag.org/content/337/6097/984.full.p
       df)

445.   Peelen, M. V., Fei-Fei, L., & Kastner, S. (2009, 2 Jul).
       Neural mechanisms of rapid natural scene categorization
       in human visual cortex. *Nature, 460*(7251), 94–97.

(Http://www.nature.com/nature/journal/v460/n7251/pdf/
nature08103.pdf)

446. Persson, A. (2001, Oct). Intimacy Among Strangers: On
mobile telephone calls in public places. *Journal of Mundane
Behavior, 2*(3).

447. Peshek, D., Semmaknejad, N., Hoffman, D., & Foley, P.
(2011). Preliminary Evidence that the Limbal Ring
Influences Facial Attractiveness. *Evolutionary
Psychology, 9*(2), 137–146.
(Http://www.epjournal.net/filestore/EP09137146.pdf?utm
_source=MadMimi&utm_medium=email&utm_content=Ma
y+2011+Newsletter&utm_campaign=May+2011+Newslett
er&utm_term=Preliminary+evidence+that+the+limbal+rin
g+influences+facial+attractiveness_)

448. Pessoa, L. (2004, 12 Mar). Seeing the World in the Same
Way. *Science, 303*(5664), 1617–1618.
(Http://www.sciencemag.org/cgi/reprint/303/5664/1617.p
df)

449. Peter J. Rentfrow, Samuel D. Gosling, & Jeff Potter.
(2008). A Theory of the Emergence, Persistence, and
Expression of Geographic Variation in Psychological
Characteristics. *Perspectives on Psychological
Science, 3*(5), 339–369.
(Http://www3.interscience.wiley.com/cgi-
bin/fulltext/121394239/PDFSTART)

450. Petranker, J. (2003). Inhabiting Conscious Experience.
Journal of Consciousness Studies, 10(12), 3–23.
(Http://docserver.ingentaconnect.com/deliver/connect/im
p/13558250/v10n12/s1.pdf?expires=1417388603&id=800
52364&titleid=3956&accname=Joseph+Carrabis&checksu
m=265FC200995D7F31F7B4FB285CE5E13E)

451. Phillips, D. (2008). The Psychology of Social Media.
Journal of New Communications Research, 3(1), 79–85.

452. Phillips, M. L. (2009, 12 Mar). Of owls, larks and alarm
clocks. *Nature, 458*(7235), 142–144.
(Http://www.nature.com/news/2009/090311/pdf/458142a
.pdf)

453. Poizner, H., Klima, E. S., & Bellugi, U. (1990). *What the Hands Reveal About the Brain.* Cambridge, MA: MIT Press.

454. Poulet, J. F. A., & Hedwig, B. (2002, 22 Aug). A corollary discharge maintains auditory sensitivity during sound production. *Nature, 418*(6900), 872–876. (Http://www.nature.com/nature/journal/v418/n6900/pdf/nature00919.pdf)

455. Powell, R. M. Using Traditional Gender Norms to Expand Gender: A Qualitative Study of Old Time Dance Communities. *Journal of Mundane Behavior, 3*(1).

456. Prut, Y., & Fetz, E. E. (1999, 7 Oct). Primate spinal interneurons show pre-movement instructed delay activity. *Nature, 401*(6753), 590–594. (Http://www.nature.com/nature/journal/v401/n6753/pdf/401590a0.pdf)

457. Puce, A., McNeely, M. E., Berrebi, M., Thompson, J. C., Hardee, J. E., & Brefczynski-Lewis, J. (2013, 14 Jun). Multiple faces elicit augmented neural activity. *Frontiers in Human Neuroscience, 7.* (Http://www.frontiersin.org/Journal/DownloadFile.ashx?pdf=1&FileId=260526&articleId=32917&Version=1&ContentTypeId=21&FileName=fnhum-07-00282.pdf)

458. Puts, D., McDaniel, M., Jordan, C., & Breedlove, S. (2008-02-01). Spatial Ability and Prenatal Androgens: Meta-Analyses of Congenital Adrenal Hyperplasia and Digit Ratio (2D:4D) Studies. *Archives of Sexual Behavior, 37*(1), 100–111. Springer Netherlands.

459. Quoidbach, J., Gilbert, D. T., & Wilson, T. D. (2013, 4 Jan). The End of History Illusion. *Science, 339*(6115), 96–98. (Http://www.sciencemag.org/content/339/6115/96.full.pdf)

460. Ramachandran, V. S., & Hubbard, E. M. (2001). Synaesthesia - AWindow Into Perception, Thought and Language. *Journal of Consciousness Studies, 8*(12), 3–34.

461. Ramachandran, V., & Hirstein, W. (1999). The Science of Art - A Neurological Theory of Aesthetic Experience.

Journal of Consciousness Studies, 6(6–7), 15–51.
(Http://www.ingentaconnect.com/content/imp/jcs/1999/0
0000006/F0020006/949)

462.   Ramirez, G., & Beilock, S. L. (2011, 14 Jan). Writing About
Testing Worries Boosts Exam Performance in the
Classroom. *Science, 331*(6014), 211–213.
(Http://www.sciencemag.org/content/331/6014/211.full.p
df)

463.   Ramsden, S., Richardson, F. M., Josse, G., Thomas, M. S.
C., Ellis, C., Shakeshaft, C., et al. (2011, 3 Nov). Verbal
and non-verbal intelligence changes in the teenage brain.
Nature, 479(7371), 113–116.
(Http://www.nature.com/nature/journal/v479/n7371/pdf/
nature10514.pdf)

464.   Ravassard, P., Kees, A., Willers, B., Ho, D., Aharoni, D.,
Cushman, J., et al. (2013, 14 Jun). Multisensory Control of
Hippocampal Spatiotemporal Selectivity.
Science, 340(6138), 1342–1346.
(Http://www.sciencemag.org/content/340/6138/1342.full.
pdf)

465.   Reardon, S. (2013, 27 Feb). Monkey brains wired to share.
Nature, 506.
(Http://www.nature.com/polopoly_fs/1.14765!/menu/mai
n/topColumns/topLeftColumn/pdf/506416a.pdf)

466.   Rees, G., Russell, C., Frith, C. D., & Driver, J. (1999, 24
Dec). Inattentional Blindness Versus Inattentional Amnesia
for Fixated But Ignored Words. *Science, 286*(5449), 2504–
2507.
(Http://www.sciencemag.org/content/286/5449/2504.full.
pdf)

467.   Reilly, C. A. (2011, 3 Jan). Teaching Wikipedia as a
mirrored technology. *First Monday, 16*(1).
(Http://firstmonday.org/htbin/cgiwrap/bin/ojs/index.php/f
m/article/view/2824/2746)

468.   Rendell, L., Boyd, R., Cownden, D., Enquist, M., Eriksson,
K., Feldman, M. W., et al. (2010, 9 Apr). Why Copy
Others? Insights from the Social Learning Strategies

Tournament. *Science, 328*(5975), 208–213.
(Http://www.sciencemag.org/content/328/5975/208.full.p
df)

469. Rennie, J., & Zorpette, G. (2011, June). The Social Era of
the Web Starts Now. *ieee Spectrum.*
(Http://spectrum.ieee.org/telecom/internet/the-social-era-
of-the-web-starts-now)

470. Reyna, V. F. (2013, 7 Nov). Good and bad news on the
adolescent brain. *Nature, 503*(7474), 48–49.
(Http://www.nature.com/nature/journal/v503/n7474/pdf/
nature12704.pdf)

471. Richmond, B. J., Liu, Z., & Shidara, M. (2003, 11 Jul).
Predicting Future Rewards. *Science, 301*(5630), 179–180.
(Http://www.sciencemag.org/cgi/reprint/sci;301/5630/17
9.pdf)

472. Rigotti, M., Barak, O., Warden, M. R., Wang, X.-J., Daw, N.
D., Miller, E. K., et al. (2013, 30 May). The importance of
mixed selectivity in complex cognitive tasks.
Nature, 497(7451), 585–590.
(Http://www.nature.com/nature/journal/v497/n7451/pdf/
nature12160.pdf)

473. Riley, S. (2006, Feb). Password Security: What Users
Know and What They Actually Do. *Usability News
(Software Usability Research Laboratory (SURL) at Wichita
State University), 8*(1).
(Http://www.surl.org/usabilitynews/81/pdf/Usability%20N
ews%2081%20-%20Riley.pdf)

474. Roberts, S. C., Owen, R. C., & Havlicek, J. (2010).
Distinguishing between perceiver and wearer effects in
clothing color-associated attributions. *Evolutionary
Psychology, 8*(3), 350–364.

475. Robertson, E. M., Press, D. Z., & Pascual-Leone, A. (2005,
6 Jul). Off-Line Learning and the Primary Motor Cortex.
The Journal of Neuroscience, 25(27), 6372–6378.
(Http://www.jneurosci.org/content/25/27/6372.full.pdf+ht
ml)

476.   Robins, R. W. (2005, 7 Oct). The Nature of Personality:
        Genes, Culture, and National Character.
        Science, 310(5745), 62–63.
        (Http://www.sciencemag.org/cgi/reprint/310/5745/62.pdf
)
477.   Rochefort, C., Arabo, A., Andrea, M., Poucet, B., Save, E.,
        & Rondi-Reig, L. (2011, 21 Oct). Cerebellum Shapes
        Hippocampal Spatial Code. *Science, 334*(6054), 385–389.
        (Http://www.sciencemag.org/content/334/6054/385.full.p
        df)
478.   Rodriguez, A., & Laio, A. (2014, 27 Jun). Clustering by fast
        search and find of density peaks.
        Science, 344(6191), 1492–1496.
        (Http://www.sciencemag.org/content/344/6191/1492.full.
        pdf)
479.   Roy Luria, N. M. (2005, Oct). Increased Control Demand
        Results in Serial Processing. *Psychological
        Science, 16*(10), 833–840.
        (Http://www3.interscience.wiley.com/cgi-
        bin/fulltext/118661668/PDFSTART)
480.   Rule, N. O., Ambady, N., & Hallett, K. C. (2009, Nov).
        Female sexual orientation is perceived accurately, rapidly,
        and automatically from the face and its features. *Journal
        of Experimental Social Psychology, 45*(6), 1245–1251.
        (Http://www.sciencedirect.com/science?_ob=MImg&_imag
        ekey=B6WJB-4WVF6W2-1-
        7&_cdi=6874&_user=10&_orig=search&_coverDate=11%
        2F30%2F2009&_sk=999549993&view=c&wchp=dGLzVlz-
        zSkWb&md5=1e560928c3a34ba2cb43df6195b7a251&ie=/
        sdarticle.pdf)
481.   Russell, C., Li, K., & Malhotra, P. A. (2013, 6 Jun).
        Harnessing motivation to alleviate neglect. *Frontiers in
        Human Neuroscience, 7.*
        (Http://www.frontiersin.org/Journal/DownloadFile.ashx?pd
        f=1&FileId=253681&articleId=49322&Version=1&Content
        TypeId=21&FileName=fnhum-07-00230.pdf)

482. Russell, M. C. (2003, Jul). A Comparison of Face-to-Face and Computer-Mediated Student Project Teams. *Usability News (Software Usability Research Laboratory (SURL) at Wichita State University), 6*(2). (Http://www.surl.org/usabilitynews/52/pdf/Usability%20N ews%2052%20-%20Russell.pdf)

483. Russell, M. C. (2005, Jul). Hotspots and Hyperlinks: Using Eye-tracking to Supplement Usability Testing. *Usability News (Software Usability Research Laboratory (SURL) at Wichita State University), 7*(2). (Http://www.surl.org/usabilitynews/72/pdf/Usability%20N ews%2072%20-%20Russell.pdf)

484. Russell, M. (2005, Feb). Using Eye-Tracking Data to Understand First Impressions of a Website. *Usability News (Software Usability Research Laboratory (SURL) at Wichita State University), 7*(1). (Http://www.surl.org/usabilitynews/71/pdf/Usability%20N ews%2071%20-%20Russell.pdf)

485. Sahin, N. T., Pinker, S., Cash, S. S., Schomer, D., & Halgren, E. (2009, 16 Oct). Sequential Processing of Lexical, Grammatical, and Phonological Information Within Broca's Area. *Science, 326*(5951), 445–449. (Http://www.sciencemag.org/cgi/reprint/326/5951/445.pd f)

486. Salazar, R. F., Dotson, N. M., Bressler, S. L., & Gray, C. M. (2012, 23 Nov). Content-Specific Fronto-Parietal Synchronization During Visual Working Memory. *Science, 338*(6110), 1097–1100. (Http://www.sciencemag.org/content/338/6110/1097.full)

487. Salganik, M. J., Dodds, P. S., & Watts, D. J. (2006, 2/10). Experimental Study of Inequality and Unpredictability in an Artificial Cultural Market. *Science, 311*(5762), 854–856. (Http://www.sciencemag.org/cgi/reprint/311/5762/854.pd f)

488. Sandberg, A., & Soderberg, R. (1997). Computer Generation: Visions and Demands. Military Applications of

Synthetic Environments and Virtual Reality, MASERV'97.
Sweden.

489. Sander L. Koole, Jeff Greenberg, & Tom Pyszczynski.
(2006, Oct). Introducing Science to the Psychology of the
Soul: Experimental Existential Psychology. *Current
Directions in Psychological Science, 15*(5), 212–216.
(Http://www3.interscience.wiley.com/cgi-
bin/fulltext/118584099/PDFSTART)

490. Sanes, J., Donoghue, J., Thangaraj, V., Edelman, R., &
Warach, S. (1995, 23 Jun). Shared neural substrates
controlling hand movements in human motor cortex.
Science, 268(5218), 1775–1777.
(Http://www.sciencemag.org/cgi/reprint/sci;268/5218/17
75.pdf)

491. Saper, C. B., Scammell, T. E., & Lu, J. (2005, 27 Oct).
Hypothalamic regulation of sleep and circadian rhythms.
Nature, 437(7063), 1257–1263.
(Http://www.nature.com/nature/journal/v437/n7063/pdf/
nature04284.pdf)

492. Sapolsky, R. (1995). Ego Boundaries, or the Fit of My
Father's Shirt. *Discover, 16,* 62–67.
(Http://discovermagazine.com/1995/nov/egoboundariesor
t586/?searchterm=ego%20boundaries,%20or%20the%20f
it%20of%20my%20father's%20shirt)

493. Sargolini, F., Fyhn, M., Hafting, T., McNaughton, B. L.,
Witter, M. P., Moser, M.-B., et al. (2006, 5 May).
Conjunctive Representation of Position, Direction, and
Velocity in Entorhinal Cortex. *Science, 312*(5774), 758–
762.
(Http://www.sciencemag.org/cgi/reprint/312/5774/758.pd
f)

494. Saxena, M., & Rana, S. (2000, July). Beyond the
Transactional Exchange: The Coming Era of Collaborative
Commerce.

495. Scheffran, J., Brzoska, M., Kominek, J., Link, P. M., &
Schilling, J. (2012, 15 May). Climate Change and Violent
Conflict. *Science, 336*(6083), 869–871.

(Http://www.sciencemag.org/content/336/6083/869.full.p df)

496. Schick, A., Wessa, M., Vollmayr, B., Kuehner, C., & Kanske, P. (2013, 12 Jun). Indirect assessment of an interpretation bias in humans: Neurophysiological and behavioral correlates. *Frontiers in Human Neuroscience, 7.* (Http://www.frontiersin.org/Journal/DownloadFile.ashx?pd f=1&FileId=257340&articleId=44420&Version=1&Content TypeId=21&FileName=fnhum-07-00272.pdf)

497. Schilling, M. F. (1990). The Longest Run of Heads. *The College Mathematics Journal, 21*(3), 196–207. (Http://gato-docs.its.txstate.edu/mathworks/DistributionOfLongestRun. pdf)

498. Schmidt, C., Collette, F., Leclercq, Y., Sterpenich, V., Vandewalle, G., Berthomier, P., et al. (2009, 24 Apr). Homeostatic Sleep Pressure and Responses to Sustained Attention in the Suprachiasmatic Area. *Science, 324*(5926), 516–519. (Http://www.sciencemag.org/cgi/reprint/324/5926/516.pd f)

499. Schooler, J. W., & Schrieber, C. A. (2004, 2004). Experience, Meta-consciousness, and the Paradox of Introspection. *Journal of Consciouness Studies, 11*(7–8), 17–39.

500. Schultz, T. F., & Kay, S. A. (2003, 18 Jul). Circadian Clocks in Daily and Seasonal Control of Development. *Science, 301*(5631), 326–328. (Http://www.sciencemag.org/cgi/reprint/sci;301/5631/32 6.pdf)

501. Schulz, L. (2015, 3 Apr). Infants explore the unexpected. *Science, 348*(6230), 42–43. (Http://www.sciencemag.org/content/348/6230/42.full.pd f)

502. Schuster, D., & Undreiu, A. Cognition of an expert tackling an unfamiliar conceptual physics problem. Michigan State University; University of Michigan;.

(Http://physics2.sciencecommunity.wikispaces.net/file/vie
w/cognition+of+an+expert+tackling+an+unfamiliar+probl
em.pdf)

503.   Schwartz, A. B., Moran, D. W., & Reina, G. A. (2004, 16
        Jan). Differential Representation of Perception and Action
        in the Frontal Cortex. *Science, 303*(5656), 380–383.
        (Http://www.sciencemag.org/cgi/reprint/303/5656/380.pd
        f)

504.   Schwartz, H., Eichstaedt, J., Dziurzynski, L., & Ramones,
        S. (2013, 25 Sep). Personality, Gender, and Age in the
        Language of Social Media: The Open-Vocabulary Approach.
        PLoS One, 8(9).
        (Http://www.plosone.org/article/fetchObject.action;jsessio
        nid=5374E28E1A87A4693F166ACB2915DD41?uri=info%3
        Adoi%2F10.1371%2Fjournal.pone.0073791&representatio
        n=PDF)

505.   Schwartz, J. (2007, 23 Jan). *IPhone Seeds Mobile
        Marketing Growth.* IMediaConnection.
        (Http://www.imediaconnection.com/content/13331.asp)

506.   Seeing through Expert Eyes. (1993, 18 July). *Science
        News,* p. 44.
        (Http://www.sciencenews.org/pages/sn_arc98/7_18_98/b
        ob2ref.htm)

507.   Serruya, M. D., Hatsopoulos, N. G., Paninski, L., Fellows,
        M. R., & Donoghue, J. P. (2002, 14 Mar). Instant neural
        control of a movement signal. *Nature, 416*(6877), 141–
        142.
        (Http://www.nature.com/nature/journal/v416/n6877/pdf/
        416141a.pdf)

508.   Shaikh, A. D., Chaparro, B. S., & Fox, D. (2009, Oct). The
        Personality of Terms and Concepts Used in Online Material.
        *Usability News (Software Usability Research Laboratory
        (SURL) at Wichita State University), 11*(1).
        (Http://www.surl.org/usabilitynews/111/pdf/Usability%20
        News%20111%20-%20Shaikh.pdf)

509.   Shaikh, A. D., & Lenz, K. (2006, Feb). Where's the Search?
        Re-examining User Expectations of Web Objects. *Usability*

News (Software Usability Research Laboratory (SURL) at Wichita State University), 8(1).
(Http://www.surl.org/usabilitynews/81/pdf/Usability%20N ews%2081%20-%20Shaikh2.pdf)

510.   Sharot, T., Riccardi, A. M., Raio, C. M., & Phelps, E. A. (2007, 1 Nov). Neural mechanisms mediating optimism bias. *Nature, 450*(7166), 102–105.
(Http://www.nature.com/nature/journal/v450/n7166/pdf/ nature06280.pdf)

511.   Sherratt, T. N., & Roberts, G. (2012, 14 Sep). When Paths to Cooperation Converge. *Science, 337*(6100), 1304–1305.
(Http://www.sciencemag.org/content/337/6100/1304.full. pdf)

512.   Shouse, B. (2001, 11 Sep). Reality TV Puts Group Behavior to the Test. *Science, 294*(5545), 1262b-1263.
(Http://www.sciencemag.org/cgi/reprint/sci;294/5545/12 62b.pdf)

513.   Shumake, J., Ilango, A., Scheich, H., Wetzel, W., & Ohl, F. W. (2010, 28 Apr). Differential Neuromodulation of Acquisition and Retrieval of Avoidance Learning by the Lateral Habenula and Ventral Tegmental Area. *The Journal of Neuroscience, 30*(17), 5876–5883.
(Http://www.jneurosci.org/content/30/17/5876.full.pdf+ht ml)

514.   Sigmund, K., De Silva, H., Traulsen, A., & Hauert, C. (2010, 12 Aug). Social learning promotes institutions for governing the commons. *Nature, 466*(7308), 861–863.
(Http://www.nature.com/nature/journal/v466/n7308/pdf/ nature09203.pdf)

515.   Silk, J. B. (2011, 10 Nov). The path to sociality. *Nature, 479*(7372), 182–183.
(Http://www.nature.com/nature/journal/v479/n7372/pdf/ 479182a.pdf)

516.   Simini, F., Gonzalez, M. C., Maritan, A., & Barabasi, A.-L. (2012, 5 Apr). A universal model for mobility and migration patterns. *Nature, 484*(7392), 96–100.

(Http://www.nature.com/nature/journal/v484/n7392/pdf/
nature10856.pdf)

517.   Slocum, J. (2005, Feb). A Breakdown of the Psychomotor
        Components of Input Device Usage. *Usability News
        (Software Usability Research Laboratory (SURL) at Wichita
        State University), 7*(1).
        (Http://www.surl.org/usabilitynews/71/pdf/Usability%20N
        ews%2071%20-%20Slocum.pdf)

518.   Smith, R. D. (2007). *Average Path Length in Complex
        Networks: Patterns and Predictions.* Bouchet-Franklin
        Research Institute: ArXiv:0710.2947v1.

519.   Solstad, T., Boccara, C. N., Kropff, E., Moser, M.-B., &
        Moser, E. I. (2008, 19 Dec). Representation of Geometric
        Borders in the Entorhinal Cortex.
        Science, 322(5909), 1865–1868.
        (Http://www.sciencemag.org/content/322/5909/1865.full.
        pdf)

520.   Song, C., Qu, Z., Blumm, N., & Barabasi, A.-L. (2010, 19
        Feb). Limits of Predictability in Human Mobility.
        Science, 327(5968), 1018–1021.
        (Http://www.sciencemag.org/cgi/reprint/sci;327/5968/10
        18.pdf)

521.   Speer, M. E., Bhanji, J. P., & Delgado, M. R. (2014, 18
        Nov). Savoring the Past: Positive Memories Evoke Value
        Representations in the Striatum. *Neuron.*
        (Http://nwkpsych.rutgers.edu/neuroscience/publications/2
        014_SpeerDelgado_Neuron.pdf)

522.   Sperling, A. J., Lu, Z.-L., Manis, F. R., Seidenberg, & Mark
        S. (2006, Dec). Motion-Perception Deficits and Reading
        Impairment: It's the Noise, Not the Motion. *Psychological
        Science, 12,* 1047–1053.
        (Http://www.psychologicalscience.org/members/goToSyne
        rgy.cfm?issn=0956-7976&date=2006&article=01825)

523.   Spielberg, J. M., Heller, W., & Miller, G. A. (2013, 17 Jun).
        Hierarchical brain networks active in approach and
        avoidance goal pursuit. *Frontiers in Human
        Neuroscience, 7.*

(Http://www.frontiersin.org/Journal/DownloadFile.ashx?pd
f=1&FileId=262222&articleId=51032&Version=1&Content
TypeId=21&FileName=fnhum-07-00284.pdf)

524. Spivey, M. J., & Dale, R. (2006, 1 Oct). Continuous
      Dynamics in Real-Time Cognition. *Current Directions in
      Psychological Science, 15*(5), 207–211.
      (Http://cdp.sagepub.com/content/15/5/207.full.pdf+html)

525. Stahl, A. E., & Feigenson, L. (2015, 3 Apr). Observing the
      unexpected enhances infants' learning and exploration.
      Science, 348(6230), 91–94.
      (Http://www.sciencemag.org/content/348/6230/91.full.pd
      f)

526. Standish, R. K. (2008). *Concept and Definition of
      Complexity.* ArXiv:0805:0685v1.

527. Steckenfinger, S. A., & Ghazanfar, A. A. (2009, 27 Oct).
      Monkey visual behavior falls into the uncanny valley.
      *Proceedings of the National Academy of
      Sciences, 106*(43), 18362–18366.
      (Http://www.pnas.org/content/106/43/18362.full.pdf+htm
      l)

528. Steenbergen, H. v., Band, G. P., & Hommel, B. (2009, 1
      Dec). Reward Counteracts Conflict Adaptation.
      Psychological Science, 20(12), 1473–1477.
      (Http://pss.sagepub.com/content/20/12/1473.full.pdf I ht
      ml)

529. Stemmler, M., Usher, M., & Niebur, E. (1995, 29 Sep).
      Lateral interactions in primary visual cortex: A model
      bridging physiology and psychophysics.
      Science, 269(5232), 1877–1880.
      (Http://www.sciencemag.org/cgi/reprint/sci;269/5232/18
      77.pdf)

530. Stensola, H., Stensola, T., Solstad, T., Froland, K., Moser,
      M.-B., & Moser, E. I. (2012, 6 Dec). The entorhinal grid
      map is discretized. *Nature, 492*(7427), 72–78.
      (Http://www.nature.com/nature/journal/v492/n7427/pdf/
      nature11649.pdf)

531.   Sternberg, R. J., & Gordeeva, T. (1996, 1 Mar). The
       Anatomy of Impact: What Makes an Article Influential?
       Psychological Science, 7(2), 69–75.
       (Http://pss.sagepub.com/content/7/2/69.full.pdf+html)
532.   Sternberg, R. J., Grigorenko, E. L., & Zhang, L.-f. (2008, 1
       Nov). A Reply to Two Stylish Critiques: Response to Hunt
       (2008) and Mayer (2008). *Perspectives on Psychological
       Science, 3*(6), 516–517.
       (Http://pps.sagepub.com/content/3/6/516.full.pdf+html)
533.   Sternberg, R. J., Grigorenko, E. L., & Zhang, L.-f. (2008, 1
       Nov). Styles of Learning and Thinking Matter in Instruction
       and Assessment. *Perspectives on Psychological
       Science, 3*(6), 486–506.
       (Http://pps.sagepub.com/content/3/6/486.full.pdf+html)
534.   Sternberg, R. J., & Grigorenko, E. L. (2007, 1 Jun). The
       Difficulty of Escaping Preconceptions in Writing an Article
       About the Difficulty of Escaping Preconceptions:
       Commentary on Hunt and Carlson (2007). *Perspectives on
       Psychological Science, 2*(2), 221–223.
       (Http://pps.sagepub.com/content/2/2/221.full.pdf+html)
535.   Sternberg, R. J., & Lubart, T. I. (1992, 1 Feb). Buy Low
       and Sell High: An Investment Approach to Creativity.
       Current Directions in Psychological Science, 1(1), 1–5.
       (Http://cdp.sagepub.com/content/1/1/1.2.full.pdf+html)
536.   Sternberg, R. J., & Wagner, R. K. (1993, 1 Feb). The g-
       ocentric View of Intelligence and Job Performance Is
       Wrong. *Current Directions in Psychological
       Science, 2*(1), 1–4.
       (Http://cdp.sagepub.com/content/2/1/1.full.pdf+html)
537.   Sternberg, R. J. (1994, 1 Mar). 468 Factor-Analyzed Data
       Sets: What They Tell Us and Don't Tell Us About Human
       Intelligence. *Psychological Science, 5*(2), 63–63.
       (Http://pss.sagepub.com/content/5/2/63.1.full.pdf+html)
538.   Sternberg, R. J. (1995, 1 Sep). For whom the Bell Curve
       Tolls: A Review of The Bell Curve. *Psychological
       Science, 6*(5), 257–261.
       (Http://pss.sagepub.com/content/6/5/257.full.pdf+html)

539. Sternberg, R. J. (2013, 17 May). The Intelligence of Nations: Smart but not Wise - A Comment on Hunt (2012). *Perspectives on Psychological Science, 8*(2), 187–189.
(Http://pps.sagepub.com/content/8/2/187.full.pdf+html)

540. Sternberg, R. J. (2014, 1 Sep). Introduction: Adopted at Last! *Psychological Science in the Public Interest, 15*(1), 1–2.
(Http://psi.sagepub.com/content/15/1/1.2.full.pdf+html)

541. Sterne, M. J. (2008, 1 Aug). How Locality, Frequency of Communication and Internet Usage Affect Modes of Communication Within Core Social Networks. *Information, Communication & Society, 11*(5), 591–618.
(Http://www.academia.edu/attachments/84419/download_file)

542. Stirling, A. (2010, 23 Dec). Keep it complex. *Nature, 468*(7327), 1029–1031.
(Http://www.nature.com/nature/journal/v468/n7327/pdf/4681029a.pdf)

543. Sugre, L. P., Corrado, G. S., & Newsome, W. T. (2004, 18 June). Matching Behavior and the Representation of Value in the Parietal Cortex. *Science, 304,* 1782–7.

544. Sugrue, L. P., Corrado, G. S., & Newsome, W. T. (2004, 18 June). Matching Behavior and the Representation of Value in the Parietal Cortex. *Science, 304*(5678), 1782–1787.
(Http://www.sciencemag.org/cgi/reprint/sci;304/5678/1782.pdf)

545. Sui, J., & Han, S. (2007, 1 Oct). Self-Construal Priming Modulates Neural Substrates of Self-Awareness. *Psychological Science, 18*(10), 861–866.
(Http://pss.sagepub.com/content/18/10/861.full.pdf+html)

546. Szolnoki, A., & Perc, M. (2010). *Reward and cooperation in the spatial public goods game.* EconoPhysics Forum.
(Http://www.unifr.ch/econophysics/paper/download/id/10 10.5771/format/pdf)

547.   Tan, J., Ma, Z., Gao, X., Wu, Y., & Fang, F. (2011, 24
       May). Gender Difference of Unconscious Attentional Bias in
       High Trait Anxiety Individuals. *PLoS ONE, 6*(5).
548.   Tanenhaus, M. K., Spivey-Knowlton, M. J., Eberhard, K.
       M., & Sedivy, J. C. (1995, 16 June). Integration of Visual
       and Linguistic Information in Spoken Language
       Comprehension. *Science, 268,* 1632–1634.
       (Http://www.sciencemag.org/cgi/reprint/268/5217/1632.p
       df)
549.   Taylor, D. M., Tillery, S. I. H., & Schwartz, A. B. (2002, 7
       Jun). Direct Cortical Control of 3D Neuroprosthetic
       Devices. *Science, 296*(5574), 1829–1832.
       (Http://www.sciencemag.org/cgi/reprint/sci;296/5574/18
       29.pdf)
550.   Taylor, K. (2001). Applying Continuous Modeling to
       Consciousness. *Journal of Consciousness
       Studies, 8*(2), 45–60.
       (Http://www.ingentaconnect.com/search/download?pub=i
       nfobike%3a%2f%2fimp%2fjcs%2f2001%2f00000008%2f0
       0000002%2f1079&mimetype=application%2fpdf&exitTarg
       etId=1335633929520)
551.   Taylor, P. D., & Day, T. (2004, 8 Apr). Cooperate with thy
       neighbour? *Nature, 428*(6983), 611–612.
       (Http://www.nature.com/nature/journal/v428/n6983/pdf/
       428611a.pdf)
552.   ter Bogt, T., Engels, R., Bogers, S., & Kloosterman, M.
       (2010–12–01). "Shake It Baby, Shake It": Media
       Preferences, Sexual Attitudes and Gender Stereotypes
       Among Adolescents. *Sex Roles, 63*(11), 844–859. Springer
       Netherlands.
553.   Terracciano, A., Abdel-Khalek, A. M., Adam, N.,
       Adamovova, L., Ahn, C.-k., Ahn, H.-n., et al. (2005, 7
       Oct). National Character Does Not Reflect Mean Personality
       Trait Levels in 49 Cultures. *Science, 310*(5745), 96–100.
       (Http://www.sciencemag.org/cgi/reprint/310/5745/96.pdf
)

554. Thalia Wheatley, J. H. (2005, Oct). Hypnotic Disgust Makes Moral Judgments More Severe. *Psychological Science, 16*(10), 780–784. (Http://www3.interscience.wiley.com/cgi-bin/fulltext/118661660/PDFSTART)

555. Thellefsen, T., Sorensen, B., & Andersen, C. (2006). Significance-effects, Semiotics and Brands. *Cybernetics And Human Knowing., 13*(3–4), 111–134. (Http://www.ingentaconnect.com/search/article?journal=Cybernetics++Human+Knowing&journal_type=words&year_from=2006&year_to=2006&database=1&pageSize=20&index=7)

556. Thiele, A., Henning, P., Kubischik, M., & Hoffmann, K.-P. (2002, 29 Mar). Neural Mechanisms of Saccadic Suppression. *Science, 295*(5564), 2460–2462. (Http://www.sciencemag.org/cgi/reprint/sci;295/5564/2460.pdf)

557. Thomaes, S., Bushman, B. J., Castro, B. O. d., Cohen, G. L., & Denissen, J. J. (2009, 1 Dec). Reducing Narcissistic Aggression by Buttressing Self-Esteem: An Experimental Field Study. *Psychological Science, 20*(12), 1536–1542. (Http://pss.sagepub.com/content/20/12/1536.full.pdf+html)

558. Thompson, K. G., Biscoe, K. L., & Sato, T. R. (2005, 12 Oct). Neuronal Basis of Covert Spatial Attention in the Frontal Eye Field. *Journal of Neuroscience, 25*(41), 9479–9487. (Http://www.jneurosci.org/cgi/reprint/25/41/9479)

559. Travis, J. (1996, 17 Feb). Biological stopwatch found in the brain. *Science News, 149,* 7.

560. Troiani, V., & Schultz, R. T. (2013, 6 Jun). Amygdala, Pulvinar & Inferior Parietal Cortex Contribute to Early Processing of Faces without Awareness. *Frontiers in Human Neuroscience, 7.* (Http://www.frontiersin.org/Journal/DownloadFile.ashx?pdf=1&FileId=252846&articleId=42110&Version=1&ContentTypeId=21&FileName=fnhum-07-00241.pdf)

561. Tsao, D. (2006, 6 Oct). A Dedicated System for Processing Faces. *Science, 314.*

562. Tuan, Y.-F. (1977). *Space and Place.* Minneapolis: University of Minnesota Press.

563. Vallesi A., Binns M., & Shallice T. (2008). An effect of spatial-temporal association of response codes: Understanding the cognitive representations of time. *Cognition, 107*(2), 501–527.

564. Vallesi A., Stuss D.T., McIntosh A.R., & Picton T.W. (2009). Age-related differences in processing irrelevant information: Evidence from event-related potentials. *Neuropsychologia, 47*(2), 577–586.

565. Van Der Steen, M. C., & Keller, P. E. (2013, 10 Jun). The Adaptation and Anticipation Model (ADAM) of sensorimotor synchronization. *Frontiers in Human Neuroscience, 7.* (Http://www.frontiersin.org/Journal/DownloadFile.ashx?pdf=1&FileId=255047&articleId=50227&Version=1&ContentTypeId=21&FileName=fnhum-07-00253.pdf)

566. van Ee, R., & Erkelens, C. J. (2010, 13 Aug). Stereo-Vision: Head-Centric Coding of Retinal Signals. *Current biology: CB, 20*(13), R567-R568. (Http://download.cell.com/current-biology/pdf/PIIS0960982210005622.pdf)

567. Van Gelder, R. N., Herzog, E. D., Schwartz, W. J., & Taghert, P. H. (2003, 6 Jun). In the Loop at Last. *Science, 300*(5625), 1534–1535. (Http://www.sciencemag.org/cgi/reprint/300/5625/1534.pdf)

568. van Straaten, I., Engels, R., Finkenauer, C., & Holland, R. (2008-12-01). Sex Differences in Short-term Mate Preferences and Behavioral Mimicry: A Semi-Naturalistic Experiment. *Archives of Sexual Behavior, 37*(6), 902–911. Springer Netherlands.

569. VanBoskirk, S. (2005). *Integrated Marketing Grows Up.* Forrester Research.

570. Vannini, P. (2002, June). Waiting Dynamics: Bergson, Virilio, Deleuze, and the Experience of Global Times. *Journal of Mundane Behavior, 3*(2).

571. Vaughn, J. E., Bradley, K. I., Byrd-Craven, J., & Kennison, S. M. (2010, Sep). The Effect of Mortality Salience on Women's Judgments of Male Faces. *Evolutionary Psychology, 8*(3), 477–491. (Http://www.epjournal.net/filestore/EP07477491.pdf?utm_source=MadMimi&utm_medium=email&utm_content=September+2010+Newsletter&utm_campaign=September+2010+Newsletter&utm_term=The%2Beffect%2Bof%2Bmortality%2Bsalience%2Bon%2Bwomen_E2_80_99s%2Bjudgments%2Bof%2Bmale%2Bfaces_)

572. Verosky, S. C., & Todorov, A. (2010, 1 Jun). Generalization of Affective Learning About Faces to Perceptually Similar Faces. *Psychological Science, 21*(6), 779–785. (Http://pss.sagepub.com/content/21/6/779.full.pdf+html)

573. Villeval, M. C. (2014, 4 Dec). Professional identity can increase dishonesty. *Nature, 516*(7529), 48–49. (Http://www.nature.com/nature/journal/v516/n7529/pdf/nature14068.pdf)

574. Viswanathan, G. M., Buldyrev, S. V., Havlin, S., da Luz, M. G. E., Raposo, E. P., & Stanley, H. E. (1999, 28 Oct). Optimizing the success of random searches. *Nature, 401*(6756), 911–914. (Http://www.nature.com/nature/journal/v401/n6756/pdf/401911a0.pdf)

575. Voermans, N. C., Petersson, K. M., Daudey, L., Weber, B., van Spaendonck, K. P., Kremer, H. P., et al. (2004, 5 Aug). Interaction between the Human Hippocampus and the Caudate Nucleus during Route Recognition. *Neuron, 43*(3), 427–435. (Http://linkinghub.elsevier.com/retrieve/pii/S0896627304004349)

576. Vohs, K. D., Baumesiter, R. F., Schmeichel, B. J., Twenge, J. M., Nelson, n. M., & Tice, D. M. (2008). Making Choices

Impairs Subsequent Self-Control: A Limited-Resource Account of Decision Making, Self-Regulation, and Active Initiative. *Journal of Personality and Social Psychology, 94*(5), 883–898. (Http://www.apa.org/journals/releases/psp945883.pdf)

577. Walker, R., & Callaghan, B. (2007). . RMIT University.

578. Walton, G. M., & Cohen, G. L. (2011, 18 Mar). A Brief Social-Belonging Intervention Improves Academic and Health Outcomes of Minority Students. *Science, 331*(6023), 1447–1451. (Http://www.sciencemag.org/content/331/6023/1447.full.pdf)

579. Wang, F., Moreno, Y., & Sun, Y. (2006). *The Structure of Peer-to-Peer Social Networks.* ArXiv:physics/0603222v1.

580. Wang, P., Gonzalez, M. C., Hidalgo, C. A., & Barabasi, A.-L. (2009, 22 May). Understanding the Spreading Patterns of Mobile Phone Viruses. *Science, 324*(5930), 1071–1076. (Http://www.sciencemag.org/cgi/reprint/sci;324/5930/1071.pdf)

581. Wargo, E. (2011, Apr). Beauty is in the Mind of the Beholder. *APS Observer, 24,* 4. (Http://www.psychologicalscience.org/index.php/publications/observer/2011/april-11/beauty-is-in-the-mind-of-the-beholder.html)

582. Warren, C., & Karrer, R. (1984). Movement-related potentials during development: A replication and extension of relationships to age, motor control, mental status and IQ [Brain and information: Event Related Potentials]. *International Journal of Neuroscience, 24,* 81–96.

583. Warren, C., & Karrer, R. (1984). Movement-related potentials in children: A replication of waveforms and their relationships to age, performance, and cognitive development [Brain and information: Event Related Potentials]. *International Journal of Neuroscience, 425.*R. Karrer, J. Cohen & P. Tueting (Eds.).

584. Watson, K. K., Ghodasra, J. H., & Platt, M. L. (2009, 14 Jan). Serotonin Transporter Genotype Modulates Social

Reward and Punishment in Rhesus Macaques. *PLoS ONE, 4*(1).
(Http://www.plosone.org/article/info%3Adoi%2F10.1371 %2Fjournal.pone.0004156)

585.   Watts, D. J., Dodds, P. S., & Newman, M. E. J. (2002, 17 May). Identity and Search in Social Networks. *Science, 296*(5571), 1302–1305.
(Http://www.sciencemag.org/cgi/reprint/296/5571/1302.p df)

586.   Watts, D. J. (2002, 22 Jul). On average, how many degrees apart is any one person in the world from another? *Scientific American.*
(Http://www.scientificamerican.com/article.cfm?id=on-average-how-many-degre)

587.   Watts, D. J. (2003). *Six Degrees of Interconnection.*
(Http://www.cecl.com.pt/redes/pdf/sixdegrees.pdf)

588.   Weaver, K., Garcia, S. M., Schwarz, N., & Miller, D. T. (2007, May). Inferring the Popularity of an Opinion From Its Familiarity: A Repetitive Voice Can Sound Like a Chorus. *Journal of Personality and Social Psychology, 92*(5), 13.
(Http://psycnet.apa.org/journals/psp/92/5/821.pdf)

589.   Webster, M. A., Kaping, D., Mizokami, Y., & Duhamel, P. (2004, 1 Apr). Adaptation to natural facial categories. *Nature, 428*(6982), 557–561.
(Http://www.nature.com/nature/journal/v428/n6982/pdf/ nature02420.pdf)

590.   Wegner, D. M. (2009, 30 Jul). How to Think, Say, or Do Precisely the Worst Thing for Any Occasion. *Science, 325*(5936), 48–50.

591.   Weikum, W. M., Vouloumanos, A., Navarra, J., Soto-Faraco, S., Sebastian-Galles, N., & Werker, J. F. (2007, 25 May). Visual Language Discrimination in Infancy. *Science, 316,* 1159.
(Http://www.sciencemag.org/cgi/reprint/316/5828/1159.p df)

592.   Weinberger, D. (1998, December). Defenses, Personality
       Structure, and Development: Integrating Psychodynamic
       Theory into a Typological Approach. *Journal of
       Personality, 66*(6), 1061–1080.
593.   Weinberger, S. (2011, 31 Mar). Web of war.
       Nature, 471(7340), 566–568.
       (Http://www.nature.com/news/2011/110330/pdf/471566a
       .pdf)
594.   Weisbuch, M., Pauker, K., & Ambady, N. (2009, 18 Dec).
       The Subtle Transmission of Race Bias via Televised
       Nonverbal Behavior. *Science, 326*(5960), 1711–1714.
       (Http://www.sciencemag.org/cgi/reprint/sci;326/5960/17
       11.pdf)
595.   Wentworth, C. (1995). *Sample Size and Sampling Error.*
       (Http://www.msearch.com/pdfs/SampleSizeError.pdf)
596.   Wentworth, C. (2010). *Sample Size and Sampling Error in
       Social Media.* Society for New Communications Research.
       (Http://www.msearch.com/pdfs/SampleSizeError.pdf)
597.   West, S. A., Pen, I., & Griffin, A. S. (2002, 5 Apr).
       Cooperation and Competition Between Relatives.
       Science, 296(5565), 72–75.
       (Http://www.sciencemag.org/cgi/reprint/sci;296/5565/72.
       pdf)
598.   Whitney, D., Westwood, D. A., & Goodale, M. A. (2003, 19
       Jun). The influence of visual motion on fast reaching
       movements to a stationary object.
       Nature, 423(6942), 869–873.
       (Http://www.nature.com/nature/journal/v423/n6942/pdf/
       nature01693.pdf)
599.   Wickelgren, I. (1999, 12 Mar). Memory for Order Found in
       the Motor Cortex. *Science, 283*(5408), 1617–1619.
       (Http://www.sciencemag.org/cgi/content/full/sci;283/540
       8/1617)
600.   Wickelgren, I. (2003, 24 Jan). Tapping the Mind.
       Science, 299(5606), 496–499.
       (Http://www.sciencemag.org/cgi/reprint/sci;299/5606/49
       6.pdf)

601. Wickelgren, I. (2004, 9 Jul). Monkey See, Monkey Think
      About Doing. *Science, 305*(5681), 162a-163.
      (Http://www.sciencemag.org/cgi/reprint/305/5681/162a.p
      df)

602. Winchester, M., & Romaniuk, J. (2001, 5 Dec). Do
      Negative Brand Image Attributes Display Evaluative and
      Descriptive Patterns? Australian and New Zealand
      Marketing Academy. Massey University, Auckland, NZ.
      (Http://smib.vuw.ac.nz:8081/WWW/ANZMAC2001/anzma
      c/AUTHORS/pdfs/Winchester.pdf)

603. Wolfe, J. M., Horowitz, T. S., & Kenner, N. M. (2005, 26
      May). Rare items often missed in visual searches.
      Nature, 435, 439–40.
      (Http://www.nature.com/nature/journal/v435/n7041/pdf/
      435439a.pdf)

604. Wolpert, D., Ghahramani, Z., & Jordan, M. (1995, 29 Sep).
      An internal model for sensorimotor integration.
      Science, 269(5232), 1880–1882.
      (Http://www.sciencemag.org/cgi/reprint/sci;269/5232/18
      80.pdf)

605. Wong, W., & Barlow, H. (2000, 27 Apr). Tunes and
      templates. *Nature, 404*(6781), 952–953.
      (Http://www.nature.com/nature/journal/v404/n6781/pdf/
      404952a0.pdf)

606. Wright, K. (2002, 1 Jun). Six Degrees of Speculation: Even
      in a Small World, There's Room for Disagreement.
      Discover.

607. Wu, B., Ooi, T. L., & He, Z. J. (2004, 4 Mar). Perceiving
      distance accurately by a directional process of integrating
      ground information. *Nature, 428*(6978), 73–77.
      (Http://www.nature.com/nature/journal/v428/n6978/pdf/
      nature02350.pdf)

608. Yair Bar-Haim, T. Z., Dominique Lamy. (2006, Feb).
      Nature and Nurture in Own-Race Face Processing.
      Psychological Science, 17(2), 159–163.
      (Http://www3.interscience.wiley.com/cgi-
      bin/fulltext/118597334/PDFSTART)

609.   Yantis, S. (2003, 3 Jan). To See Is to Attend.
       Science, 299(5603), 54–56.
       (Http://www.sciencemag.org/cgi/reprint/sci;299/5603/54.
       pdf)
610.   Yao, M., Mahood, C., & Linz, D. (2010–01–01). Sexual
       Priming, Gender Stereotyping, and Likelihood to Sexually
       Harass: Examining the Cognitive Effects of Playing a
       Sexually-Explicit Video Game. *Sex Roles, 62*(1), 77–88.
       Springer Netherlands.
611.   Ybarra, O. (2012). On-line Social Interactions and
       Executive Functions. *Frontiers in Human Neuroscience, 6.*
       (Http://www.frontiersin.org/Journal/DownloadFile.ashx?pd
       f=1&FileId=88660&articleId=21535&Version=1&ContentT
       ypeId=15&FileName=fnhum-06-00075.pdf)
612.   Yeshurun, Y., Rotshtein, P., Fried, I., Ben-Bashat, D., &
       Hendler, T. (2002, 14 Mar). The Role of the Amygdala in
       Signaling Prospective Outcome of Choice.
       Neuron, 33(6), 983–994.
       (Http://download.cell.com/neuron/pdf/PIIS089662730200
       6268.pdf)
613.   Zabet, F.-D. (2012). Playing Together And Ritualisation In
       Online Games. Cantebury: Kent.
614.   Zaghloul, K. A., Blanco, J. A., Weidemann, C. T., McGill,
       K., Jaggi, J. L., Baltuch, G. H., et al. (2009, 13 Mar).
       Human Substantia Nigra Neurons Encode Unexpected
       Financial Rewards. *Science, 323*(5920), 1496–1499.
       (Http://www.sciencemag.org/cgi/reprint/323/5920/1496.p
       df)
615.   Zell, E., & Alicke, M. D. (2009, Jan). Self-evaluative effects
       of temporal and social comparison. *Journal of
       Experimental Social Psychology, 45*(1), 223–227.
       (Http://www.sciencedirect.com/science?_ob=MImg&_imag
       ekey=B6WJB-4TJTXDC-4–
       3&_cdi=6874&_user=10&_orig=search&_coverDate=01%
       2F31%2F2009&_sk=999549998&view=c&wchp=dGLbVtz-
       zSkzV&md5=7b19a1821f9a6dc9c600478a201d8ae8&ie=/s
       darticle.pdf)

616. Zhang, J., Kaasik, K., Blackburn, M. R., & Lee, C. C.
      (2006, 19 Jan). Constant darkness is a circadian metabolic
      signal in mammals. *Nature, 439*(7074), 340–343.
      (Http://dx.doi.org/10.1038/nature04368)
617. Zhang, Z.-L., Cantor, C. R., & Schor, C. M. (2010, 13
      Aug). Perisaccadic Stereo Depth with Zero Retinal
      Disparity. *Current biology: CB, 20*(13), 1176–1181.
      (Http://download.cell.com/current-
      biology/pdf/PIIS0960982210007037.pdf)
618. Zinoviev, D. (2008). *Topology and Geometry of Online
      Social Networks.* ArXiv:0807.3996v1.
619. Zirnsak, M., Steinmetz, N. A., Noudoost, B., Xu, K. Z., &
      Moore, T. (2014, 27 Mar). Visual space is compressed in
      prefrontal cortex before eye movements.
      Nature, 507(7493), 504–507.
      (Http://www.nature.com/nature/journal/v507/n7493/pdf/
      nature13149.pdf)

Glossary

A

adaptation method - how the repeated action of something leads to less cognitive effort being required to perform the action

afferent - going inwards

anchoring - applying (often non-conscious) significance to some thing or event such that a psycho-cognitive, - spiritual, - emotional or -physical state can be re-experienced by simply remembering or being in the presence of the thing or event

anonymity levels - what we're not willing to let others know about us, usually demonstrated thrugh various Personalities

audience knowledgeable design - having an in-depth knowledge of your audience's psycho-cognitive, - spiritual, -emotional or -physical limits, boundaries, abilities, experiences, et cetera, and applying this knowledge to your design work

C

chinese general solicitation - a 2nd difference investigation into some desired quality. For example, if you're evaluating candidates for a high level position and all the candidates know each other, ask them individually who should get the job if something happens to the individual. Whoever gets the consensus opinion should get the job.

core - an individual's emotional, physical, spiritual and psychological center

D

digital entitlement - a sense that because I can access it I own it or have rights to it

efferent - going outwards

E

ego identification - the subsumation of an individual's own identity into some other identity to which the individual assigns greater cultural meaning

exafferent - signals external to the body that go inward. Watching TV is exafferent because there's no interaction with the information such that a change in the observer's state causes a change in the TV program's state (we're not considering changing channels because the TV show sucks)

exaptation - when one process or method that achieves one goal is co-opted to another process or method to achieve a different goal

executive function - how the brain manages cognitive processes, reasoning, the various memories, solves problems and performs solutions to problems. Executive function is also known as "the modeler", "cognitive control" and "supervisory attentional system"

F

fair-exchange - a psycho-cognitive, -emotive, -spiritual and -physical state that occurs when you give as good as you get in an exchange and all parties involved are multi-dimensionally satisfied with the exchange

I

identity - the emotional, physical, spiritual and psychological layer that exists outside the core and inside the personality. The Identity's job is to strengthen and maintain an individual's personalities while constantly protecting the Core from harm

Identity levels - what we're willing to let others know about us, usually demonstrated through various Personalities

invariant features - the elements of a system that do not change

M

meaningful noise - anything that draws an individual's attention away from what they were focusing on to something they start focusing on when the individual doesn't want to relinquish their primary focus of attention

P

personality - the outermost layer of an individual's emotional, physical, spiritual and psychological being. The Personality is what is projected into the world to interact with others. The Personality's job is to make sure the Identity remains whole despite changes in the environment that may require modifications to the Personality itself

polarity response - two extreme and opposing states to a single event

primary modality channel - the sensory system an individual uses most often to gather information about their environment

probability solids - a multidimensional manifold that is the boundary for what can happen and what can't happenprotention - an anticipation of a future event

psychomotor behavioral cuing - the minute adjustments the brain makes to the body in response to internal and external stimuli

Q

QBist - a subjective approach to quantum theory. People who adhere a Bayesian aspect to quantum mechanical properties and events

R

reafferent - signals generated by the body that are directed towards an external object. Playing a game, online or off, is highly reafferent because the game changes based on the player's changes

S

semiotics - the study of signs and symbols and the relationships they create

spatial relationships - how two or more structures are related in space

T

temporal relationships - how two or more structures are related in time

time-phase learning loop - the time it takes for an individual to become desensitized to environmental information

Index

About the Author[a]

Joseph Carrabis is Founder and Chief Research Officer of The NextStage Companies and helps clients understand how people think and react to marketing, leveraging that information to improve marketing efforts. He has been awarded patents for NextStage's Evolution Technology, creating a new, disruptive field of technology and applications. Evolution Technology allows any programmable device to understand human thought and respond accordingly.

He has designed, developed and delivered over 100 tools that analyze everything from group and individual social behaviors to product design and development to community development and monitoring to consumer psychology to resume analysis and improvement to finding compatible life-partners to personal growth to training measurement for governments, businesses and individuals worldwide.

He is a Senior Research Fellow at the University of Southern California's Annenberg Center for the Digital Future; a Senior Research Fellow and Board Advisory Member for the Society for New Communications Research; a Founder, Senior Researcher and Director of Predictive Analytics for the Center for Adaptive Solutions; a member of Scientists Without Borders; has served as Chief Neuroscience Officer and currently advises the event industry about the neuroscience of events, conferences, conventions and trainings.

Joseph has authored over 25 books, including *Reading Virtual Minds Volume I: Science and History* and *Tales 'Told Round Celestial Campfires*.

---

[a] – And deep thanks to Dolores "Hawkeye" Fallon for stating the obvious here

NextStage Evolution Live and Webinar Trainings

Much of the material covered in this book is available as both live and webinar trainings and classes. For that matter, there's a whole lot of stuff not covered in this book that's available as live and webinar trainings and classes.

Seriously, contact us at 603-791-4925 or info@nextstagevolution.com. Tell us what you want to learn. Chances are we already have a training on it, can modify an existing training to suit your exact needs or design a new training specific to your goals and desires.

Most frequently requested trainings can be found at http://nlb.pub/G. A training schedule is available at http://nlb.pub/I.

Comments from Live and Web Training Participants

"A MAGICAL TRIP! ... a phantasmagoric rollercoaster ride through our neural networks, showing us places we didn't know existed. And leaving us limp, giddy and exhilarated. ... push you to the wild fringe of your imagination and beyond. Race. Race. Race. Push your mind as far as it can go. MORE! We all wanted more." – Vienna, VA

"Put down your guard, stop thinking you know what you're doing, keep quiet, watch, learn, listen. Carrabis gave us 500 things if he gave us five and each one paid off a million fold." – St. John, NB

"...someone whose insights, talent and generosity with their time turned out to make a big difference in the quality of our work. ... You were a real find...and I wanted you to know that we are grateful to you." – Bedford, NH

"Carrabis is a wonderfully articulate speaker who draws on a lot of different images to makes things clear to people of many backgrounds." – Waltham, MA

"We didn't know what we didn't know until working with NextStage." – Bedford, MA

"I was unprepared for the amount of learning Carrabis packed into a one-day session." – Rothesay, NB

"Of all the tips and tricks that I learned, none proved more effective than the many I received from Mr. Carrabis in regards to the tone, inflection and proper nomenclature to be used in my pitch to the client. In fact, after one specific sitting with him I was able to improve my results 500%." – Burlington, MA

"Taking a NextStage seminar is rather like having the top of your skull surgically removed, turned around backwards and reattached. It's like trying to tell someone all the things you always believed were true, then finding those things sound silly even to you. It's like taking what you know and turning it inside out and upside down and backwards, and suddenly realizing it looks better that way. Taking a NextStage seminar will stretch your mind if your mind is capable of stretching without breaking. What are Carrabis' methods? I can't tell you, because the methods used in the seminars I attended probably won't be the ones he uses in yours. Carrabis suits the method to his current purpose, as far as I can tell, and you never know exactly what's going to happen until it already has, (believe me, I saw it time after time) you end all of a sudden with a clear understanding of something you didn't even know existed before you started. And it turns out to be something that's important to you! Amazing." – Columbia, SC

"I am not exaggerating: Everybody who has trained me has been excellent, but you are the best, really." – Burlington, MA

"I've worked with Joseph for three years and still find myself surprised by his truly unique perspective and insight. At the recent iMedia Brand Summit, his workshop was a big hit— both enlightening and entertaining the participants." – Los Angeles, CA

"...seeing your insights in action (especially with the relationship website and some of your ideas on how to present copy, deal with someone who is in pain, remove blame by replacing 'your relationship' with 'the relationship' – that was really cool. ... my favorite part of the time was discussing male versus female humor. ... Considering so many advertisers use humor in their ads, this is a super relevant subject." – NYC

"Ever since I met Joseph several years ago I was always fascinated by his ability to be so attentive to one's thoughts, emotions and physical messages. Since I do more speaking appearances and often meet with executives, I asked if he could coach me a little. The experience was revealing - it allowed me to uncover little things that will help me improve my verbal and non-verbal communication skills and even become more aware of others." – Stephane Hamel, Director of Innovation, Cardinal Path

"I've been lucky enough to have experienced one of the intensive individual trainings and it was simply mind-blowing/life-altering/universe-opening." – Dan Linton, Group Director Analytics at MRM // McCann

"An excellent investment of time. Joseph not only provided "how to interpret" but also gives actionable advice on 'how to respond'." – June Li, Managing Director, ClickInsight - Online Marketing Optimization Consulting

"This was a fabulous session with Joseph and the team on the moves that matter." – Dr. Amy Price, CEO at Empower2Go

"WOW, what an impressive webinar, thanks so much for opening the door, the cheek and the conversation. If you haven't had the pleasure of spending sometime with Joseph, you should start today. Different levels of information that fit just about every level of interaction. Take some time out and see if there is any room in his future classes well worth the time and energy plus you walk away ready to take on every level of interaction with a new approach. A must for businesspeople wanting to better understand the emotions and subliminal references from their perspective business relationships." – Spencer Wade, Trusted Digital Media Adviser, Google Partner, Google Partners Ambassador, City Expert

"Impressive, informative content presented to our group of volunteers in an interactive approach. Each attendee brought a different perspective on how we were reading Joseph's facial expressions and hand gestures while exhibiting traits of our personality.

"By interpreting and better understanding the behavioral patterns encountered in business settings, we learned how to generate better outcomes by counteracting with different measures overseen in the training session.

"Joseph was great! We had lots of fun practicing in real time using a new set of tools to influence whoever we were interacting with by modifying our hand gestures and facial expressions. We all enjoyed our time together sharing thoughts and perceptions on issues encountered in our everyday life.

"Each of us will definitely perform and achieve better results. Thanks Joseph and each participant in our training session." – Lyn Demers, Business Development, Product Development, E-Marketing Strategies, CHINA LOGISTICS

"My 'Know how someone is thinking' training with Joseph and Susan was life altering. A year ago, I embarked on 'the journey' with them for two days in a conference room in New Hampshire. The training focused on them observing me, me observing them, and me observing myself. Through the repetition of observations they put the information into my 'deep memory'. After which, and for about two weeks, my brain underwent a process that literally 'hurt'. Thankfully, after that period, my brain continued to work on it subconsciously and with no pain.

"I was initially concerned I wouldn't remember what I'd learned, but to my delight, a year later, I've noticed that I'm even more skilled at reading people's micro-expressions than I was immediately after the training. I have used the knowledge and new brain wiring I have in various circumstances to my advantage; be it new business pitches, presentations to large and small audiences, negotiations with clients, management of my staff, as well as general interpersonal relationships.

"Knowing what they are thinking allows me to tailor myself and my communication to the needs of the situation be it putting someone at ease, or putting myself in a position of authority. I would and have, recommended this to anyone in a leadership, management or a sales position." – Shaina Boone, Managing Director, Marketing Decision Sciences at OMD USA

Contact Northern Lights Publishing

Did you enjoy Joseph Carrabis' *Reading Virtual Minds Volume II: Experience and Expectation*? We hope so and would be interested in your thoughts on what worked and what didn't, and if you'd be interested in reading anything else by Joseph Carrabis or some of our other authors.

Other Northern Lights Books include:

Reading Virtual Minds Volume I: Science and History,
available on Amazon[b] and with other fine retailers
Tales Told Round Celestial Campfires, available on
Amazon[c] and with other fine retailers

You can email us with your comments at feedback@northernlightspublishing.com.

----

[b] – http://nlb.pub/RVMV14th
[c] – http://nlb.pub/TalesV1

www.ingramcontent.com/pod-product-compliance
Lightning Source LLC
Chambersburg PA
CBHW060129200326
41518CB00008B/974